# TO YOUR TENTS, O ISRAEL!

# CULTURE AND HISTORY OF THE ANCIENT NEAR EAST

EDITED BY

B. HALPERN, M. H. E. WEIPPERT

TH. P.J. VAN DEN HOUT, I. WINTER

VOLUME 12

# TO YOUR TENTS, O ISRAEL!

*The Terminology, Function, Form, and Symbolism of Tents
in the Hebrew Bible and the Ancient Near East*

BY

MICHAEL M. HOMAN

BRILL
LEIDEN · BOSTON · KÖLN
2002

This book is printed on acid-free paper.

## Library of Congress Cataloging-in-Publication Data

Homan, Michael M.
    To your tents, O Israel! : the terminology, function, form, and symbolism of tents in the Hebrew Bible and the ancient Near East / by Michael M. Homan.
      p.  cm.—Culture and history of the ancient Near East; v. 12)
Includes bibliographical references and index.
ISBN 9004126066
    1.Tents in the Bible. 2. Bible. O.T.—Criticism,. interpretation, etc. 3. Tents—Middle East. 4. Middle East—Antiquities. 5. tabernacle. I. Title. II. Series.

BS1199.T42 H66 2002
221.9'5—dc21

2002025414

## Die Deutsche Bibliothek – CIP-Einheitsaufnahme

Homan, Michael M. :
To your tents, O Israel! : the terminology, function, form and symbolism of tents in the Hebrew Bible and the Ancient Near East / by Michael M. Homan. – Leiden ; Boston ; Köln : Brill, 2002
(Culture and history of the ancient Near East ; Vol. 12)
ISBN 90-04-12606-6

ISSN   1566-2055
ISBN   90 04 12606 6

PRINTED IN THE NETHERLANDS

# DEDICATION

This book is dedicated to my family, whom I immensely appreciate. My feelings echo the alewife Siduri's advice to the forlorn Gilgamesh:

> As for you, Gilgamesh, let your belly be full. Dance and be merry by day and night, by night and day make a feast of rejoicing, day and night dance and play. Let your garments be white, your head washed, bathe in water. Cherish the little child that holds your hand. Let your spouse delight in your embrace. For this too is the lot of mankind.
>
> (*Gilgamesh*, OB, X:III:6-14)

I wish to thank my father William for his work ethic, my mother Julie for her spontaneity, my sister Chris and brother Jim for their friendship, my daughter Kalypso for her imagination, my son Gilgamesh for his promise of future, and my wife Therese Fitzpatrick for her love, support, enthusiasm, and all these years of imposed frugality. I love you all very much.

# TABLE OF CONTENTS

# ABBREVIATIONS

| | |
|---|---|
| 1 Chr | 1 Chronicles |
| 1 Kgs | 1 Kings |
| 1 Sam | 1 Samuel |
| 1 Chr | 1 Chronicles |
| 2 Chr | 2 Chronicles |
| 2 Kgs | 2 Kings |
| 2 Sam | 2 Samuel |
| *AASOR* | *Annual of the American Schools of Oriental Research* |
| AB | Anchor Bible |
| *ABD* | *Anchor Bible Dictionary*, D. N. Freedman, ed. |
| *AJSL* | *American Journal of Semitic Languages and Literature* |
| *ANEP* | *Ancient Near East in Pictures*, J. B. Pritchard, ed. |
| *ANET* | *Ancient Near Eastern Texts*, J. B. Pritchard, ed. |
| *AOAT* | *Alter Orient und Altes Testament* |
| *ARE* | *Ancient Records of Egypt,* J. H. Breasted, ed. |
| *ARM* | *Archives royales de Mari* |
| *ASAE* | *Annales du Service des antiquités de l'Égypte* |
| *ASORDS* | *American Schools of Oriental Research Dissertation Series* |
| AV | Authorized Version |
| *BA* | *Biblical Archaeologist* |
| *BAR* | *Biblical Archaeology Review* |
| *BASOR* | *Bulletin of the American Schools of Oriental Research* |
| BCE | Before the Common Era |
| *Bib* | *Biblica* |
| *BN* | *Biblische Notizen* |
| CahRb | Cahiers de la Revue biblique |
| *CAD* | *The Assyrian Dictionary of the Oriental Institute of the University of Chicago* |
| *CAT* | *The Cuneiform Alphabetic Texts* (Revised and Enlarged *KTU*) |

| | |
|---|---|
| *CBQ* | *Catholic Biblical Quarterly* |
| CE | Common Era |
| *CIH* | *Corpus inscriptionum semiticarum, pars IV, inscriptiones himyariticas et sabaeas continens.* |
| *CMHE* | *Canaanite Myth and Hebrew Epic,* Frank M. Cross, Jr. |
| *CTA* | *Corpus des tablettes en cunéiformes alphabétiques,* A. Herdner |
| Dan | Daniel |
| Deut | Deuteronomy |
| *DJD* | *Discoveries in the Judaean Desert* |
| *DMOA* | *Documenta et Monumenta Orientis Antiqui* |
| *EANE* | *The Oxford Encyclopedia of Archaeology in the Near East,* E. Meyers, ed. |
| EB | Early Bronze |
| Exod | Exodus |
| Ezek | Ezekiel |
| fig(s). | figure(s) |
| Gen | Genesis |
| HB | Hebrew Bible |
| *HSM* | *Harvard Semitic Monographs* |
| *HTR* | *Harvard Theological Review* |
| *HUCA* | *Hebrew Union College Annual* |
| *Ibid.* | *ibidem*, in the same place |
| *IBOT* | *Istanbul Arkeoloji Müzelerinde Bulunan Bogaköy Tabletleri* |
| *ICC* | *International Critical Commentary* |
| *IDB* | *Interpreter's Dictionary of the Bible,* G. A. Buttrick, ed. |
| *IEJ* | *Israel Exploration Journal* |
| Isa | Isaiah |
| *JANES* | *Journal of the Ancient Near East Society* |
| *JAOS* | *Journal of the American Oriental Society* |
| *JARCE* | *Journal of the American Research Center in Egypt* |
| *JBL* | *Journal of Biblical Literature* |
| *JCS* | *Journal of Cuneiform Studies* |
| *JEA* | *Journal of Egyptian Archaeology* |
| Jer | Jeremiah |

| | |
|---|---|
| *JESHO* | *Journal of the Economic and Social History of the Orient* |
| Jn | John |
| *JNES* | *Journal of Near Eastern Studies* |
| Josh | Joshua |
| *JPS* | *Jewish Publication Society* |
| *JQR* | *Jewish Quarterly Review* |
| *JSOT* | *Journal for the Study of the Old Testament* |
| JSOT SS | Journal for the Study of the Old Testament Supplement Series |
| *JTS* | *Journal of Theological Studies* |
| Judg | Judges |
| *KAH* | *Keilschrifttexte aus Assur historischen Inhalts* |
| KJV | King James Version |
| *KTU* | *Keilalphabetische Texte aus Ugarit*, vol. 1. M. Dietrich, O. Loretz, and J Sanmartin, eds. |
| *KUB* | *Keilschrifturkunden aus Boghazköi* |
| LB | Late Bronze |
| Lev | Leviticus |
| Lk | Luke |
| LXX | Septuagint |
| MB | Middle Bronze |
| *MDIK* | *Mitteilungen des deutschen archäologischen Instituts, Kairo* |
| MK | Middle Kingdom |
| Mt | Matthew |
| MT | Masoretic Text |
| *MVAG* | *Mitteilungen der vorderasiatischen Gesellschaft* |
| N | Number |
| n(n). | note(s) |
| *NEAEHL* | *The New Encyclopedia of Archaeological Excavations in the Holy Land*, E. Stern, ed. |
| NK | New Kingdom |
| NRSV | New Revised Standard Version |
| Num | Numbers |
| OBO | Orbis biblicus et orientalis |
| OK | Old Kingdom |
| *OLP* | *Orientalia lovaniensia periodica* |
| *Or* | *Orientalia* |

| | |
|---|---|
| *OTL* | *Old Testament Library* |
| p(p). | page(s) |
| *PE* | *Praeparatio evangelica,* Eusebius |
| PEF | Palestine Exploration Fund |
| *PEQ* | *Palestine Exploration Quarterly* |
| pl(s). | plate(s) |
| *PRU* | *Le Palais Royal d'Ugarit,* C. F. Schaeffer and J. Nougayrol, eds. |
| Ps(s) | Psalm(s) |
| *PWCJS* | *Proceedings of the . . . World Congress of Jewish Studies* |
| *RB* | *Revue biblique* |
| *RHA* | *Revue hittite et asiatique* |
| *RHR* | *Revue de l'histoire ecclésiastique* |
| RSV | Revised Standard Version |
| *SAM* | Sheffield Archaeological Monographs |
| *SJOT* | *Scandinavian Journal of the Old Testament* |
| *SSEA* | *Society for the Study of Egyptian Antiquities* |
| *TDOT* | *Theological Dictionary of the Old Testament* |
| *UF* | *Ugarit-Forschungen* |
| *Urk* | *Urkunden des ägyptischen Altertums* |
| *VT* | *Vetus Testamentum* |
| *VTSup* | *Vetus Testamentum Supplements* |
| WFD | Wadi Fidan |
| *ZA* | *Zeitschrift für Assyriologie* |
| *ZÄS* | *Zeitschrift für Ägyptische Sprache und Altertumskunde* |
| *ZAW* | *Zeitschrift für die alttestamentliche Wissenschaft* |
| *ZDMG* | *Zeitschrift der deutschen morgenländischen Gesellschaft* |
| *ZDPV* | *Zeitschrift des deutschen Palästina-Vereins* |
| Zec | Zechariah |

## LIST OF FIGURES

LIST OF PLATES

# ACKNOWLEDGEMENTS

This book owes much to the inspirations and efforts of my two mentors: William H. C. Propp and Thomas E. Levy. Concerning the former, I wish to acknowledge his time, encouragement, and unsurpassed erudition not only in the preparation of this work, but for teaching me the Hebrew Bible in its ancient Near Eastern historical and linguistic contexts. I thank the latter for his supervision in all areas pertaining to archaeology and anthropology, his camaraderie in the field, and his encouragement at my attempts to narrow the widening gap between text and artifact.

Richard Elliott Friedman assisted me with Tabernacle sections and methodology; more important, he best taught me how to teach. David Noel Freedman deserves accolades for teaching me biblical Hebrew and establishing a record of publications. David M. Goodblatt ensured that my knowledge of ancient Israel transcended the Babylonian exile. Further thanks are owed to Jeffrey C. Geoghegan for optimism and fraternity in the face of Herculean tasks; he has become a cherished friend.

I wish to thank my colleagues at Xavier University of Louisiana: Mary Ann Stachow, Gerald Boodoo, Jerry Farmer, Phillip Linden, Mark Gstohl, and Keith Lee. I am forever indebted to my friend and mentor Richard Freund who opened for me the doors of academia. Much needed and appreciated financial assistance came from the Dita Gumpel Graduate Student Fellowship, the Wexler Family Trust Fellowship in Honor of David Noel Freedman, the Samuel H. Kress Fellowship at the Albright Institute of Archaeological Research, and United States Information Agency fellowships at the American Center of Oriental Research in Amman and at the Albright Institute.

Lastly, I wish to express my gratitude to Baruch Halpern who edited the book, and to Patricia Radder who helped produce the final volume.

CHAPTER ONE

INTRODUCTION

It would be difficult to overstate the importance of tents in the
Hebrew Bible. To begin with, they provide the dominant
habitation throughout the Torah, sheltering such famous
personages as Noah, Shem, Abraham, Sarah, Lot, Isaac, Rebekah,
Jacob, Rachel, Leah, Moses, Aaron, and Joshua.[1] Even Yahweh
inhabits a tent from Sinai until the construction of Solomon's
Temple; accordingly, a tent is pictured as ancient Israel's cultic
center during its formative period.[2] Tents are intimately
connected to the judgeships of Deborah and Samuel, as well as the
monarchy under David and his successors.[3] Later Israelite and
Judahite prophets romanticize and idealize their tent heritage,
even praising nomadic contemporaries who forgo urban trappings
in favor of the perceived superior lodging provided by tents.[4] The
tent in the Hebrew Bible serves as a metaphor for God, life, the
universe, Israel, and Judah.[5] Moreover, the use of tents transcends
the domestic and religious spheres. Tents are closely associated
with the military, often used by ancient Israel and her enemies
during campaigns and sieges.[6] They are also employed in
weddings, apparently both in the ceremony and as a consummation chamber.[7] Tents surpass in importance all other structures
in Israelite society.

---

[1] On the use of tent homes by these and other biblical figures, see pp. 29-34.

[2] Yahweh's terrestrial and celestial Tabernacles are examined below, p. 34.
The long-range impact of the sacred tent in Judaism can be seen in the New
Testament, where "the Word became flesh and tented (εσκηνωσεν) among us"
(Jn 1:14). Also, Peter seeks to construct tents to shelter Moses, Elijah and Jesus
during the Transfiguration (Mt 17:4; Mk 9:5; Lk 9:33).

[3] For details, see pp. 35; 76-77; 82-83; 85-87.

[4] E.g., the Rechabites and Kenites. See below, pp. 35-38.

[5] On these and other metaphorical uses of "tent," see pp. 7-9.

[6] Military tents are explored below in chapter 5 (pp. 61-78).

[7] See chapter 6 (pp. 79-87) for the use of tents in marital and other sexual
settings.

*Reasons for Their Neglect*

Despite the enormous significance of tents in the Hebrew Bible, modern scholarship has paid surprisingly little attention to the topic. This was not the case previously, at least not for one tent in particular. The riddle of the Tabernacle's form has lured many of humanity's sharpest minds, including Josephus, Philo, Origen, Jerome, Augustine, Bede, Maimonides, Rashi, and even Sir Isaac Newton.[8] Yet the advent of Higher Criticism meant hard times for the Tabernacle. Karl Graf's theory of biblical authorship, masterfully and influentially argued by Julius Wellhausen, reduced the priestly Tabernacle to a post-exilic invention to give credence to a fictitious period of desert wanderings.[9] For Wellhausen and his many adherents, the author of P fraudulently created the Tabernacle by halving the dimensions of the Jerusalem Temple.[10] Many subsequent scholars hold opinions similar to that of Wellhausen: the Tabernacle as described by P is a fictitious model of the Temple;[11] even if an early tent shrine played a role in the pre-Solomonic cult of ancient Israel, it was far more austere than P's tent.[12]

---

[8] Josephus, *Antiquities* 3.102-87; Philo, *On the Life of Moses* 2.71-135; *Questions and Solutions in Exodus* 2.51-124; Origen, *Homiliae in Exodum* 9.13; *De principiis* 4.2.2; Jerome, *Epistula* 64; Augustine, *Quaestiones in Exodum* 104-40, 168-77; *Locutiones in Exodum* 114-27, 145-69; Bede, *De tabernaculo* 1-139; *Homiliae* 2.1, 2.24, 25 (For further references to these and other Christian exegetes, see Arthur G. Holder, "The Mosaic Tabernacle in Early Christian Exegesis," *Studia Patristica* 25 [1993]: pp. 101-06); Maimonides, *Dalalāt al-Ḥairin* (The Guide for the Perplexed); Rashi, Commentary on Exodus 26; Isaac Newton, *The Temple of Solomon* (London, 1702).

[9] Karl H. Graf, *Die geschichtlichen Bücher des Alten Testaments* (Leipzig, 1866): p. 30; Julius Wellhausen, *Prolegomena zur Geschichte Israels* (Berlin, 1883): p. 39.

[10] For references, see p. 89 n. 1.

[11] This includes both Solomon's Temple and the Temple of Zerubbabel, which Wellhausen assumed was modeled on its predecessor and owned the 60:20:30 cubit measurements described in 1 Kgs 6:2.

[12] Examples of scholars believing the Priestly author's Tabernacle is based (at least in part) on the Jerusalem Temple include Ralph W. Klein, who states the Priestly description of the Tabernacle represents an idealized version of a simpler tent, which "surely incorporates in some fashion aspects of Solomon's temple" ("Back to the Future: The Tabernacle in the Book of Exodus," *Interpretation* 50 [1996]: pp. 264-65). Similarly, G. Henton Davies: "it is almost universally supposed that P's tabernacle is based on Solomon's temple"

While Wellhausen and Higher Criticism severely damaged the Tabernacle's credibility already in the nineteenth century, in the twentieth century archaeology has cast doubt on the Bible's account of Israel's tent-dwelling nomadic past. For example, a literal reading of the P Exodus narrative of Israel's migration is considered impossible, for if 603,550 adult non-Levitical males and their families inhabited tents at Qadesh-Barnea for 38 years, one would expect ample material evidence of their encampment, for which there is currently none.[13] But inflated numbers are not the only obstacle to verifying this tent-dwelling heritage for ancient Israel.

Two considerations have restricted archaeological investigation of tents and tent-dwelling. First, tents leave little trace in the material record. Until recently, archaeological discoveries of fabric, poles, pole-holes, tent-outlines, ropes, pegs, or other vestiges of tent-life were quite rare, though finding tents in the archaeological landscape is becoming increasingly feasible.[14]

-----

("Tabernacle," *IDB* IV [1962]: p. 504). So, too, Martin Noth: "The sanctuary . . . is in P quite clearly orientated on the picture of the later temple at Jerusalem. The only question is whether the model is the temple of Solomon . . . or the temple of Zerubbabel" (*Exodus* [Philadelphia, 1962]: p. 201). Ronald E. Clements writes that the Tabernacle is a "description of a temple under the guise of a portable tent sanctuary," (*God and Temple* [Philadelphia, 1965]: p. 111). For more extreme views, see John Van Seters, *Abraham in History and Tradition* (New Haven, 1975): pp. 14, 310, who claims that not only tent shrines, but tents in general were lacking until they were popularized by Arabs in the first millennium B.C.E. Even some of the greatest advocates for an actual Tabernacle concede that in actuality it stood in a simpler form than the elaborate tent described in the P text: Frank M. Cross, Jr., writes that the Priestly description was "perhaps too complex and richly ornamented" ("The Priestly Tabernacle in the Light of Recent Research," *Temples and High Places in Biblical Times* [Jerusalem, 1981]: p. 169; *From Epic to Canon* [Baltimore, 1998]: p. 85). So, too, Menahem Haran writes, "It is evident that as depicted in P the tabernacle is largely imaginary and never existed in Israel" ("Shiloh and Jerusalem, *JBL* 81 [1962]: p. 14). Others, including Th. A. Busink, have argued that the Tabernacle is a fiction due to the unfeasibility of construction (*Der Tempel von Jerusalem* [Leiden, 1970]: pp. 602-03. For more detailed information concerning the state of the field of Tabernacle historicity, see pp. 129-85 below.

[13] Num 1:46 provides the population. On the absence of archaeological confirmation, see Rudolph Cohen, "Excavations at Kadesh-barnea," *BA* 44 (1981): pp. 93-107. The chronology of 38 of 40 years at Qadesh-Barnea is discussed in n. 24 pp. 134-35.

[14] The recent improvements in camp-site excavations are examined in

Second, even when practicable, excavating tent fragments and elliptical settlement patterns is less romantic and fruitful in both publications and fundraising than digging a massive urban center. Thus, while biblical houses, palaces, and temples have been treated at length in modern scholarship, tents have for the most part been neglected.

Nevertheless, the topic of tents, in both the Hebrew Bible and the ancient Near East, has attracted a small but increasing contingent of scholars, beginning in 1947 with Frank M. Cross Jr.'s article on the Tabernacle, which remains the most influential rebuttal to Wellhausen.[15] Prior to Cross, those arguing for the reality of an ancient Israelite cultic tent focused on portable Bedouin shrines that bore limited resemblance to the Tabernacle.[16] Cross, however, drew on verbal and pictorial records from Phoenicia, Ugarit, Egypt, and Mesopotamia to show the actuality and antiquity of the Tabernacle, which Cross suggested was modeled on 500-year-old written documentation of the tent David erected for the Ark upon its initial entry into Jerusalem.[17] Since Cross's work, ensuing studies have amassed data on ancient Near Eastern tents, generally by focusing on a specific class of tent or cultural area.[18] Yet a comprehensive and detailed

---

chapter 4, pp. 47-59.

[15] Frank M. Cross, Jr., "The Tabernacle: A Study from an Archaeological and Historical Approach," *BA* 10 (1947): pp. 45-68; revised and reprinted as "The Priestly Tabernacle," *The Biblical Archaeologist Reader* I (New York, 1961): pp. 201-28.

[16] For these Bedouin and proto-Bedouin parallels to the Tabernacle (including the *ʿutfah, maḥmal,* and *qubba*), see pp. 90-93.

[17] David's tent is not the only Tabernacle prototype to be proposed. On David's tent and the tent shrine of Shiloh as P's model, see below, pp. 133-37.

[18] The most comprehensive studies on biblical and ancient Near Eastern tents thus far include Kenneth Kitchen, "The Tabernacle-A Bronze Age Artefact," *Eretz-Israel* 24 (1993): pp. 119-29, "The Desert Tabernacle," BR 16.6 (2000): pp. 14-21, and James K. Hoffmeier, "Tents in Egypt and the Ancient Near East," *SSEA Newsletter* vol. 7, no. 3 (May, 1977): pp. 13-28. Both gather primarily Egyptian pictorial and written records, Kitchen to provide a Late Bronze setting for the Tabernacle, Hoffmeier to disprove John Van Seter's claim of the absence of tents in the 2nd millennium B.C.E. (see n. 12 pp. 2-3 above). Cross has reexamined his previous studies in "The Priestly Tabernacle in the Light of Recent Research," pp. 169-80. Another noteworthy contribution is Albrecht Alt, "Zelt und Hütten," *Kleine Schriften zur Geschichte des Volkes Israel*, vol. 3 (München, 1959): pp. 233-42.

examination of the Hebrew Bible's broad range of tents, including the Tabernacle, has been conspicuously lacking.

## Principle Aims of the Current Study

This book will strengthen the case for Israel's tent-dwelling past. Certainly not *all* of ancient Israel stemmed from a nomadic exodus from Egypt.[19] Ancient Israel was composed of many elements, but we shall see that much, if not most, of her heritage involved living in tents. Similarly, the actuality of the Priestly Tabernacle will be advocated. Although I began this enterprise as a skeptic, the many parallels collected to the Tabernacle's form and function have convinced me that an elaborate tent served as the focal point for Israelite religion until the completion of Solomon's Temple. If this tent-shrine did not correspond exactly to the description in Exodus 25-27, it came very close. The many other uses of tents will be explored, especially their role in warfare and in wedding ceremonies.

The title of this book, "To your tents, O Israel!" is a call to rebellion twice evoked in the Hebrew Bible's early monarchical history. Sheba sounds it first in 2 Sam 20:1, expressing dissatisfaction with Israel's membership in the Davidic united kingdom. Two generations later, Rehoboam hears the same phrase after alienating his northern Israelite subjects (1 Kgs 12:20= 2 Chr 10:16). The reason for invoking tents in a period dominated by house-dwelling urbanism is somewhat enigmatic.[20] Our final chapter will examine this call in light of the many previously explored functions of tents. Comparison with similar expressions from cultures neighboring ancient Israel will show that the

---

[19] The term "nomad" best fits the Exodus account, as "semi-nomad" implies limited sedentarization and farming. Perhaps even more realistic is Michael B. Rowton's term, "enclosed nomadism," discussed in "Economic and Political Factors in Ancient Nomadism," *Nomads and Sedentary Peoples* (Mexico, 1981): pp. 25-36. For further discussion, see Anatoly M. Khazanov, *Nomads and the Outside World* (Cambridge, 1984): pp. 17-25, 53-59; revised edition with expanded introduction (Madison, WI, 1994): xxix-lix; 17-25; 53-59; and Roger Cribb, *Nomads in Archaeology* (Cambridge, 1991): pp. 15-22.

[20] On the many interpretations of "To your tents, O Israel!" see below, pp. 187-92.

summons "To your tents, O Israel!" is part of a widespread creed for disbanding councils, both divine and secular.

The subject of the following chapter is the terminology associated with tents. The large number of terms, and the Hebrew Bible's tendency to blend terms for tents and houses, will strengthen the case for a heritage of ancient Israel in which tents played a vital role.

# CHAPTER TWO

# TENT TERMINOLOGY: THE MANY WORDS FOR TENTS AND THEIR INTERCHANGEABILITY

> This chapter examines the many terms designating "tents" in the Hebrew Bible. It will show that these expressions are not always distinct, as biblical terms for "tent," "house," and other domiciles blend in usage. This phenomenon seems to exist as a result of the large impact of tents on the culture and heritage of ancient Israel.

Balaam's oracle in Num 24:5 begins by blessing the Israelite tribes: "How goodly are your *tents*, O Jacob, your *tabernacles*, O Israel." The two words for tent-related architecture (אֹהֶל, מִשְׁכָּן) are among 13 used to designate tents in the Hebrew Bible. When one compares this with the fact that there is only one word for tent in the LXX (σκηνή), one realizes the importance of tents in the culture of ancient Israel.[1] Tent-related nomenclature transcends portable dwellings, as even permanent structures are often designated "tent" or "tabernacle," while at the same time portable abodes are called "house" and "temple." This chapter will examine individually the many tent designations in the Hebrew Bible, to show how domiciliary terms are used interchangeably, and to explore the underlying socio-historical reasons behind this phenomenon.

## 1. TENT (אֹהֶל)

The most common Hebrew word for tent is אֹהֶל. Derivatives of אהל appear 347 times in the Hebrew Bible, but not always in

---

[1] For a further discussion of the Greek translation of "tent," see Russell D. Nelson, *Studies in the Development of the Text of the Tabernacle Account*, Harvard Dissertation (Cambridge, 1986): p. 49; David W. Gooding, *The Account of the Tabernacle: Translation and Textual Problems of the Greek Exodus* (Cambridge, 1959); Craig R. Koester, *The Dwelling of God: The Tabernacle in the Old Testament, Intertestamental Jewish Literature, and the New Testament* (Washington, 1989): pp. 19-20.

reference to portable architecture. The false-cognate אֲהָלִים //
אֲהָלוֹת occurs in at least three verses, always in parallel with myrrh
and other aromatic spices, and is identified with *Aquilaria
agallocha*, a nonmedicinal aromatic aloe.[2] The plant is
indigenous to China and India, and the name derives not from
Semitic *ʾhl*, but from Sanskrit *aghal*.[3] One other passage employs
אהל in a manner not related to tents: Job 25:5 uses יַאֲהִיל to
connote the moon's shining. As this verb is parallel to the stars
being "bright" (זַכּוּ), several commentators believe the א in יַאֲהִיל
to be superfluous, as elsewhere Job utilizes the root הלל in the
hiphil to denote shining.[4]

The remaining 343 times, אהל denotes domiciles, mostly
portable. Three passages utilize the root אהל verbally, with the
meaning "to pitch one's tent."[5] The majority of nominal uses
(148) refer to the Tabernacle, most frequently designated "tent of
the appointed time" (אֹהֶל מוֹעֵד), but also "the tent of the
covenant" (אֹהֶל הָעֵדוּת), "the tent of Yahweh" (אֹהֶל יהוה) and

---

[2] The word אֲהָלִים occurs in Prov 7:17; אֲהָלוֹת in Ps 45:9; Cant 4:14. The MT of
Num 24:6 also reads אֲהָלִים, but this is problematic, as the LXX, Vulgate, Syriac,
and Targum Pseudo-Jonathan all read "tents" (אֹהָלִים), favored by the context
within Balaam's oracle, especially vss. 5-6. Others prefer "oaks" (אֵלִים) for Num
24:6, as the word is parallel to "cedars." See John C. Trevor, "Aloes," *IDB* I
(Nashville, 1962): p. 88; Marvin H. Pope, *Song of Songs*, AB 7c (Garden City,
NY, 1977): p. 494. The confusion seems to arise from the verb נָטַע "to plant."
Admittedly, נָטַע is most often connected to flora, but elsewhere it is used with
"tents" (Dan 11:45, and perhaps Isa 51:16) and more frequently "people" (Exod
15:17; 2 Sam 17:10=1 Chr 17:9; Jer 24:6; 32:41; Ezek 36:36; Amos 9:15). The
similarities of driving a tent peg and planting are apparent, as is the
homophony of נָטַע "plant" and נָטָה "pitch a tent." See William H. C. Propp,
*Exodus 1-18*, AB 2a (New York, 1999): p. 541.
[3] Thus English agal-wood, eagle-wood, or wood-aloe (xylaloe); αγαλλοχον
in Greek. See Chaim Rabin, "The Song of Songs and Tamil Poetry," *Studies in
Religion* 3 (1973): pp. 205-219; Marvin H. Pope, *Song of Songs*, p. 28,
Michael Zohary, *Plants of the Bible* (Cambridge, 1982): p. 204. However, D. J.
Wetzstein in F. Delitzsch's *Die poetischen Bücher des Alten Testaments*
(Leipzig, 1875): pp. 167-70 identifies the plant with cardamum, Arabic *hyl*
(هيل) from *ʾhyl* "little tent," because of the three-cornered shape of the plant's
capsules.
[4] Job 31:26 (יַהֵל); 41:10 (תָּהֶל). See Marvin H. Pope, *Job,* AB 15 (Garden City,
NY, 1965): pp. 163-64, who translates יַאֲהִיל in Job 25:5 as "bright," and
compares Job 4:17; 15:15; and Ps 8:3-4.
[5] Qal וַיֶּאֱהַל in Gen 13:12, 18; piel יַהֵל (a contraction of a putative יַאֲהֵל) in Isa
13:20.

simply "the tent" (הָאֹהֶל).⁶ At times the heavens are conceived of as a tent stretched out by Yahweh.⁷ Tents also symbolize life.⁸

The root אהל is common in Semitic languages. Like Hebrew אֹהֶל, Ugaritic *ahl* and Aramaic אהלא mean simply "tent."⁹ However, other languages employ אהל more broadly. For example, Akkadian *ālu(m)<\*ahlum* refers to a city, and *aʾlu*, a loanword from Aramaic, refers to "a people" or "a family," as do Arabic *ʾahl* (أهل) and Syriac *yahlā*.¹⁰ Likewise, in the Hebrew Bible, אֳהֳלֵי אֱדוֹם refers to the Edomites in Ps 83:7, אָהֳלֵי יַעֲקוֹב to the inhabitants of Judah in Jer 30:18, Zec 12:7, and Mal 2:12, and אָהֳלֵי בַת־צִיוֹן to the inhabitants of Jerusalem in Lam 2:4.

## 2. BOOTH (סֻכָּה)

The word סֻכָּה, alternately spelled שֵׂכָה, is used 38 times in the Hebrew Bible, most often not for tents, but for temporary shelters constructed of gathered foliage. Hence "booth" is a slightly more accurate English translation than "hut."¹¹ The root סכך is common in Semitic languages, most often meaning "to cover," or "to weave." Arabic *škk* indicates covering or weaving, suggesting an ultimate derivation from proto-Semitic *\*śkk*.¹²

---

⁶ Num 9:15; 17:22, 23; 18:2; 2 Chr 24:6 use אֹהֶל הָעֵדֻת; we find אֹהֶל יהוה in 1 Kgs 2:28-30; and הָאֹהֶל in Exod 33:7-11; Num 12:5, 10; Deut 31:14-15, etc.

⁷ Isa 40:22; Ps 19:5-6. Note also Plate 50a—a Mesopotamian tent hosts the sun disk.

⁸ Isa 38:12; Note also 2 Cor 5:1, where life is symbolized by a tent, and eternal life by a heavenly house.

⁹ For Ugaritic, see *CAT* 1.15.III.18; 1.17.V.32; 1.19.IV.50-52, 60. For Aramaic, see Michael Sokoloff, *A Dictionary of Jewish Palestinian Aramaic* (Jerusalem, 1990): p. 37; Marcus Jastrow, *Talmudic Dictionary* I (New York, 1903): p. 20.

¹⁰ For Akkadian, see Wolfram von Soden, *Akkadisches Handwörterbuch* I, p. 39; *CAD* I:1, pp. 379-91. For Arabic, see Edward W. Lane, *Arabic-English Lexicon* I:1 (London, 1863): p. 121. For Syriac, see Carl Brockelmann, *Lexicon Syriacum*, 2nd ed. (Göttingen, 1928): p. 299; *Grundriss der vergleichenden Grammatik der semitischen Sprachen*, I (Berlin, 1908-1913): pp. 194, 242.

¹¹ "Hut" derives from Old English *hȳd* (hide, skin), while "booth" denotes a simple roofed structure built of any material at hand, often in the context of animal husbandry or harvest (*Webster's Third New International Dictionary* [1971]).

¹² Edward W. Lane, *Arabic-English Lexicon* I:4, pp. 1582-83.

Aramaic שׁוכא/סוכא and Syriac *swkt³/swk³* are usually rendered "bough" or "branch," but also "booth."[13]

In the Hebrew Bible, the Ark dwells in a סֻכָּה when the Israelites are at war; so do Israelite and Syrian soldiers.[14] Jacob builds סֻכּוֹת for his cattle, providing the etymology for the Transjordanian town Succoth near the mouth of the Jabbok River.[15] Clouds are occasionally described as booths constructed by Yahweh to shade the earth.[16] Most often סֻכָּה refers to a temporary hut constructed for shelter during the harvest.[17] Hence they became the namesake of the fall harvest festival Sukkoth, previously named "the Festival of Ingathering," during which one week is spent in booths to commemorate the dwellings of the Exodus (Plate 1a).[18] Also, סֻכָּה can also be used metaphorically for the prosperity of the kingdom. Thus, סֻכַּת דָּוִיד in Amos 9:11 refers to the desired restoration of David's kingdom. In like manner, Yahweh's destruction of a שֻׂכָּה symbolizes the end of all appointed holidays in Lam 2:6. Finally, the root *skk* can be used verbally with the

---

[13] Marcus Jastrow, *Talmudic Dictionary* II, pp. 963-64; J. Payne Smith, *Syriac Dictionary* (Oxford, 1903): p. 365; Michael Sokoloff, *A Dictionary of Jewish Palestinian Aramaic of the Byzantine Period* (Jerusalem, 1990): p. 370.

[14] 2 Sam 11:11; 1 Kgs 20:12, 16. These are indeed booths, and not the town of Succoth, *pace* Yigael Yadin, "Some Aspects of the Strategy of Ahab and David," *Bib* 36 (1955): pp. 332-51; *The Art of Warfare in Biblical Lands* (New York, 1963): pp. 274-75. See Michael M. Homan, "Booths or Succoth?- A Response to Yigael Yadin," *JBL* 118 (1999): pp. 691-97. Jacob's building shelters for cattle with 2 Chr 14:14, which refers to "cattle-tents."

[15] Gen 33:17.

[16] 2 Sam 22:12=Ps 18:12; Job 36:29. See also Isa 4:5-6, where סֻכָּה is parallel to חֻפָּה. Note the photographs of early 20th century Palestinian booths erected to watch crops, in Gustaf Dalman, *Arbeit und Sitte in Palästina* (Hildesheim, 1928): 2.11-16.

[17] E.g., Isa 1:8; Job 27:18.

[18] Neh 8:16 and Josephus, *Wars* 6.V.3, mention that booths were set up in the Temple courtyard. Lev 23:39-43 commands that branches of four types be gathered and applied to the booths: fruit of a majestic tree (פְּרִי עֵץ הָדָר), branches of palm trees (כַּפֹּת תְּמָרִים), bough of a leafy tree (עֲנַף עֵץ־עָבֹת), and willows of a brook (עַרְבֵי־נָחַל). However, cf. Neh 8:14-17, which prescribes branches of olive (זַיִת), tree of oil (עֵץ שֶׁמֶן), myrtle (הֲדַס), palm (תְּמָרִים), and leafy tree (עֵץ־עָבֹת). Less descriptive references to the Sukkoth festival include Lev 23:34; Deut 16:13-16; 31:10; Zec 14:16-19; Ezra 3:4. On the festival after the Babylonian Exile, see Jeffrey L. Rubenstein, *The History of Sukkot in the Second Temple and Rabbinic Periods* (Atlanta, 1995).

general meaning of "to cover," as in Exod 40:3, which instructs that one cover (סַכֹּתָ) the Ark with the Paroket (פָּרֹכֶת).[19]

## 3. TABERNACLE (מִשְׁכָּן)

The word מִשְׁכָּן appears 139 times in Hebrew Bible, most often applied by the Priestly author to the Tabernacle. However, at times, secular Israelite abodes, as well as those of foreign nations, are designated as מִשְׁכָּנוֹת in non-Priestly strata.[20] Twice מִשְׁכָּן designates a tomb (Isa 22:16; Ps 49:12) and once the abode of a wild ass (Job 39:6). All other occurrences refer to the Tabernacle. The word is qualified in various forms as מִשְׁכַּן יהוה (the Tabernacle of Yahweh), מִשְׁכַּן אֹהֶל מוֹעֵד (the Tabernacle of the tent of the appointed time), מִשְׁכַּן הָעֵדֻת (the Tabernacle of the covenant), מִשְׁכַּן כְּבוֹדֶךָ (the Tabernacle of your glory), מִשְׁכַּן שְׁמֶךָ (the Tabernacle of your name), and מִשְׁכַּן בֵּית הָאֱלֹהִים (the Tabernacle of the house of God).[21] The word מִשְׁכָּן is derived from the root שׁכן (to dwell), a common verb virtually synonymous with גור and יׁשב, although the latter often implies inhabiting a more permanent nature.[22]

Hebrew מִשְׁכָּן has many Semitic cognates.[23] Ugaritic *mškn* refers to a tent, and the verb *škn* means "to dwell."[24] Among the several

---

[19] For the Tabernacle's מָסָךְ, see below, pp. 158-59.

[20] Num 16:24, 27, for example, speaks of the tabernacle (מִשְׁכָּן) of Korah, Dathan, and Abiram, which is alternately called a tent (אֹהֶל) in verse 27. Three other examples (Num 25:4; Isa 54:2; Jer 30:18) find מִשְׁכָּן as a secular Israelite dwelling, but all are in poetry and all are parallel to אֹהֶל. For the tabernacles of foreign nations, see Jer 51:30; Ezek 25:4; Hab 1:6.

[21] The phrase מִשְׁכַּן יהוה occurs in Lev 17:4; Num 16:9; 17:28; 19:13; etc.; מִשְׁכַּן אֹהֶל מוֹעֵד in Exod 39:32; 40:2, 6, 29; 1 Chr 6:17; מִשְׁכַּן הָעֵדֻת in Exod 38:21; Num 1:50, 53; 9:15; 10:11; 17:23; 18:2), מִשְׁכַּן כְּבוֹדֶךָ in Ps 26:8; מִשְׁכַּן שְׁמֶךָ in Ps 74:7; מִשְׁכַּן בֵּית הָאֱלֹהִים in 1 Chr 6:33.

[22] For verbal usage of שׁכן, see for example Lev 16:16, where the tent of the appointed time "tabernacles" (שֹׁכֵן), and Num 9:18, 22, where Yahweh's cloud "dwells" (יִשְׁכָּן) over the Tabernacle as an indication that the camp should stay put.

[23] Semitic *škn* may also shed light on the etymology of Greek σκηνή, a word first attested immediately following the Persian invasion of Greece (c. 490 B.C.E.). Earlier, Homer had called the portable dwellings of the Achaian soldiers κλισίη; these more resemble huts than tents (e.g. *Iliad* 24: 448-453). But the Persian army's ornate tents, especially those of Darius and Xerxes, greatly impressed the Greeks, as attested by Herodotus, *Histories*, VII.119, IX.70, and Xenophon, *Cyropaedia*, II.i.25-28; IV.ii.11; VIII.v.2-16; Alexander too would later construct an opulent tent, described in Quintus Curtius Rufus, *History of*

definitions of Akkadian *maškanu* are "tent," "house," "can-opy," and "sanctuary."[25] Similarly *šakānu,* a verb with the gen-eral meaning "to put, set, place," can also be used idiomatically meaning "to pitch camp," and it is used in reference to setting up a ritual tent at Mari.[26] Aramaic and Syriac employ *mašk°nā°* for "tent," while the verb *škn* means "to dwell."[27] Later Aramaic uses משכן to designate a general holy place, not just a tent shrine, as in the 2$^{nd}$ century C.E. inscription from Hatra.[28]

The use of משכן for "tent" at Ugarit, and in the Oracles of Balaam (Num 24:5), as well as the verb שכן in the Noachic Oracle (Gen 9:27), Jacob's Blessing (Gen 49:13), the Blessing of Moses (Deut 33:12, 16, 28), and the Song of Deborah (Judg 5:17), all point to the archaic usage of this root in Northwest Semitic languages.[29] Some have seen a deliberately archaic connotation of nomadism in P's preference for שכן over ישב and גור to describe Yahweh's terrestrial dwelling.[30]

---

*Alexander* 10.5-6, and Athenaeus's *Deipnosophistae*. In fact, the first attestation of σκηνή occurs in Aeschylus's *The Persians,* line 1000, designating Persian tents. Thereafter, σκηνή also came to denote the theatrical stage (whence English "scene"). Aramaic, the official language of the Persian empire, would likely have referred to the emperor's ornate tent as משכן, ultimately evolving into Greek σκηνή. Syriac *mašk°nā°* too denotes both a tent and the stage of a theater. See J. Payne Smith, *A Compendious Syriac Dictionary,* pp. 306-07. On previous attempts at an Indo-European etymology, see Wilhelm Michaelis, "σκηνή," *Theological Dictionary of the New Testament,* p. 368.

[24] For *mškn* as tent, see *CAT* 1.15.III.19; 1.17.V.32-33; 4.335.28. For Ugaritic *škn* "to dwell," see 2.3.20; 2.33.23, 2.39.6, 4.245.I.3, etc.

[25] *CAD* 10:1: pp. 369-73.

[26] *CAD* 17:1: pp. 116, 127. For the ritual tent at Mari, see pp. 179-81.

[27] Marcus Jastrow, *Talmudic Dictionary* II, pp. 855, 1575. J. Payne Smith, *A Compendious Syriac Dictionary,* pp. 306-07; Michael Sokoloff, *A Dictionary of Jewish Palestinian Aramaic,* p. 334.

[28] *KAI* 247. See Delbert R. Hillers, "MŠKN 'Temple' in Inscriptions from Hatra," *BASOR* 206 (1972): pp. 54-56.

[29] On the archaic character of these poems, see Frank M. Cross, Jr., and David N. Freedman, *Studies in Ancient Yahwistic Poetry* (Missoula, 1975). Also note the use of the verb *šakānum* for setting up a ritual tent at Mari (see pp. 116-18).

[30] E.g., Frank M. Cross, Jr., "The Priestly Tabernacle," *The Biblical Archaeologist Reader,* pp. 224-27.

*Ten Additional Designations* (טֶרֶה, נָוֶה, יְרִיעָה, שַׁפְרִיר, חֻפָּה, דֹּק, קֻבָּה, צֵל, סֵתֶר, חַנָּה)

4. (קֻבָּה) The Tabernacle, or a specific part of it, is referred to as the קֻבָּה in Num 25:8, where Phinehas pursues an Israelite man and a Midianite woman into the Tabernacle and executes them for defiling the sacred tent. The word parallels Syriac *qbbʾ/qwbtʾ* (vaulted tent) and Arabic *qubba* (tent).[31] The Priestly author's use of this hapax legomenon may be playing on a following word: Phinehas thrusts a spear through "her belly" (קֵבָתָהּ).[32]

5. (דֹּק) Another word applied to tents is דֹּק, from the root דקק (thin), used in Isa 40:22b:

הַנּוֹטֶה כַדֹּק שָׁמַיִם
וַיִּמְתָּחֵם כָּאֹהֶל לָשָׁבֶת

he who stretches out the heavens like a דֹּק,
and spreads them like a tent to live in.


The use of דֹּק parallel to אֹהֶל, as well as the verb נוֹטֶה, both suggest a meaning, perhaps "curtain."[33]

6. (חֻפָּה) Similar in nature is חֻפָּה, a word now commonly applied to canopies in Jewish wedding ceremonies. Isa 4:5-6 predicts that Zion will be protected by a סֻכָּה and a חֻפָּה. Joel 2:16 uses חֻפָּה in the context of a wedding, as does Ps 19:5-6, where חֻפָּה is parallel to אֹהֶל.

7. (שַׁפְרִיר) Another hapax legomenon used for a tent is found in Jer 43:10, where Jeremiah predicts the overthrow of Egypt, prophesying that Nebuchadnezzar will place his throne and stretch his שַׁפְרִיר near Pharaoh's palace.[34] The verb נָטָה (to stretch out) as well as the Akkadian cognate *šuparruru* (spread out)

---

[31] On the pre-Islamic *qubba* tent shrine, see pp. 92-93.

[32] Here the Syriac simply repeats *baqqubbāh*, so the couple is pierced inside the tent. It is not clear whether the word קֻבָּה refers to the Tabernacle as a whole or a specific part of it. Perhaps it is the פָּרֹכֶת, if Richard E. Friedman is correct in understanding it as a square tent and not a screen (see below, pp. 156-58).

[33] For דֹּק as a "curtain," see Claus Westermann, *Isaiah 40-66* (Philadelphia, 1969): p. 56; alternatively, John L. McKenzie translates דֹּק as "veil" (*Second Isaiah* [AB 20; Garden City, NY, 1968]: pp. 21-22.

[34] The *qʾrê* is שַׁפְרִירוֹ, while the *kʾtîb* is שַׁפְרוּרוֹ.

indicate a tent-related nature for שַׁפְרִיר.[35] Likely, שַׁפְרִיר is the king's canopy as seen in reliefs and the bases of which were discovered in Tel Dan's gate complex.

8. (יְרִיעָה) Another word affiliated with tents is יְרִיעָה (curtain). The panels of fine linen and goat hair which compose the Tabernacle's coverings are designated יְרִיעָה in Exodus 26 and 36. David complains in 1 Chr 17:1 that while he lives in a house, the Ark dwells תַּחַת יְרִיעוֹת "under curtains." The corresponding verse in 2 Sam 7:2 uses בְּתוֹךְ הַיְרִיעָה "in the midst of the curtain." Ps 104:2 also uses יְרִיעָה with the verb נוֹטֶה, likening the sky to a tent.

9. (נָוֶה) The noun נָוֶה is frequently used for the abode of shepherds and their flocks. The word is parallel to אֹהֶל in Job 5:24; 18:15, and Isa 33:20. Furthermore, נָוֶה is used in reference to the tent David erects to house the Ark in 2 Sam 15:25.[36] Akkadian *nawû/namû* likewise refers to the land inhabited by nomads, most often the Amorites.[37] It seems that נָוֶה is the filed in which tents are pitched.

10. (טִרָה) Elsewhere a group of tents is referred to as טִרָה, a term used most often to refer to the encampments of Arabian nomadic groups.[38] The tent association is clear from Ps 69:26, which uses טִרָה in parallel with אֹהֶל.

11. (חַוָּה) Yet another term for a collection of tents is חַוָּה, used in reference to the encampments captured by Jair of Manasseh in Gilead.[39] The root is similarly used in Arabic for a collection of tents (*ḥiwā'a*).

12. (סֵתֶר) סֵתֶר "hiding place" is used for shelters, in parallel with "booth" in Ps 18:12=2 Sam 22:12, and Ps 27:5. Moreover, Ps 27:5 uses it in construct with tent (סֵתֶר אָהֳלוֹ). The root is also found verbally, referring to both tents and booths in Pss 27:5 and 31:21.

---

[35] Akkadian *šuparruru* is often found in the context of textiles. See *CAD* 17:3: pp. 317-18.

[36] Note also that נָוֶה is used for Yahweh's abode in Exod 15:13 and for Yahweh Himself in Jer 50:7.

[37] *CAD* 11:1: p. 249; E. O. Edzard, "Altbabylonische *nawûm*," *ZA* 53 (1959): pp. 168-73.

[38] Gen 25:16 (Ishmaelites); Num 31:10 (Midianites), and Ezek 25:4 (Qedemites).

[39] Num 32:41; Deut 3:14; Josh 13:30; Judg 10:4; 1 Kgs 4:13; 1 Chr 2:23.

13. (צֵל) צֵל "shade" is naturally associated with tent. Isa 4:6 predicts God's creation of a heavenly canopy in order to give relief from the day's heat. Both סֵתֶר and צֵל, as well as מְרָה, likely referred originally to the arrangement of tents and then the term became used metaphorically for a group of tents.

14. (חַיָּה) חַיָּה is used of war camps in 2 Sam 23:11 and Ps 68:11.

Less certain to be tent-related is an enigmatic architectural feature, designated עָב in 1 Kgs 7:6, located in front of Solomon's palace. Some have interpreted the structure as a pavilion or canopy, given its association with pillars. However, this is unlikely, since Ezek 41:25-26 speaks of a *wooden* עָב in Ezekiel's temple vision.

*Tent Accessories*

In addition to these 13 direct tent designations, there are many words in the Hebrew Bible for tent accessories. Isa 33:20 refers to Jerusalem as "an immovable tent, whose stakes (יְתֵדֹתָיו) will never be taken up, and all of its cords (חֲבָלָיו) will not be broken." Similarly, Isa 54:2 predicts the end of a woman's barrenness: "Enlarge the place of your tent, and let the curtains of your tabernacles be stretched out; hold not back, lengthen your cords (מֵיתָרַיִךְ) and strengthen your stakes (יְתֵדֹתַיִךְ)."[40] In addition to יָתֵד, חֶבֶל, and יֶתֶר/מֵיתָר, other tent accessories are included in the plans for the Tabernacle: "pillar" (עַמּוּד), "loops" (לֻלָאֹת), "hooks" (קְרָסִים), "boards" (קֶרֶשׁ), "tenon" (יָד), and "socket" (אֶדֶן).[41]

*Tent Verbs*

Apart from the aforementioned verbal aspects of שָׁכַן, סָכַךְ, אָהַל, and סָתַר, there are additional verbs associated with tents. The most common is חָנָה, meaning "to encamp." For example, in Num 1:50-53, the root appears five times where the Levites are instructed to pitch the Tabernacle and camp around it. In several

---

[40] A similar metaphor is found in Jer 10:12, 20, where a destroyed tent and broken tent-cords symbolize desolation. Additional usages of יָתֵד include: Exod 27:19; 35:18; 38:20, 31; Num 3:37; 4:32; Deut 23:14; Judg 4:21-22 and 5:26 (as the weapon used by Jael); 16:14; Zec 10:4. The words יֶתֶר/מֵיתָר for a tent-cord can be found in Exod 35:18; 39:40; Num 3:26, 37; 4:26, 32; Job 4:21.

[41] See Exodus 26 and 36. For their role in the Tabernacle's construction, see below, pp. 137-59.

places the verb has clear military connotations, where armies
encamp against opposing forces.[42] The verb is not reserved for
humans, as locusts are said to be encamping (הַחֹנִים) on hedges in
Nah 3:17. The root חנה also occurs nominally in reference to
encampments (מַחֲנֶה), including the place names מַחֲנֵה־דָן (camp of
Dan) and מַחֲנָיִם (two camps).[43]

Another verb referring to tents is נטה, with the general meaning
of "to stretch out." Thus Abraham stretches (וַיֵּט) his tent just east
of Beth-El in Gen 12:8.[44] Likewise, Moses stretches out the
אֹהֶל מוֹעֵד in Exod 33:7, and David does the same for his tent in
Jerusalem in 2 Sam 6:17=1 Chr 16:1. This verb also describes
Yahweh's stretching out the heavens in Jer 10:12, 20 and Ps
104:2.[45]

## Ambiguity in Hebrew Terms for Dwellings

As we have seen, the variety of designations for tents attests to
their importance in the Hebrew Bible. Moreover, there is
considerable fluidity in terminology associated with biblical
domiciles in general, both permanent and portable. In the Hebrew
Bible, not only can a tent be designated by אֹהֶל, מִשְׁכָּן, סֻכָּה, קֻבָּה, דֹּק,
חֻפָּה, שַׁפְרִיר, יְרִיעָה, נָוֶה, טִרָה, חַוָּה, סֵתֶר, and צֵל, but also by terms
typically reserved for non-portable dwellings, such as "house"
(בַּיִת) and "palace" (הֵיכָל). Moreover, this transfer of terminology
is not uni-directional; i.e., solid structures are frequently referred
to by tent-related designations.

## Portable Terminology for Permanent Dwellings - אֹהֶל for בַּיִת

The terms בַּיִת and אֹהֶל are used in parallel in Judg 20:8; Ps 84:11;
Job 21:28, and Prov 14:11, which suggests similar, if not
interchangeable, definitions. Moreover, often אֹהֶל is used where
one would expect to find בַּיִת or הֵיכָל. In the following 12

---

[42] Num 10:31; Josh 4:19; 5:10; 10:5, 31, 34; Judg 6:4; 20:19; 1 Sam 4:1;
11:1; 13:5, 16; 2 Sam 12:28; 23:23; 1 Kgs 16:15; 2 Kgs 25:1; etc.

[43] On מַחֲנֵה־דָן, see Judg 13:25; 18:12. On מַחֲנָיִם, see Gen 32:3; Josh 13:26, 30;
21:36; 2 Sam 2:8, 12, 29; 17:24, 27; 19:33; 1 Kgs 2:8; 4:14; 1 Chr 6:65.
Perhaps חנה derives from an Afro-Asiatic root ḥny; cf. Egyptian ḥn for "tent."

[44] For similar usage of נטה, see Gen 26:25; 33:19; 35:21; Judg 4:11.

[45] See also Job 26:7.

examples,[46] אֹהֶל is used in an expression meaning "to go home."[47]

1) *Judg 19:9.* A man offers his Levite son-in-law hospitality by asking him to spend the night. The father-in-law then suggests, "you shall rise early tomorrow for your journey, and you shall go to your tent (לְאֹהָלֶךְ)." It is possible that the Levite has been traveling with a tent, but it is not mentioned elsewhere in the passage. The best explanation is that the phrase "go to your tent" here means "go to your home."

2) *1 Kgs 8:66.* Following the weeklong celebration of the Temple's dedication, the people bless their king and "go to their tents (לְאָהֳלֵיהֶם)."[48] Again the expression apparently means "go to their homes," as tents are not mentioned elsewhere in this context.

3) *1 Sam 4:10.* Israel loses the battle and the Ark to the Philistines. The text states that after the fighting, "they [Israel] fled, each to his tent(s) (לְאֹהָלָיו)."

4) *2 Sam 18:17.* The Israelite supporters of Absalom return home following the usurper's death, "and all Israel fled, each to his tent(s) (לְאֹהָלָיו)."

5) *2 Sam 19:9.* David stops mourning and goes to the city gate. The text repeats that "all Israel had fled, each to his tent(s) (לְאֹהָלָיו)."

6) *2 Kgs 14:12* (= *2 Chr 25:22*). Amaziah, the king of Judah, is defeated by Israel under King Jehoash. After the battle, "they fled each man to his tent(s) (וַיָּנֻסוּ אִישׁ לְאֹהָלָיו)." The subject of נוס must be Judah, since only the defeated would "flee."

7) *2 Sam 20:22.* Joab lays siege to Abel-Beth-Maacah, until the head of Sheba is thrown over the wall. Joab blows the shofar, "and they dispersed (וַיָּפֻצוּ) from about the city, each man to his

---

[46] Two cases in Chronicles mirror passages in Kings; hence, there are actually 14 examples.

[47] There are many examples where the phrase "to go home" utilizes the expected בַּיִת, (see for example: Deut 20:5-8; 1 Sam 15:34; 2 Sam 11:9; 12:15; etc.). However, both RSV and JPS translate the Hebrew phrase "to go to one's tent" in the first nine of the following examples as "to go home"; the last two they translate literally.

[48] In this and the following examples, "tents" is used in the plural whenever the subject is collective.

tent(s) (לְאֹהָלָיו).'' The subject of פוץ is the Judahite army under Joab.

8) *Judg 7:8*. Gideon is facing the Midianites, and of his 32,000 troops he lets 22,000 go. Ten thousand are still too many, so the 300 who lap water from their hands remain, while the rest "h e sent away, every man of Israel, each to his tent(s) (לְאֹהָלָיו).''

9) *1 Sam 13:2*. Saul chooses 3,000 men out of Israel, and the rest of the people "he sent each man to his tent(s) (לְאֹהָלָיו).''

10) *Judg 20:8*. After a Levite's concubine is fatally raped, the enraged Israelite nation tells him "we will not go each to his tent (לְאָהֳלוֹ), and we will not return each to his house (לְבֵיתוֹ).'' Here one might argue that בַּיִת and אֹהֶל are distinguishable: neither the people who inhabit tents nor those who live in houses shall return to their residences. However, in light of the 11 other examples presented here, as well as archaeological data suggesting that Iron Age Israel's urban population vastly outnumbered seminomadic pastoralists, it seems more likely that the two terms are simply used in synonymous parallelism.[49] Consequently, both expressions mean the same thing: "we will not go home.''

11) *2 Sam 20:1*. Shortly after Absalom's revolt is quelled, Sheba blows the shofar and says, "There is no portion for us in David, and no inheritance for us in the son of Jesse. Each man to his tent(s), O Israel! (אִישׁ לְאֹהָלָיו יִשְׂרָאֵל).'' The reasons behind this call to tents, as with the following example, are complicated, and will be treated at length in this book's final chapter. For our purposes here, it should be noted that tents are not mentioned elsewhere in the passage, and Sheba's main goal appears to be the dismissal of the council to their homes.

12) *1 Kgs 12:16* (= *2 Chr 10:16*). Rehoboam ignores the advice of his wiser counselors and acts harshly towards his northern subjects. Israel sends word back to the king, saying,

> "What portion is there for us in David? And no inheritance in the son of Jesse. To your tent(s), O Israel! (לְאֹהָלֶיךָ יִשְׂרָאֵל). Now see to your house, O David (בֵּיתְךָ דָּוִד)!'' And all Israel (each man) went to his tents (לְאֹהָלָיו).

---

[49] For archaeological information on the urban nature of Iron Age Israel, see below, pp. 47-52.

Once again, the exhortation to go to tents suggests that the assembly simply goes home.

Ten of the 12 examples above are directly associated with the military. Despite the natural association between tents and warfare,[50] the 10 examples listed above *follow* battles, and as the majority of troops were house-dwellers, it remains peculiar that they should return *to* their tents. Rather they should be going home *from* their tents.

Curiously, in nine of the 12 passages above, when the group that returns to their "tent(s)" is specified, it is always Israel as opposed to Judah.[51] It is possible that the usage of אֹהֶל in the sense "to go home" is an expression reserved to the northern tribes. More likely perhaps in the majority of cases, however, the name Israel refers to all the tribes, including Judah. Still, not only does 1 Kgs 12:16 use אֹהֶל twice specifically in reference to Northern Israel returning home, but the charge to David to "see to your own house" is followed in verse 24 by Shemaiah's order that the troops from Judah "return each man to his house" (שֻׁבוּ אִישׁ לְבֵיתוֹ). This correspondence of בַּיִת to Judah and אֹהֶל to Israel might be directly related to the Ark's transition from an amphictyonic tent sanctuary to a permanent home in Solomon's Temple.[52]

In addition to the 12 examples listed above, we find "tent" in place of the expected "house" five other times.

1) *Isa 16:5.* Isaiah prophesies vindication following Moabite oppression:

---

[50] See chapter 5, pp. 61-78. Note also that the tent-dwelling Rechabites not only fought with Jehu (9th century B.C.E.), but were still around in Jeremiah's time (7-6th century B.C.E.).

[51] Examples 2, 3-5, and 8-12.

[52] See below, pp. 133-37. Ps 78:60-70, which legitimates Mount Zion as Yahweh's permanent home, illustrates that housing the Ark in anything but a transportable tent must have been quite controversial. Note also the symbolic correspondence between בַּיִת and אֹהֶל in Ps 132:3, where David himself claims to live in a tent, while the Ark lacks a tent. Thus the tent is a claim of impermanency, while the בַּיִת is a dynasty. In fact, Judah is called "house of David" in Isa 7:13, the Tel Dan Inscription, and perhaps the Moabite Stone. Northern Israel lacked such a permanent dynasty. Only once the house of David is gone can it be described as סֻכָּה and אֹהֶל, terms associated with destruction and impermanence. Perhaps the tent David erects for the Ark in 2 Samuel 6 is a necessary transition from the tribal alliance, as the structure remains tent-related but no longer moves from city to city.

And a throne shall be established in mercy,
and he [the prince] shall sit on it in stability
in the tent of David (אֹהֶל דָּוִד),
judging and seeking justice and swift in righteousness.

The tent in the above passage might refer to the royal house of David's descendants (cf. Arabic ʾahl "family") or possibly David's military tent mentioned in 1 Sam 17:54. However, the latter seems unlikely, given references to throne (כִּסֵּא) and justice (מִשְׁפָּט). The expression "tent of David" could perhaps refer to all of Judah, just as "tents of the daughters of Zion" describes Jerusalem.[53] However, in the several cases where אֹהֶל refers to specific regions and their populations, it consistently appears in plural construct (אָהֳלֵי), whereas here "tent of David" is in the singular.[54] More to the point, Judah and Jacob are all names of nations, not people. Another possibility is the tent David erects for the Ark in 2 Sam 6:17, as if David judged in Yahweh's own abode. More likely, given the context, the verses describe an outdoor pavilion, in which David sits to judge the accused.[55] A final possibility is that "tent" may be a poetic description of David's palace. In any case, אֹהֶל is here used ambiguously in a context where one might expect בַּיִת.

2) *Num 19:14-16.* This passage contains a law for when a man dies in a tent. Presumably, the law applies to houses too, but P is attempting to avoid anachronism by placing the statute in its wilderness setting. P's consciousness of the difference between the pastoral lifestyle of the desert and sedentary habitation is clear in Lev 14:34, where the procedure for dealing with a "leprous" house is prefaced by "when you come into the land which I am giving you."

3) *Ps 132:3.* This psalm claims David will lead an austere life until he finds a home for Yahweh. Verse 3 states, "I [David] will not go to the tent of my house (בְּאֹהֶל בֵּיתִי), or go up to the couch of my

---

[53] Lam 2:4.

[54] See "tents of Judah" (Zech 12:7), "tents of Jacob" (Jer 30:18; Mal 2:2), "tents of Edom" (Ps 83:7), and "tents of Kedar" (Ps 120:5).

[55] Note the base of such a pavilion discovered at the gate of Dan (Plate 50b), a common location for deciding legal cases (Avraham Biran, *Biblical Dan* [Jerusalem, 1994]).

bed (עֶרֶשׂ יְצוּעָי)." The expression "tent of my house" is unique, and seems again to be a case where אֹהֶל is equivalent to בַּיִת. Admittedly, Mitchell Dahood claims אֹהֶל is here a canopy or baldachin, comparing Prov 7:17,[56] but אֲהָלִים in Proverbs most likely refers to aloe. It would rather seem that, just as "couch of my bed" (עֶרֶשׂ יְצוּעָי) employs two synonyms in construct, the same holds true for "tent of my house." Psalm 132 describes both David and Yahweh as inhabiting tents, on some level modeling the king on the deity, just as Solomon will build solid palaces for both himself and God.[57] Similarly, in vv. 8 and 14, David's bed parallels Yahweh's מְנוּחָה.[58]

4) *Ps 15:1*. Yahweh is asked "Who shall reside in your tent? Who shall tabernacle on your holy hill?" At the time of composition, likely in the sixth-fifth centuries B.C.E., many centuries had passed with a temple or the remains of a temple on Mount Zion's summit.[59] Apparently, the phrase is metaphoric,[60] and Yahweh's tenting is traced by Cross to El imagery.[61] The issue is complicated by the apparent belief of several ancient authors that the Tabernacle was in the Temple.[62] But in any event "tent" is used where we would expect either "house" or "temple."

5) *Ps 27:4-6*. Three verses refer to the Temple, as בַּיִת, הֵיכָל, סֻכָּה, and אֹהֶל:

> 4 I have asked one thing from Yahweh; that I will seek: That I may dwell in the *house* of Yahweh all the days of my life;
> To behold the beauty of Yahweh, and to inquire in His *temple*.
> 5 For He will hide me in his *booth* in a bad day;

---

[56] Mitchell Dahood, *Psalms III,* AB 17a (Garden City, NY, 1970): p. 243.

[57] As suggested to me by William H. C. Propp.

[58] Alternatively "the tent of my house" may refer to a tent erected on the roof to sleep under; cf. Absalom's tent on the palace roof discussed on p. 119-21, and a picture of a 18th Dynasty Egyptian house from the tomb of Thotnefer in which a bed under a canopy seems to be prepared on the uppermost of three stories (Dan Svarth, *Egyptisk Møbelkunst Fra Faraotiden* [Denmark, 1998]: p. 21).

[59] On the dating of Psalm 15, see Charles A. Briggs, *The Book of Psalms,* ICC (New York, 1906): pp. 112-16.

[60] Compare the reference to the Temple as the "house of the tent" in 1 Chr 9:23, the meaning of which is discussed below, pp. 173-77.

[61] See below, pp. 94-99.

[62] See below, pp. 173-77.

He will hide me in the hidden place of His *tent*, He will set me high
upon a rock.
[6]And now my head will be lifted above my enemies all around me,
and I will sacrifice in His *tent* sacrifices of joy;
I will sing and I will praise Yahweh.


Admittedly, this is poetry and so the language may be more
evocative than precise. Nevertheless, these two verses illustrate the
fluidity of residential terminology.[63]

*Portable Terminology for Permanent Dwellings -* מִשְׁכָּן *for* בַּיִת *and*
הֵיכָל

Similarly, the Temple is often referred to as a מִשְׁכָּן. This is
perhaps not as surprising as the אֹהֶל designation, since מִשְׁכָּן most
frequently means "tabernacle," but also occasionally implies a
more general "dwelling." There are six examples of such an
interchange.
1) *Ps 26:8*. Yahweh's house, the Temple, is said to be the place of
His glory's "tabernacle" (מִשְׁכָּן).
2) *Ps 43:3*. The subject asks God to bring him to "your holy hill
and to your Tabernacle(s) (מִשְׁכְּנוֹתֶיךָ)."[64]
3) *Ps 46:5*. God's city, presumably Jerusalem, is referred to as
"the holy Tabernacle of the Most High."
4) *Ps 74:7*. The psalm laments the destruction of the Temple,
stating: "They set your sanctuary on fire; to the ground they
desecrated the Tabernacle of your name."[65]
5) *Ps 132:5-7*. David vows he will not rest until he finds מִשְׁכָּנוֹת for
Yahweh. As Yahweh previously occupied the Tabernacle, at least
according to the Primary History, the use of מִשְׁכָּן here is
somewhat surprising. Even so, again the terms "temple" or
"house" might be expected, although David does make a tent for
Yahweh.

---

[63] The context is again military, as in verse 3 enemies encamp. The Temple
is called a "tent" also in the Wisdom of Solomon 9:8.

[64] The plural may connote grandeur or complexity. Compare Ugaritic *bhtm* as
an elaborate *bt* "house."

[65] God is also said to שָׁכַן on Mt. Zion in verse 2.

6) *Ezek 37:27*. Ezekiel's visionary Temple is referred to as "My [Yahweh's] Tabernacle (מִשְׁכָּנִי)".

Again, the above six examples of מִשְׁכָּן can be understood as "dwelling." But given the overwhelming use of מִשְׁכָּן to denote God's tent, its association with permanent dwellings is slightly unusual.

## Permanent Domiciliary Terminology for Portable Dwellings

Up to this point we have seen that אֹהֶל and מִשְׁכָּן are often found where one might expect either בַּיִת or הֵיכָל. Conversely, at times בַּיִת and הֵיכָל can be used for a tent structure. For example, we find two anomalous references to houses in Genesis, both in the Patriarchal narratives. Abraham, Isaac, and Jacob are explicitly described as tent-dwellers.[66] Nevertheless, Gen 27:15 states that "Rebekah took the clothes of Esau her elder son, the costly ones that were with her in the *house*, and she clothed her younger son Jacob."[67] Moreover, Gen 33:17 places Jacob in a house at the site of Succoth.[68]

Another possible case of this phenomenon is 2 Kgs 23:7. As part of Josiah's religious reforms, "he destroyed the ritual houses that were in the house of Yahweh, where the women were weaving houses for Asherah." As the root ארג (to weave) is at no other time associated with house construction, it seems that the women are manufacturing fabric.[69] Godfrey R. Driver invokes an Arabic cognate (*batt*) meaning "vestments."[70] However, this definition is not found elsewhere in the Hebrew Bible, and there is little reason to doubt that בָּתִּים simply means homes, which here happens to be tents.

Similarly, the tent David erects in Jerusalem to house the Ark is referred to as בֵּית יהוה in 2 Sam 12:20, as elsewhere the phrase

---

[66] See below, pp. 29-31.

[67] However, בַּיִת may here mean "inside," i.e. in her part of the tent.

[68] It is clear this really is a house, as the verb is בנה, not נטה.

[69] This verse was seen as problematic over 2000 years ago, as the LXX apparently sought to transliterate בַּיִת rather than translate, yielding a corrupt χεττιειν. See Mordechai Cogan and Hayim Tadmor, *II Kings*, AB 11 (Garden City, NY, 1988): p. 286.

[70] Godfrey R. Driver, "Supposed Arabisms in the Old Testament," *JBL* 55 (1936): p. 107.

בֵּית יהוה is applied to the Tabernacle,[71] which is also called
בֵּית־הָאֱלֹהִים in Judg 18:31 and הֵיכָל in 1 Sam 1:9; 3:3.[72] These
passages are frequently seen as anachronistic and examples of the
authors' ineptitude. However, in light of the frequency with which
domiciliary terms interchange, this need not be the case.[73]

Perhaps בַּיִת is not a house per se, but a place where something
is found, a residence or container. Such seems to be the case in
Gen 28:17-19 and 35:14-15, where Jacob pours oil on a standing-
stone (מַצֵּבָה) at Luz, and subsequently changes the name of the
place to Bethel (the house of God). Parallel to this is Philo of
Byblos's euhemeristic account of the battle between Ouranos and
his son Kronos. Ouranos is said to have made βαιτυλια, which
Philo claims are animate rocks (λιθους εμψυχους).[74] A stone is
clearly not a house, but it contains the spirit of God.

The usage of בַּיִת to denote a place where an object can be
found may explain the anomalous case of 1 Chr 9:23, where
house is used in construct with tent: "And they [the Levitical
gatekeepers] and their sons (were) over the gates of the house of
Yahweh to the house of the tent (לְבֵית הָאֹהֶל) by watches." Thus
the phrase בֵּית הָאֹהֶל may simply mean the building where the tent
is found, namely: the Temple.[75]

*Sociohistorical Reasons for Fluidity in Terminology*

The interchange of terms discussed above is more than a curiosity
of metaphorical language. It reflects an important sociohistorical
process: the sedentarization of nomads. As pastoralists abandon
transportable domiciles and settle in cities, domiciliary terms for
portable and permanent architecture grow increasingly synon-

---

[71] Josh 6:24; Judg 15:17, 24; 19:18.

[72] Note the shrine at Shiloh is called "the tent of the appointed time" in 1
Sam 2:22; on the nature of Shiloh's structure, see below, pp. 203-09. Josephus,
*Antiquities*, 3.6.1, also calls the Tabernacle a temple (ναος).

[73] See further below, pp. 133-37.

[74] Philo of Byblos 810:28. For a commentary see Albert Baumgarten, *The
Phoenician History of Philo of Byblos* (Leiden, 1981): p. 202.

[75] It could also mean the house that is *symbolically* a tent. Another explanation might be that the author of Chronicles is attempting to avoid anachronism
by using אֹהֶל for David's appointment of the gatekeepers prior to Solomon's
construction of the Temple. Nevertheless, other passages in Chronicles suggest
that this author envisions the Tabernacle as residing within the Temple; see
below, pp. 173-77.

ymous.[76] Thus in Arabic not only are there many words for tents and their accessories, but also domiciliary terminology can be used interchangeably. Arabic *bayt ša'r* ( بيت شعر ) "*house* of hair" refers to tents.[77] Less common, but still attested, is the employment of *bayt* alone for a tent.[78]

It is widely assumed that the Semites in general, and Northwest Semites in particular, had nomadic antecedents.[79] At Ugarit, El's abode receives the tent-related designations *ahl* "tent," *mškn* "tabernacle," *dd* "domed-tent," and *qrš* "tent-frame," as well as the non-tent-related *mṭb* "dwelling," *mẓll* "shelter," *bt* "house," and *hkl* "temple."[80]

Cuneiform tablets from Mari also refer to a tent shrine.[81] Furthermore, Akkadian *bītu* "house" can refer to an encampment of nomads, and we have already seen that the term for city, *ālu*, etymologically means "tent."[82]

The interchange of portable and permanent domiciliary terminology is paralleled outside of the Semitic world. For example, in the original Tatar and Mongol languages, "yurt" (*IOPT*) is the word for "house," since the yurt was the primary

---

[76] Many Bedouin began settling in urban areas as early as the mid-19th century as recorded by Claude R. Conder, *Tent Work in Palestine* (London, 1878): 2.271.

[77] Edward W. Lane, *Arabic-English Lexicon* I, pp. 280.

[78] *Ibid.* Note also that Arabic *bayt* can refer to portable Islamic tent-shrines, and the sacred symbols inside (Herbert G. May, "The Ark-A Miniature Temple," *AJSL* 52 [1936]: p. 229). The terms for these tent shrines (*qubba, maḥmal, 'utfah*) also blend in usage (Julian Morgenstern, "The Ark, the Ephod, and the 'Tent of Meeting,'" *HUCA* 17 [1942]: pp. 191-92).

[79] See below, pp. 94-99; 116-18.

[80] El's tent is designated *ahl* in *CAT* 1.15.III.18-19, and perhaps *CAT* 1.19.IV.50-60; *mškn* in 1.15.III.17-19; *dd* and *qrš* in 1.1.III.23-24; 1.4.IV.23-24; 1.6.I.34-36; *mṭb* and *mẓll* in 1.4.I.13-19; IV.52-57; *bt* in 1.17.I.32-33; II.4-5, 21-22; 1.114.12 (although Hebrew צל has tent-related connotations, discussed above p. 19); and *hkl* in 1.21.8 and perhaps 1.3.V.21. Other Ugaritic words, such as *ḫmt*, designate tents. See p. 94 n. 24, p. 99 n. 46.

[81] See pp. 116-18.

[82] *CAD* 2: pp. 282-96. Perhaps related to this is the fact that several Amorite rulers boast of a nomadic heritage of tent-dwelling, including Hammurapi of Babylon and the 17 tent-dwelling ancestors of the Assyrians. See Donald J. Wiseman, "They Lived in Tents," *Biblical and Near Eastern Studies*, Essays in Honor of W. S. Lasor (Grand Rapids, 1978): pp. 195-200, and Jean-Robert Kupper, *Les nomades en Mésopotamie au temps des rois de Mari* (Paris, 1957): pp. XIV ff.

residential shelter while the Tatars maintained a nomadic lifestyle.[83] "Yurt" further designated a specific territory allocated to the members of the ruling family.[84] However, "yurt" is defined more narrowly by sedentary peoples, translating "tent" or "camp."[85] After many Tatars sedentarized in the 13th century, the word "yurt" and the local term for house blended in usage in the Tatar language.[86]

*A Few Further Remarks on the Fluidity in Terms for Dwellings*

Though "house" and "tent" may seem dichotomous, possibly the ambiguity is greater for our 21st century post-Enlightenment minds than it was for the Israelites. Paradoxical domiciliary imagery also appears in Ps 104:2b-3a, which describes Yahweh as "stretching out (נוֹטֶה) the heavens like a curtain (יְרִיעָה); laying beams (הַמְקָרֶה) in the waters of his upper rooms." This Psalm mentions neither אֹהֶל nor בַּיִת explicitly, but the terms נטה and יריעה are otherwise reserved for tent-related structures, while the verb קרה is consistently used in house construction.[87] Apparently, the lines that separate tent and house dwelling are often blurred.

Even today many Near Eastern house-dwelling urbanites erect tents adjoining or on the roofs of their houses and flats, especially as a means to cope with the heat of summer.[88] Also, many houses in the Near East incorporate tent-fabric into their roofs, as seen in two homes (Plates 1b, 2a) and one public building (Plate 2b) in northern Syria. So too are tents reinforced with housing material (Plate 3a), in contrast to the more traditional goat-hair tent (Plate

---

[83] See Vladimir N. Basilov and O. Naumova, "Yurts, Rugs, and Felts" in *Nomads of Eurasia* (Seattle, 1989): p. 101.

[84] For example, Genghis Khan divided the territory of his empire into four yurts for each of his legitimate sons, as told to me by Anatoly M. Khazanov.

[85] I.e., in Russian and several Turkic languages. To Russian and Turkish urbanites, "yurt" means a round tent, and not a permanent house.

[86] See Vladimir N. Basilov and O. Naumova, "Yurts, Rugs, and Felts," p. 101. See also Anatoly M. Khazanov, *Nomads and the Outside World* (Cambridge, 1984): pp. 233-63.

[87] For the association of נטה with tents, see Gen 12:8; 26:25; 33:19; Exod 33:7; Judg 4:11; Isa 54:2-3; Jer 43:10. For the use of קרה in house construction, see 2 Chr 34:11.

[88] As witnessed by the author in Tyre, Damascus, and Amman. Note that 19th century Bedouin inhabit tents in the winter and reed huts in the summer (Claude R. Conder, *Tent Work in Palestine*, 2.276).

3b). However, the extent to which this was practiced in antiquity remains unknown.

The following two chapters explore the domestic use of tents by ancient Israel and her neighbors. Chapter three examines the issue by focusing on historical sources, while chapter 4 investigates the archaeology of pastoral nomadic societies in which tents provide the dominant form of habitation. All of these next chapters will strengthen the case for ancient Israel's tent-dwelling heritage.

# TENT HOMES: THE TEXTUAL CASE FOR ANCIENT ISRAEL'S TENT-DWELLING HERITAGE

> The biblical authors claim a non-sedentary tent-dwelling heritage. This is manifest in genealogies, narratives about the patriarchs and matriarchs and Israel's desert wanderings, as well as perceived relations with their nomadic contemporaries. Their claim is supported by the accumulation of biblical evidence and historical references to Late Bronze tent-dwelling pastoralists. While ancient Israel's background was surely mixed, there is little reason to doubt that many, if not most, of their ancestors lived in tents as seminomads, as will be shown here and in the following chapter, which addresses this issue from the perspective of archaeology.

## Ancient Israel's Tent-Dwelling Heritage: The Evidence from Genesis

According to Gen 9:21, humans universally descend from a tent-inhabiting ancestor, as Noah lives in a tent after the flood. However, the situation rapidly diversifies in the next generation. Unlike his brothers Ham and Japheth, Israel's ancestor Shem alone is said to possess tents (Gen 9:27). So begins the Hebrew Bible's claim that tents were the principal habitation for ancient Israel prior to the settlement of Canaan.

Tents are very prominent in the patriarchal period. Abraham inhabits a tent throughout his journeys (Gen 12:8; 13:3, 18; 18:1-2), with Sarah's tent pitched nearby (Gen 18:6, 9, 10; 24:67). Tents similarly house Lot (Gen 13:5, 12), Isaac (Gen 26:25), and Jacob (Gen 25:27; 31:25, 33; 33:18-19; 35:21). The Hebrew Bible's conception of the patriarchal encampment is elaborated in Gen 31:33, where separate tents are allotted to Jacob, Rachel, and Leah, while a single tent is apparently shared by the two maidservants Bilhah and Zilpah.

A few more details concerning tents can be gleaned from the narratives of Genesis. Tents were pitched in a variety of terrains and environs, ranging from isolated mountains (12:8; 31:25) to urban outskirts (33:18). The tent-door twice proves an auspicious setting: once as a place for Abraham to seek refuge from the day's heat (18:1) and once as a location for Sarah's auspicious eavesdropping (18:10). Apparently baking wares and ingredients are stored in Sarah's tent (18:6), and after her death, Sarah's tent passes on to the newlyweds Isaac and Rebekah (24:67).

This conceived Israelite tent-dwelling heritage is further expressed in genealogies. The Israelites generally claim kindred relations to non-sedentary tent inhabitants, while distancing themselves from house-dwelling urbanites. Groups that are the epitomy of tent-dwelling nomads in the Hebrew Bible, such as the Ishmaelites, Midianites, and Edomites, are all closely related to Israel, being either uncles (Ishmael and Midian) or a fraternal twin (Edom) (Figure 1).[1]

---

[1] Ishmael's birth is recorded in Gen 16:15; Midian's in Gen 25:2; Edom's and Israel's (Esau and Jacob) in Gen 25:25-26. Ishmael's affinity for tents is mentioned in Gen 25:16 and Ps 83:7. Midian's use of tents is established in Num 31:10; Judg 7:1, 8, 13; Hab 3:7. Midian's relation with Israel is made more intimate through the marriage of Moses to Zipporah, the daughter of the Midianite priest (Exod 2:21). The Bible again recalls the relationship to Edom in Deut 23:8, "You shall not abhor an Edomite, for he is your brother." Edomite tent usage is mentioned in Ps 83:6, and also the records of Rameses III, who claims to have pillaged the tents (*ʾhr*) of Seʿir (*ANET*, p. 262). For further discussion of Edom in Egyptian sources, see Kenneth A. Kitchen, "The Egyptian Evidence on Ancient Jordan," *Early Edom and Moab* (Sheffield, 1992): pp. 21-34. Further evidence for Israel's affiliation with tent-dwelling peoples can be seen from the Hivites, a group closely related if not synonymous with Edom. The very name "Hivite" (*hiwwî*) seems to mean "tent-dweller" (see above, p. 14), and a Hivite woman named Oholibamah, "my tent is a high place," marries Esau, the ancestor of Edom. See Cyris H. Moon, *A Political History of Edom*, Emory Dissertation (1971): pp. 27-28. Archaeological evidence of these non-Israelite tent-dwellers is examined below, chapter 4, pp. 47-59.

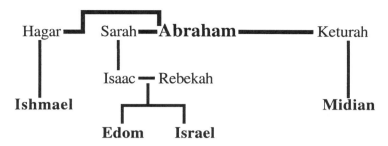

Figure 1 – Conceived Genealogies of Israel and Her Neighbors

Moreover, like the Israelites, the tent-dwelling Ishmaelites, Midianites, and Edomites appear to be tribally organized.[2] Conversely, non-tribal groups purported to be house-dwellers, such as the Egyptians, Canaanites, and Philistines, all descend from Ham according to Genesis 10.[3] These urban-based cultures, according to the authors of the biblical genealogies, could not be less related to ancient Israel, because the only common ancestor is Noah.

---

[2] Gen 25:16 seems to indicate that like Israel, Ishmael contained 12 tribes. Midian's tribal organization is suggested in Num 25:15. Edom's genealogy in Genesis 36 has also been argued to consist of 12 tribes, although this is less certain. See Cyris H. Moon, *A Political History of Edom*, pp. 16-20. Israel's tribal organization can be seen as early as the second half of the 12th century B.C.E. in the Song of Deborah (Judges 5). See David N. Freedman, "Early Israelite Poetry and Historical Reconstructions," *Symposia for ASOR's 75th Anniversary* (Cambridge, MA, 1979): p. 88; Baruch Halpern, *The Emergence of Israel in Canaan* (Chico, 1983): pp. 146-49, and Lawrence E. Stager, "Archaeology, Ecology, and Social History: Background Themes to the Song of Deborah," *VTSup* 49 (1987): pp. 221-34; "The Song of Deborah," *BAR* 15 (1989): 50-64.

[3] For the urbanism in Egypt, Canaan, and Philistia, see Mason Hammond, *The City in the Ancient World* (Cambridge, 1972): pp. 70-91. The emphasis on cities from ancient Egypt can further be seen from the Egyptians' contempt for nomads (see p. 36 n. 18), and such passages as Gen 41:48, Ezek 29:12. Canaanite urbanism is highlighted in Josh 11:10. The importance of cities for Philistia is shown by their city-state government (Josh 13:3; 15:46). However, the dichotomy between tent- and house-dwelling is blurred in Ps 78:51, which calls Egypt "the tents of Ham"—here, "tents" may connote "clans" (see above, p. 9).

*Ancient Israel's Tent-Dwelling Heritage: The Period of Wanderings*

Tent homes, so prevalent in the patriarchal period, reappear in the Israelite historical narrative following the Exodus. After an interval of house-dwelling servitude, Israel returns to the tent throughout the generation of wanderings until the settlement in Canaan. The first thing Balaam notices while surveying the Israelites from atop a Moabite hill is "How goodly are your tents, O Jacob, your tabernacles, O Israel" (Num 24:5). Numerous other passages record the encampments of the Israelites in the wilderness (e.g. Exod 16:7, 16; 18:7; 33:8; Lev 14:8; Num 11:10; 16:26-27; 19:14; 24:2; Deut 1:27; 5:30; 11:6; 16:7; Josh 3:14; 7:21; 22:4, 6-8; Ps 78:55).[4] The authors of the Hebrew Bible emphatically believed that ancient Israel descended from a tent-dwelling, non-sedentary people.[5]

The ancient Israelite encampments recorded in Numbers are arranged by genealogical proximity, a practice closely mirroring the layout of contemporary nomadic camps in the Levant.[6] This is apparent in JE, which states that "Israel encamped according to his tribes" (Num 24:2). It is even more clearly developed in P: not only do the Israelites encamp by tribe, but there is a direct relationship between the degree of kinship and camp proximity. That is to say, the more closely related the tribes, the more likely they are to encamp next to one another. Numbers 2 describes the maternal affiliation and camp layout as follows:

---

[4] Other passages record a non-sedentary past from which tent-dwelling might be inferred; e.g., Deut 26:5 recollects "My father was a wandering Aramaean." Similarly Ps 105:12-13 and 1 Chr 16:19-20 remember the past as follows: "When they were few in number, insignificant, and strangers in it, wandering from nation to nation, from one kingdom to another people . . . ."

[5] Contrast William G. Dever's claim that Israel knew they descended from urban Canaanite house-dwellers, examined below, pp. 50-51.

[6] William Lancaster, *The Rwala Bedouin Today* (Prospect Heights, IL, 1997): pp. 10-11.

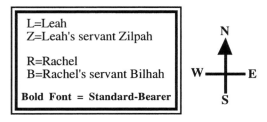

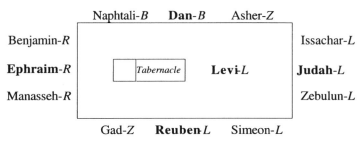

Figure 2 – Tribal Genealogy (Genesis 29-30; 35) and Encampment (Numbers 2)

Benjamin and Joseph's two sons, Ephraim and Manasseh, all claim descent from Rachel and are camped next to one another on the west side. A similar arrangement is found on the east side, where all three tribes are children of Leah. The picture is more complicated with the remaining two sides. On the north side, Dan camps in the center, but the position of Asher and Naphtali is problematic, as the text enigmatically places them with Asher "next to him [Dan]" and "then" Naphtali (Num 2:27-29). Consequently, the position of Asher and Naphtali could be reversed in the model above.[7] The same holds true for the south side, with Reuben's position fixed but those of Simeon and Gad flexible (Num 2:12-14). The encampment as depicted above places Simeon and Reuben next to their full brothers on the east, and the children of Bilhah on the north in close proximity to the tribes descending from Bilhah's mistress Rachel. The picture is admittedly problematic for Zilpah's children; in any possible reconstruction, they are separated, with one on the north (Asher), and one on the south (Gad). Nonetheless, they may be placed

---

[7] As in Jacob Milgrom's reconstruction, although the 11 remaining tribes correspond to our model exactly (*Numbers*, JPS Torah Commentary [Philadelphia, 1989]: pp. 340-41.

near the offspring of Leah, Zilpah's mistress. Much of this displacement, with Gad replacing Levi, stems from the adjustment of the geneology to create 13 tribes with Levi in the center of camp. Despite the uncertain placement of the tribes camped north and south and the separation of Zilpah's descendants, there generally exists a greater tendency to camp near one's closest relatives.

*Yahweh's Tent-Dwelling Heritage*

Equally vital to understanding the Bible's tent tradition is Yahweh's famous tent home, the Tabernacle.[8] Just as the urban Israelites claimed to have once dwelt in tents, so they believed their god originally inhabited a Tabernacle. In fact, on Sinai, Yahweh reveals a celestial prototype (תַּבְנִית) to Moses when ordering the construction of the Tabernacle (Exod 25:9).[9] That is to say, Yahweh owns and lives in two tents: one perched in heaven above Sinai, and one which moves among His terrestrial subjects.[10] According to the Bible, Yahweh inhabits the Tabernacle for nearly three centuries; it serves as the focal point of the Israelite cult until the completion of Solomon's temple.[11] Nathan's oracle in 2 Sam 7:5-6 illuminates the difficult transition:

> Thus says Yahweh: "You will build for me a house for my dwelling? For I have not dwelt in a house since the day I brought up the children of Israel from Egypt, and until this day, but I have been moving about in a tent and in a Tabernacle."

Although one generation later He opts to settle permanently, here Yahweh chooses a tent over a temple.[12]

---

[8] For an analysis of the Tabernacle's form and historicity, see below, chapter 8, pp. 129-85.

[9] Celestial prototypes are standard in ancient Near Eastern literature about temples, as displayed in Gudea (*ANET* 268-69).

[10] Admittedly, some understand תַּבְנִית as denoting a mere blueprint. However, the root בנה indicates it is something built, i.e. a three-dimensional measured model. Also, various passages describe the heavens as a celestial tent, e.g. Isa 40:22; Pss 19:4; 104:2.

[11] On the debate concerning the nature of the shrine at Shiloh, variably called a "tent," "house," "tabernacle," and "temple," see below, pp. 133-37.

[12] The struggle at Ugarit between the upstart, house-dwelling Baal and the

*Positively Connoted Tents and Their Inhabitants in the Hebrew Bible*

The majority of literature from the ancient Near East relegates tents and their inhabitants to the realm of the ignorant and barbaric. That is to say, the normative connotation for both tents and nomads is negative. This is displayed early in the historical corpus; the Sumerian *Marriage of Martu* describes an Amorite as:

> A person who digs for truffles in the highlands, who knows not how to pay homage. He eats uncooked meat, who as long as he lives has no house, and when he dies, receives no burial.[13]

The failure to live in permanent dwellings is one of the main peculiarities for which the Amorites are castigated.[14] Also, the Sumerian *Lament for the Destruction of Ur*, compares destroyed houses to "tents" and "booths" in order to emphasize their impermanence.[15] A similar disdain for tents and nomads abounds in the later literature of Assyria. We find a change only with the rise to prominence of Amorite dynasties in both Babylonia and Assyria. Now both Hammurapi and Shamshi Adad I boast of their Amorite ancestors as *ašibūt kultari*, "tent-dwellers."[16] Non-sedentary people are typically perceived in Assyrian annals as bandits posing continuous threats to trade and communication.[17]

---

patriarchal, tent-dwelling El is another illustration of the problems in transference from tent to house (see pp. 94-99). Just as Yahweh inherits epithets and attributes of both El and Baal, he appears to imitate first El and then Baal in respect of domicile. The tent is maintained as a reminder of Yahweh's and his people's seminomadic, egalitarian heritage, while the palatial house represents sedentarization and monarchy. Richard E. Friedman's theory, in which the Tabernacle was incorporated into the Temple's cult, would further highlight the difficulty in the total abandonment of a tent-dwelling lifestyle (see pp. 173-77).

[13] Translation from Jerrold S. Cooper, *The Curse of Agade* (Baltimore, 1983): pp. 30-33. See also Samuel N. Kramer, *Sumerian Mythology* (Philadelphia, 1972): pp. 99-101.

[14] Note also the Sumerian contempt for the seminomadic Gutians, in Jerrold S. Cooper, *The Curse of Agade*, pp. 30-33.

[15] *ANET*, p. 457.

[16] The tent-dwelling origins of Assyria's first 17 kings, and the similar heritage of the First Dynasty of Babylon, are described in Jacob J. Finkelstein, "The Genealogy of the Hammurapi Dynasty," *JCS* 20 (1966): p. 95-118.

[17] See J. Nicholas Postgate, "Nomads and Sedentaries in the Middle Assyrian Sources," *Nomads and Sedentary Peoples* (Mexico, 1981): pp. 47-56; Israel

Similar views come from Egypt as well, where tents are mostly reserved for those perceived to be uncultured and ignorant.[18]

We expect such views from the literature of the Mesopotamian and Egyptian literate, urban elite. It is all the more surprising that tents and pastoral nomadism are for the most part positively connoted in the Hebrew Bible, even though it, too, must have been composed by and for cultured urbanites. Already in Genesis 4, the fruits of Abel's pastoral efforts are preferred to those of his farming brother.[19] Nothing negative stems from the tent-dwelling heritage associated with the patriarchs and the period of wanderings; rather, there is a fondness in these recollections, and nomadism is even celebrated.[20] For example, the annual construction of booths during Sukkot pays homage to Israelite ancestors who wandered the wilderness in impermanent structures (Plate 1a).[21] This temporary return to a tent heritage is in some ways paralleled by the Muslim Haj, when tent-cities are set up on the plain of Arafat (Plate 4a)[22], and to a lesser extent, tent mosques which shade worshippers (Plate 4b).

---

Eph'al, *The Ancient Arabs* (Leiden, 1982): pp. 150-53, 174-75; Donald J. Wiseman, "They Lived in Tents," pp. 195-200.

[18] Thus, the Amarna Letters complain about tent-dwelling *ḫapiru* and *Shasu* raiders; see *ANET,* pp. 487-90; Raphael Giveon, *Les bédouins Shosou des documents égyptiens*, DMOA 22 (Leiden, 1971): documents 11 and 36. Perhaps related is the Egyptian disdain for the Hyksos, likely to be of Amorite tent-dwelling stock (Aharon Kempinski, "Some Observations on the Hyksos [XVth] Dynasty and its Canaanite Origins," *Pharaonic Egypt, the Bible and Christianity* [Jerusalem, 1985]: pp. 129-38; William A. Ward, "Some Personal Names of the Hyksos Period Rulers and Notes on the Epigraphy of Their Scarabs," *UF* 8 [1975]: pp. 353-65).

[19] Note that in Gen 4:20, Cain's descendant Jabal is said to be the father of tent-dwellers. Apparently, the line of Jabal replaces the extinguished Abel.

[20] Israel's "nomadic ideal" was first promulgated by Karl Budde, "The Nomadic Ideal in the Old Testament," *The New World*, 4 (1895): pp. 726-45. See also John W. Flight, "The Nomadic Ideal in the OT," *JBL* 42 (1923): pp. 158-226; Paul A. Riemann, *Desert and Return to Desert in the Pre-Exilic Prophets*, Harvard Dissertation (1964). Contrast Shemaryahu Talmon, who dismisses the desert ideal in "The 'Desert Motif' in the Bible and in Qumran Literature," *Biblical Motifs*, ed. Alexander Altmann (Cambridge, MA, 1966): pp. 31-63, and William G. Dever, "Israelite Origins and the 'Nomadic Ideal': Can Archaeology Separate Fact from Fiction*?"*, *Mediterranean Peoples in Transition* (Jerusalem, 1998): pp. 220-37.

[21] See above, pp. 9-11.

[22] The tents erected at Korazim to house the Christian pilgrims during Pope John Paul II's visit to Israel in March of 2000 also reflect a return to tents.

Another aspect of the Hebrew Bible's affinity for tents and their inhabitants is the biblical authors' admiration for those who forwent the urban house-based lifestyle and remained in tents. One example is the Kenite people, most clearly seen in Judges 4 and 5. The defeated Canaanite general Sisera flees the Israelite forces, seeking refuge at the tent of Jael, the wife of Heber the Kenite. The story is full of irony. Sisera, representative of the Canaanite city-states, uses Jael's tent to hide, an action further emphasized when Jael covers him with a blanket (Judg 4:18-19). Although Sisera envisions the tent as his salvation, it proves to be his undoing. The tent itself is even the murder weapon, as Jael hammers a tent-peg into Sisera's head (Judg 4:22). Unlike other literatures of the ancient Near East dealing with nomads, Judges 4-5 positively portrays the Kenites and their tents.

An even clearer case in which tents and their associated way of life are fondly portrayed concerns the Rechabites in Jeremiah 35. Jeremiah tells how the Rechabite ancestor, Jonadab ben Rechab, had essentially commanded that his descendants remain nomadic, specifically forbidding houses, the consumption of wine, and farming (Jer 35:7).[23] Jeremiah's point seems to be admiration for the Rechabites' steadfastness in the face of adversity, but along the way, their tents and tent-dwelling are again positively featured.

Tents also bear positive connotations in Prov 14:11: "The house of the wicked will be destroyed, and the tent of the righteous will flourish." Similarly, Cant 1:5 uses tents as a metaphor for beauty, as does Balaam's oracle in Num 24:5. Nevertheless, the Hebrew Bible's use of tents is not always positive. Two antagonists in Job twice use negatively-connoted tents in explaining their theodicy.[24] Bildad the Shuhite in Job 8:22 predicts the destruction of the "tent of the wicked," and Eliphaz the Temanite in 22:23 speaks of removing iniquity far from one's tent (though this could be seen as positive).[25] Ps

---

However, this was a practical matter, while the use of tents at Arafat seems highly symbolic.

[23] This portrayal of the Rechabites bears many similarities to the description of the Nabataeans by Diodorus of Sicily 19:94. See David F. Graf, "The Origin of the Nabataeans," *Aram* 2:1 (1990): p. 52.

[24] Yet, the book of Job as a whole evinces a romanticization of tent-dwelling pastoral nomadism.

[25] Also see Job 11:14; 12:16; 15:34; 18:15.

84:10 also contrasts the "house of my God" with the "tents of wickedness." Other negative connotations naturally occur when tents are associated with Israel's enemies.[26] Even so, it remains striking that ancient Israel's portrayal of tent-homes, be they of the patriarchs, those escaped from Egyptian bondage, contemporary neighbors, or even the home of Yahweh, is most often positive, a rare phenomenon in the ancient Near East.

*Arabian Tents of the Past Remembered Fondly: A Case-Study from Modern Jordan*

A tent-dwelling nomadic heritage is likewise often vaunted within the Arab world.[27] Islam's holiest shrine, the Ka'ba, is believed originally to have been a tent.[28] Similar to the biblical holiday Sukkot, several Islamic celebrations, including *Id 'al-'Adḥā* (the feast of sacrifice), celebrate a tent-dwelling past.[29] However, consistent with the normal ancient Near Eastern contempt for tent dwellings, various Islamic governments have ridiculed and disapproved of tents and their inhabitants. Such is the situation in many documents from the Ottoman period, which resemble those from ancient Egypt and Mesopotamia, equating tent-dwellers with uncivilized barbarians unaware of the superiority of urban living.[30] Thus the Bible's positive inclination towards tents and their inhabitants is all the more remarkable.

Despite the negative portrayal of tents by various Islamic powers, there exists nostalgia for tents among former nomads who have recently become sedentarized. The fond recollection of a tent-dwelling past so prominent in the Hebrew Bible is also exhibited in a field-study the author conducted in the south-

---

[26] For the use of tents in the armies of ancient Israel and her neighbors, see p. 77.

[27] Illuminating ancient Israel by examining the 19th and 20th century Arab world is a practice which has been abused (see p. 91 n. 10 below). Nevertheless, there remains merit in reserved comparison. For example, both ancient Israelite and Arab societies are patrilineal, and at least some continuation in culture can be seen in the retention of place names in Palestine and the Near East in general.

[28] See below, pp. 93-94.

[29] Gustave E. von Grunebaum, *Muhammadan Festivals* (New York, 1988): pp. 34 ff. Note also the employment of Bedouin tents in Islamic urban celebrations, most notably weddings.

[30] See Norman N. Lewis, *Nomads and Settlers in Syria and Jordan*, 1800-1980 (Cambridge, 1987): pp. 24-73.

Jordanian village of Qreiqara. The population of Qreiqara is estimated at 300 people, nearly all Bedouin, although from four separate tribes: the ʿAzazmah, ʿAmarin, Ṣayadin, and Feinan Rashayid.[31] Between February and August of 1999, over 30 of the village's elder male population were interviewed regarding their former pastoral lifestyle and memories of tents. Not only were tents and their corresponding way of life fondly recalled by all of the subjects, but many continued to occupy tents within the village, foregoing houses. All of the subjects expressed the superiority of tents over houses, although their reasons varied. Some cited the freedom inherent to tents, others their low cost in contrast with houses. The pleasant sound of the wind amplified by the tent panels was mentioned by many.

One final point of relevance reoccurred through these interviews: the line between the nomadic and sedentary is most often blurred. Not only were the majority of the subjects simultaneously living in both houses and tents, their families' subsistence included a mixture of farming and pastoralism. The knowledge of farming possessed by the occupants of the Iron IA highland settlements is often cited to discredit a pastoral heritage for ancient Israel.[32] Yet, in addition to pastoralism, these modern Jordanian tent-dwellers know a great deal about farming. They are basically tent-dwellers in the initial stages of sedentarization. Even the Rwala, considered the most nomadic of the Bedouin, incorporate houses and tents in many villages.[33] The houses are

---

[31] On the accuracy and imagination of Bedouin ethnicity, see Andrew J. Shryock, "Popular Genealogical Nationalism: History Writing and Identity among the Balqa Tribes of Jordan," *Comparative Studies in Society and History* 37 (April, 1995): pp. 325-57; Dale F. Eickelman, "Being Bedouin: Nomads and Tribes in the Arab Social Imagination," *Changing Nomads in a Changing World* (Brighton, 1998): pp. 38-49.

[32] See William G. Dever, "Cultural Continuity, Ethnicity in the Archaeological Record, and the Question of Israelite Origins," *Eretz-Israel* 24 (1993): p. 26*. Note also the agricultural components of the patriarchal narratives (including the possession of wheat, grain, grapes, lentils, and almonds) pointed out by Norman K. Gottwald, *Tribes of Yahweh* (New York, 1979): p. 452.

[33] See Roger L. Cribb, "Mobile Villagers: The Structure and Organization of Nomadic Pastoral Campsites in the Near East," *Ethnoararchaeological Approaches to Mobile Campsites* (Ann Arbor, 1991): p. 386.

not for the permanently settled; however, they are reserved for families briefly passing through.[34]

### Persian Tent-Heritages Maintained

The reluctance to part with a tent heritage can also be seen in 15th and 16th century Persia. The Timurids and Safavids adhered to their nomadic tent-dwelling past, as the ruler set up a tent-camp adjoining his stone-built palace in the capital.[35] Also, the architecture of these palaces often was modeled on the form of a royal pavilion.[36] Thus, the Timurids and Safavids celebrated and maintained their tent-dwelling past rather than abandoning it.

### Tent-Dwellers of the Bronze Age: The Amurru, Habiru, Shasu, and Israelites

The topography and climate of the non-coastal Levant are conducive to pastoralism. From history's onset, there have constantly been seminomadic tent-dwellers roaming about the region.[37] In contrast to the Mediterranean Sea area, where farming and fishing provide the main sustenance, the Sahara-Arab desert zone provides an environmental framework in which

---

[34] Despite the Rwala's possession of houses, they remained nomadic. E.g., out of 500 Rwala families at the fairly permanent encampment of Ar-Risha in 1972, only eight remained in 1979. William Lancaster, *The Rwala Bedouin Today*, 2nd edition (Prospect Heights, IL, 1997): p. 10.

[35] Monika Gonke, "The Persian Court Between Palace and Tent," *Timurid Art and Culture*, eds. Lisa Golombek and Maria Subtelny (New York, 1992): pp. 18-22.

[36] Bernard O'Kane, "From Tents to Pavilions: Royal Mobility and Persian Palace Design," *Ars Orientalis* 23 (1993): pp. 249-68.

[37] It is unknown when tents first began to be used, but evidence suggests their presence in the Neolithic period. The east Jordanian Azraq oasis revealed rows of stones most likely used to support the walls of tents, as told to me by Phil Wilke and Leslie Quintero. Several tent-camps dating from the Neolithic to EB periods exist in the Negev and Sinai (Uzi Avner, "Settlement, Agriculture and Paleoclimate in 'Uvda Valley, Southern Negev Desert, 6th-3rd Millennia BC," *Water, Environment, and Society in Times of Climatic Change*, A. S. Issar and N. Brown, eds. [Netherlands, 1998]: pp. 147-202, and Uzi Avner, Israel Carmi, and Dror Segal, "Neolithic to Bronze Age Settlement of the Negev and Sinai in Light of Radiocarbon Dating," *Late Quaternary Chronology and Paleoclimates of the Eastern Mediterranean*, Ofer Bar-Yosef and Renee S. Kra, eds. [Cambridge, MA, 1994]: pp. 265-300).

migration increases the chances of survival.[38] The population inhabiting tents at any given time is difficult to ascertain; the number is also dynamic, changing dramatically across different time periods. Such is the case with the end of the predominantly urban Early Bronze III period and the beginning of the Early Bronze IV/Middle Bronze I, when the amount of seminomadic activity greatly increased.[39] One thousand years later, the Late Bronze II period saw vast political upheaval and various mass migrations, as seminomadic tent-dwelling peoples expanded while urban-centers again declined. The emergence of the formerly-nomadic Aramaeans, Edomites, and Israelites is to be associated with these changes.[40] Shortly after the destruction of Jerusalem in 587 B.C.E., as Mesopotamian strength reached its peak, the tent-dwelling Nabataeans came to power on the fringes of the Babylonian/Persian empire, their power climaxing during the Roman era. So too did the onset of Islam in Arabia represent a

---

[38] Anatoly M. Khazanov, *Nomads and the Outside World* (Madison, 1994): pp. 85-118.

[39] The period after the abrupt end of EB III cities in Palestine c. 2300 B.C.E. was initially termed MB I. As sites demonstrating cultural continuity between MB I and EB III began to emerge (most notably Bab edh-Dhra), however, the EB IV nomenclature has gained in popularity. On the seminomadic nature of the EB IV period, see Amihai Mazar, *Archaeology of the Land of the Bible* (New York, 1990): pp. 151-73. Debates continue as to whether the EB III was ended violently by invading Amorites, or by an Egyptian campaign under Pepi II, or whether nomadic groups simply filled an existing vacuum, though it is likely to be a combination of factors rather than a single-cause.

[40] Previously, the Edomites were believed to be attested in the archaeological record beginning in the Iron II period (Crystal M. Bennett, "Excavations at Buseirah, Southern Jordan, 1974," *Levant* 7 [1975]: p. 5; "Biblical Traditions and Archaeological Results," *The Archaeology of Jordan and Other Studies* [Berrien Springs, 1986]: pp. 77, 80). Now, increasing evidence attests that there were Edomites in the Iron I period, perhaps with items of material culture paralleling ancient Israel, such as collar-rim jars. For references, see Israel Finkelstein, *Living on the Fringe* (Sheffield, 1995), pp. 127-37. For a synthesis of Edom in the Iron I period, see Piotr Bienkowski, "Iron Age Settlement in Edom: A Revised Framework," *The World of the Aramaeans* (Sheffield: in press). On some of the earliest Iron Age remains of Edomite culture, see Thomas E. Levy, Russell B. Adams, and Rula Shafiq, "The Jabal Hamrat Fidan Project: Excavations at the Wadi Fidan 40 Cemetery, Jordan (1997)," *Levant* 31 (1999): pp. 293-308, and Michael M. Homan, Russell B. Adams, and Thomas E. Levy, "The Iron Age in the Jabal Hamrat Fidan (Jordan): A Preliminary Assessment of the 1997-1999 Seasons," *Wadi Faynan Conference*, forthcoming.

period in which nomadic groups increased in number and strength.

Two of these periods (EB IV/MB II and LB II/Iron I) concern us here, as they might to correspond to biblical claims of tent-dwelling. The increase in Amorite[41] nomadization in the Early Bronze IV period, especially their presence in the Negev, led many scholars to see this as the chronological setting for the patriarchs.[42] Relevant here is the Egyptian Tale of Sinuhe, in which tent-houses are attested in Canaan.[43] Nevertheless, various aspects of the patriarchal narratives seem better placed in a MB II context, especially in light of the Mari texts.[44] It now seems that the stories of Genesis 12-50 are best understood against a wide range of periods, from the Early Bronze Age to the Iron Age.[45] The claim by John Van Seters and Thomas Thompson that the patriarchal stories have nothing to do with the history and culture of the early ancient Israelites is exaggerated, as is Van Seter's argument for a late Iron Age context for Abraham based on a supposed lack of tents in second millennium sources.[46] Tents have been documented in ancient Near Eastern historical sources

---

[41] On the appropriateness of the term "Amorite," see William G. Dever, "The Beginning of the Middle Bronze Age in Syria-Palestine," *Magnalia Dei*, eds. Frank M. Cross, Jr., Werner E. Lemke, and Patrick D. Miller, Jr. (Garden City, 1976): pp. 5-6.

[42] E.g. William F. Albright, "Abram the Hebrew," *BASOR* 163 (1961): pp. 36-54. On Bronze Age settlement in the Negev, see Rudi Cohen, "The Settlement of the Central Negev in the Light of Archaeology and Literary Sources During the $4^{th}$-$5^{th}$ Millennia BCE," Ph.D. dissertation, The Hebrew University, 1986.

[43] *ANET*, p. 20.

[44] Against the extremely late dates argued by John Van Seters, *Abraham in History and Tradition* (New Haven, 1975): p. 17, and Thomas L. Thompson, *The Historicity of the Patriarchal Narratives: The Quest for the Historical Abraham* (Berlin, 1974): pp. 85-88, William G. Dever is correct in surmising "the Mari material provides the best available data . . . for promising research on patriarchal backgrounds" based on laws, customs, and topography ("Palestine in the Second Millennium BCE," *Israelite and Judaean History*, Hayes and Miller, eds. [Philadelphia, 1977]: pp. 116-17).

[45] E.g., patriarchal activity in the Negev seems to represent EB IV; the MB II laws of Mari correspond to Abraham's adoption of Lot, while Isaac's blessing of Edom (Gen 27:40) could not have been written until Edomite independence in the mid-9th century.

[46] John Van Seters, *Abraham in History and Tradition*, p. 14.

from the onset of history until the modern period.[47] The family of Abraham's migratory tent-living may well be related to Amorite nomadization, especially those of the EB IV and MB II periods. Still, caution is advised, given the paucity of evidence.

Linking the biblical accounts of Israel's presettlement wanderings with Late Bronze extra-biblical sources concerning seminomadic tent-dwellers has been a more fruitful enterprise. Throughout the second millennium B.C.E., but especially in the Late Bronze Age, Egyptian and Mesopotamian sources record the presence of unsettled tent-dwelling people designated as *ḥapiru*.[48] The term was initially linked to עִבְרִי "Hebrew," but, while this remains linguistically possible, it is clear from extra-biblical sources that *ḥapiru* is best understood not as an ethnic group, but as a social stratum or lifestyle, something akin to "fugitive."[49] Even so, this designation by no means contradicts the Israelite self-conception.[50] The similarities in designations and lifestyles seem to transcend the realm of coincidence.

Similar in nature are the *Shasu*, although the term is limited to Egyptian sources. Like *Habiru*, *Shasu* most often refers to a social

---

[47] For tents specifically referenced in second millennium B.C.E. sources, see Victor H. Matthews, *Pastoral Nomadism in the Mari Kingdom* (ASORDS 3; Cambridge, MA, 1978), and Donald J. Wiseman, "They Lived in Tents," *Biblical and Near Eastern Studies* (Grand Rapids, 1978): pp. 195-200.

[48] Also written *ḥabiru*. For information concerning the *Habiru*, see George E. Mendenhall, *The Tenth Generation* (Baltimore, 1973): p. 138; Manfred Weippert, *The Settlement of the Israelite Tribes in Palestine* (London, 1971): pp. 63-102; Frank A. Spina, "Israelites as *gērîm*," *The Word of the Lord Shall Go Forth*, Fs for David N. Freedman (Winona Lake, Indiana, 1983): pp. 330-32. George E. Mendenhall, "The Amorite Migrations," *Mari in Retrospect* (Winona Lake, IN, 1992): pp. 233-41; Israel Eph'al, *The Ancient Arabs* (Leiden, 1982): pp. 10-11, and the works cited in the following note.

[49] The term *ḥapiru* occurs over 250 times in cuneiform sources. On its meaning, see Niels P. Lemche, "Ḥabiru, Ḥapiru," *ABD* III, pp. 6-10; Moshe Greenberg, *The Ḥab/piru* (New Haven, 1955); Nadav Na'aman, "Habiru and Hebrews: The Transfer of a Social Term to the Literary Sphere," *JNES* 45 (1986): pp. 271-288. The use of *ḥapiru* as a collective term parallels the use of "Arab," which became an all-inclusive term for nomadic peoples from the 9th century B.C.E. onward (John F. Healey, "Were the Nabataeans Arabs?" *Aram* 1:1 [1989]: p. 40).

[50] E.g. Gen 23:4 "I (Abraham) am an alien (גֵּר) and a visitor (תּוֹשָׁב) with you"; Deut 10:19 "For you were aliens (גֵּרִים) in the land of Egypt." See Frank A. Spina, "Israelites as *gērîm*," pp. 330-32.

class rather than an ethnic group.[51] *Shasu* is also applied
geographically, although the region is not consistent, ranging
from Syria to Nubia.[52] However, it is most often applied to the
area of southern Edom and to its corresponding population.[53]
The Egyptian texts recording the employment of *Shasu*
mercenaries mention their inclination to thievery, their pastoral
tent-dwelling lifestyle and tribal organization. The last two items
correspond to biblical accounts of the Israelite ancestors.[54]

Further corroborating the biblical claim of a Late Bronze Age
tent-dwelling existence is the Merneptah stele.[55] While tents are
not mentioned explicitly, "I-s-r-ʾa-a-l" is followed by the
hieroglyphic determinative for an ethnic group rather than a
country or city, implying that "Israel" is an unsettled or newly-
settled people.[56] The stele further locates the Israelite people in
Canaan, although no mention is made of their derivation from or
any connection with Egypt.[57]

---

[51] Manfred Weippert, "Semitische Nomaden des zweiten Jahrtausends. Über
die *Šꜣsw* der ägyptischen Quellen," *Bib* 55 (1974): pp. 265-80, 427-33; William
A. Ward, "Shasu," *ABD* V, pp. 1165-67.

[52] The presence of *Shasu* in Nubia has been attributed to possible migrations
from Southwest Asia (Raphael Giveon, "The Shosu of the Late XXth Dynasty,"
*JARCE* 8 [1970]: pp. 51-53). But this is not necessary, if we assume the term
primarily connotes a lifestyle.

[53] *Shasu* is equated with Se'ir (Edom) in the records of Rameses II. See
Kenneth Kitchen, "Asiatic Wars of Ramses II," *JEA* 50 (1964): pp. 66-67.

[54] Raphael Giveon, *Les bédouins Shosou des documents égyptiens* (Leiden,
1971): documents 37-38; pp. 114-115 n. 5. Papyrus Harris I, 76, 10 mentions
the Shasu's tents and livestock; Papyrus Anastasi VI refers to the Shasu's
migrations with livestock; see Kenneth A. Kitchen, "The Egyptian Evidence on
Ancient Jordan," pp. 21-34.

[55] The Victory Stele of Merneptah is dated to c. 1207 B.C.E. by Lawrence E.
Stager, "Merneptah, Israel and Sea Peoples: New Light on an Old Relief," *Eretz-
Israel* 18 (1985): pp. 56-64.

[56] Contrast places such as Gezer and Ashkelon in the Merneptah stele, which
are provided with the Egyptian determinative for "city." Gösta W. Ahlström,
however, rejects the association of Merneptah's "Israel" with a people, claiming
that the reference is geographical, in *Who Were the Israelites?* (Winona Lake,
1986).

[57] As pointed out by William G. Dever, "Israel, History of (Archaeology and
the 'Conquest')," *ABD* III, p. 546. However, it could be argued that many
Israelites never left Canaan for Egypt.

*Some Concluding Remarks on Ancient Israelite Tent Homes*

The authors of the Hebrew Bible believed their ancestors were not tied to one specific location; rather, they periodically migrated while living in tents. This assertion is corroborated on many levels: an extensive Hebrew vocabulary for things tent-related, a blended usage of terms for permanent and impermanent dwellings, a rare positive connotation for tents and nomadism in Israelite literature, and a certain amount of verisimilitude that accompanies this claim. It is unlikely that someone would invent a tent-dwelling heritage were it not true. Extra-biblical textual evidence of Bronze Age seminomadic tent-dwelling furthers the claim, providing peoples in the right place at the right time with the right tent-homes. Admittedly, not all Israelites were descended from nomads. The Israelites, like most people, were heterogeneous in origin. However, the tent-dwelling heritage, both real and exaggerated, impacted their society to an unusual degree.[58] Even their deity lived in a tent.

This claim of a tent-dwelling heritage by the authors of the Hebrew Bible is supported not only in historical sources, but also through anthropological and archaeological research. This is the subject of the following chapter.

---

[58] Niels P. Lemche seems to be the first to have suggested the term "polymorphous society" in reference to early Israel, in *Early Israel* (Leiden, 1985). William G. Dever as well subscribes to this polymorphous model, arguing that a limited number of former pastoral nomads "came to shape the literary tradition disproportionally" ("Cultural Continuity, Ethnicity in the Archaeological Record," p. 31[*]). For further discussion see chapter 4 below, pp. 47-59.

CHAPTER FOUR

# THE ARCHAEOLOGY OF TENTS AND PASTORAL NOMADS

Recent innovations in archaeological theory
and methodology have made the excavation of
pastoral settlements increasingly feasible.
Coupled with anthropological studies of
pastoral economies, archaeology sheds new
light on early Israel. The similarities in
material culture between the lowland Canaanite
urban centers and the highland settlements has
been argued to signify a common ancestry.
Nevertheless, pastoral economies by nature
accumulate artifacts from the towns with which
they must trade for survival. This chapter
explores the archaeology of pastoral nomads.
It also examines a cemetery for nomads in
southern Jordan which dates to the early Iron
Age, as well as evidence from a survey of the
Jabal Hamrat Fidan region, which reveals 24
sites with Iron Age occupations.

This book's examination of tents in the Hebrew Bible and the
ancient Near East exemplifies the importance of an interface
between history and archaeology. While independently both offer
much to the topic, it is the conglomeration of disciplines that best
illustrates the important role that tents played in antiquity. Thus,
while the previous chapter made the historical case for ancient
Israel's tent-dwelling heritage, the present chapter explores the
archaeology of societies that inhabit tents.

## Archaeological Evidence For and Against Ancient Israel's Tent-Dwelling Heritage

Apart from the possible *ḥapiru*=עִבְרִי equation, the parallels
between the *Habiru*, *Shasu*, and Merneptah's "Israel," and the
biblical "Hebrews" are of a general rather than a specific nature.
However, all three epigraphically attested groups from Southwest
Asia in the late 13th/early 12th century B.C.E. live lifestyles

similar to those recorded in the Hebrew Bible, and they all live in tents with a presumed pastoral economic base.

Attempts to find more specific parallels between the pastoral nomads recorded in the Hebrew Bible and Egyptian historical sources, however, have typically failed, as tents and encampments by nature leave few remains.[1] Still, we find indirect evidence for the presence of nomadic peoples in the archaeological record, including cemeteries, desert kites, cultic installations, and most relevant to our purposes, settlement patterns and site architecture, especially those of the Late Bronze II/Iron IA highland villages.[2] The dramatic increase in population in these areas is seen by most as archaeological evidence for the presence of early Israel.[3] Within these highland settlements, houses are typically placed one next to the other with their outer walls forming an elliptical defense-wall, a shape shared by many seminomadic Bedouin camps.[4] Between the houses is an elliptical courtyard in which to

---

[1] Contrast Israel Finkelstein's view that ". . . groups that practice subsistence economy based on hunting-gathering or on animal-husbandry—and migrate in search of food, water and good pasture—do not leave traceable remains" (Israel Finkelstein and A. Perevolotsky, "Processes of Sedentarization and Nomadization in the History of Sinai and the Negev," *BASOR* 279 [1990]: p. 68), with that of Steven A. Rosen: "It is possible not only to find the remains of such nomads, but also to reconstruct their lifeways and to place them in historical context" ("Nomads in Archaeology: A Response to Finkelstein and Perevolotsky," *BASOR* 287 [1992]: pp. 75-85). On improved methodology and the increasing feasibility of finding nomads and tent camps in the material record, see Roger Cribb, *Nomads in Archaeology* (Cambridge, 1991).

[2] These include the highland areas of Galilee, Samaria, the northern Negev, and Benjamin, as well as central and northern Transjordan. The greatest concentration, however, is in tribal areas of Manasseh and Ephraim (cf. Genesis 48). See Israel Finkelstein, *The Archaeology of the Israelite Settlement* (Jerusalem, 1988), who estimates the highland population to be 51,000 based on 45 persons per settled hectare; and David C. Hopkins, "Pastoralists in Late Bronze Age Palestine: Which Way Did They Go?" *BA* 56 (1993): pp. 200-11.

[3] E.g., Israel Finkelstein, *The Archaeology of the Israelite Settlement*. Cf. Dever's term, "proto-Israel."

[4] Claude R. Conder records that 19th century Bedouin camps placed the tents side-by-side to enclose animals (*Tent Work in Palestine*, 2.275). On Bedouin tents placed side-by-side for defensive purposes, see Finkelstein, *Living on the Fringe*, p. 47, for bibliography. Compare, however, Tel Masos, in which the houses' entrances face outward, indicating that defense was not the prime motive. Note too the disagreement between Finkelstein and his field supervisor Zvi Lederman over the context of the oval outline at ʿIzbet Ṣarṭah, in "Nomads They Never Were: A Reevaluation of Izbet Sarta'," *Abstracts, AAR/SBL 1990*, p. 238.

pen livestock, another feature common to pastoral camps.[5] Elliptical villages are a widely-attested indicator of a seminomadic lifestyle, existing in Africa, Asia, and North America.[6] Thus, the elliptical village pattern popular in the highland area lends support to the biblical assertion that prior to settlement, ancient Israel occupied tent-camps.

However, archaeology has also provided the major objection to the biblical claim of a seminomadic heritage: the ceramic profile of highland sites associated with early Israel is similar to that of the Canaanite urban lowlands.[7] Nevertheless, the assemblages are not identical: collar-rim jars are proportionately much more abundant in the highland settlements, and Philistine bichrome ware that is popular in the lowland continues to be extremely rare in the highlands.[8] Even where the assemblages do correspond, ethnoarchaeological studies have revealed that nomadic groups living in urban fringes typically possess many of the same items as their settled neighbors due to trade and exchange, even though they lead very different lifestyles.[9]

---

[5] Israel Finkelstein, *Living on the Fringe*, p. 48.

[6] See Kent V. Flannery, "The Origins of the Village as a Settlement Type in Mesoamerica and the Near East," *Man, Settlement, and Urbanism*, Peter J. Ucko, Ruth Tringham, and G. W. Dimbleby, eds. (London, 1972): pp. 23-53. Elliptical and circular camps in some areas are referred to by Arabic *duwwar* "circle" (Israel Finkelstein, *Living on the Fringe*, p. 47). For North America, see Reginald Laubin and Gladys Laubin, *The Indian Tipi: Its History, Construction and Use* (Norman, 1977): pp. 293 - 300. In Africa, note the study of the recently sedentarized Shuwa Bedouin, in Augustin Holl and Thomas Levy, "From the Nile Valley to the Chad Basin: Ethnoarchaeology of Shuwa Arab Settlements," *BA* 56:4 (1993): pp. 166-79. The notion of rectangular settlements as sedentary and elliptical as nomadic is oversimplified, however; some rectangular shapes are manifest also in pastoral camps (Finkelstein, *Living on the Fringe*, pp. 46-49).

[7] The highland remains from ʿIzbet Ṣarṭah and the lowland urban center of Gezer dominate this discussion. See Israel Finkelstein, *The Archaeology of the Israelite Settlement,* and *ʿIzbet Ṣarṭah* (Oxford, 1986), and William G. Dever's reviews in "Archaeological Data on the Israelite Settlement," *BASOR* 284 (1991): pp. 77-90.

[8] William G. Dever writes that bichrome ware is unattested at ʿIzbet Ṣarṭah, Shilo and Ebal ("Cultural Continuity, Ethnicity in the Archaeological Record and the Question of Israelite Origins," *Eretz-Israel* 24, Avraham Malamat Volume [1993]: p. 27*). Bichrome ware has been found in small quantities at Nasbeh, Bethel, and Hirbet et-Tubeqa.

[9] Michael B. Rowton's term "enclosed nomadism" is apt at describing such an existence. See "Enclosed Nomadism," *JESHO* 17 (1974): pp. 1-30; "Economic and Political Factors in Ancient Nomadism," *Nomads and Sedentary*

The highland settlers' knowledge of farming techniques, especially terracing, has likewise been cited to support their urban origins.[10] William G. Dever in particular has claimed that the occupants of these highland villagers were not recently settled nomads, but experienced farmers.[11] However, history is full of examples in which former seminomadic peoples in the process of sedentarization are capable farmers. Pastoralism does not rule out farming, as crops play a large role in the lives of many nomads.[12] For example, early Nabataeans practiced extensive farming, as did their predecessors in Edom.[13]

Dever further claims that the ancient Israelites were fully aware they originated in Canaanite urban centers, citing Ezek 16:3: "Your birth and your nativity are from the land of Canaan; your father was an Amorite, your mother a Hittite."[14] However, Dever

---

*People* (Mexico City, 1981): pp. 25-36. It must also be noted that cultural adaptations, like biological adaptations, can occur rather abruptly on the archaeological time scale. We should not expect to find evidence of the transition. See Anatoly M. Khazanov, *Nomads and the Outside World* (Madison, 1994); "Pastoralists in the Contemporary World: The Problem of Survival," *Changing Nomads in a Changing World*, Jospeh Ginat and Anatoly M. Khazanov, eds. (Portland, 1998): pp. 7-23; and Thomas E. Levy and Augustin F. C. Holl, "Israelite Settlement Processes: Archaeological and Ethno-archaeological Perspectives," paper presented at the World Archaeology Congress (New Delhi, 1994): publication forthcoming.

[10] William G. Dever, "Cultural Continuity, Ethnicity in the Archaeological Record and the Question of Israelite Origins," p. 27*. On Iron Age terracing, see Oded Borowski, *Agriculture in Iron Age Palestine* (Winona Lake, 1987): pp. 15-18.

[11] William G. Dever, "Cultural Continuity, Ethnicity in the Archaeological Record and the Question of Israelite Origins," pp. 22-33*.; "Will the Real Israel Please Stand Up?" Part I, *BASOR* 297 (1995): pp. 61-80; Part II, *BASOR* 298 (1995): pp. 37-58.

[12] Kenneth W. Russell, *Ecology and Energetics of Early Food Production in the Near East and North Africa,* University of Utah Dissertation (1986): p. 372. Russell also notes the reverse, where farmers keep herds of livestock.

[13] On Nabataean farming innovations and competency, see Avraham Negev, *Nabataean Archaeology Today* (New York, 1986): pp. 104-05; Philip C. Hammond, *The Nabataeans: Their History, Culture and Archaeology* (Gothenberg, 1973): pp. 72-73. On Edomite agriculture, see Ernst A. Knauf-Belleri, "Edom: The Social and Economic History," *You Shall Not Abhor an Edomite For He is Your Brother* (Atlanta, 1995): pp. 96-99.

[14] William G. Dever, "Cultural Continuity, Ethnicity in the Archaeological Record and the Question of Israelite Origins," pp. 22-33* (esp. 31*); "Will the Real Israel Please Stand Up?" Part 1, pp. 61-80; Part 2, pp. 37-58. Ezek 16:45 contains a similar passage.

fails to mention that the addressee is not collective Israel, but rather the city of Jerusalem. Thus it is unclear whether Ezekiel names Jerusalem as a metonym for contemporary Israel, or whether Ezekiel is recalling Jerusalem's Jebusite heritage. The latter seems likely, given the close connections between Hittites, Canaanites, Amorites, and Jebusites.[15] Hence, Ezekiel is admonishing the current inhabitants of Jerusalem for practicing the same idolatries as the original pagan inhabitants.[16]

Whether or not Dever is correct in assuming ancient Israel situated their ancestors in urban Canaan, the similarities in material culture and agricultural sophistication shared by the highland villages with the urban centers have led many archaeologists to support the Peasant Revolt model of Israelite origins.[17] Yet this theory, in which the repressed peasant farmers rebel against their taxing Canaanite overlords, too heavily relies upon 19th century Marxist ideas to the exclusion of socio-economic factors involving the anthropology of seminomadic pastoralists and urban centers.[18] The peasant revolt model, moreover, fails to account for the biblical claim of a seminomadic lifestyle. Certainly no peasant in 16th-century Germany or 20th-century Russia would have invented a fictitious tent-dwelling heritage. It is clear from the Hebrew Bible, an ethno-historical document, that Israelite mythology and tradition place their origin in pastoral nomadism of some form, while there is nothing in the biblical text to point to a peasant revolt.

---

[15] E.g. Gen 10:15-16; see Moshe Greenberg, *Ezekiel,* AB 22 (Garden City, NY, 1983): p. 274.

[16] It is unclear if "Amorite" in Ezek 16:3, 45 means an urban-Canaanite or a pastoral nomad. For a discussion of the Amorite link to a pastoral nomadic economy, see George E. Mendenhall, "Amorites," *ABD* I, pp. 199-202.

[17] First proposed by George E. Mendenhall, "The Hebrew Conquest of Palestine," *BA* 25 (1962): pp. 66-87, and later supported by Norman K. Gottwald, *The Tribes of Yahweh* (New York, 1979).

[18] See Manfred Weippert's comparison of Mendenhall's proposed revolt to the German Peasants' Revolt in the 16th century (*The Settlement of the Israelite Tribes in Palestine* [Naperville, Illinois, 1971]: p. 59), and Niels P. Lemche's review of Gottwald's theory in "Israel, History of (Archaeology and the 'Conquest')," *ABD* III, pp. 539-45. Note too Mendenhall's assertion that Merneptah's stele refers to a peasant uprising ("The Hebrew Conquest of Palestine," pp. 66-87). For the best refutations of Mendenhall, see Niels P. Lemche, *Early Israel* (Leiden, 1985), and Baruch Halpern, *The Emergence of Israel in Canaan* (Chico, 1983): pp. 50-63.

The best theory of Israelite Settlement to date appears to be the Symbiosis model initially proposed by Volkmar Fritz.[19] It accounts for the polymorphous nature of earliest Israel. Not only did seminomads maintain contact with urban centers prior to sedentarization, but the two groups continued to coexist after the former gradually abandoned their migrations, and at times former city-dwellers and seminomads even lived within the same villages. This is a widely documented characteristic of the interaction between sedentarized and pastoral peoples.[20] Certainly Dever is correct when stating "urbanites, rural agriculturalists, and pastoral nomads were all involved in the early Iron I colonization of the hill country."[21] However, the proportions of each element are disputed. Ancient Israel was composed of some farmers and some urbanites, but mostly of former pastoralists, with a heritage of tent-dwelling.[22] Lawrence E. Stager has shown in the "Song of Deborah" how the different tribes had different economic foundations (farmers, herders, and maritime traders).[23] That is why they did not all answer Deborah's war-cry. As one of the earliest poems in the Hebrew Bible (c. 1150-1100 B.C.E.),[24] it lends support to the multi-economic nature of "tribal" societies in Palestine at the time. To deny the tent-dwelling heritage claimed in the Hebrew Bible is required by neither the artifactual nor the textual evidence.

---

[19] Volkmar Fritz's self-designated "Symbiosis model" modifies Alt, Noth, and Weippert's Peaceful Infiltration Model, combining periods of sedentarization with reversion to nomadism, and the coexistence of former-nomads with those of urban heritage. However, the model itself remains underdeveloped, limited to a few paragraphs at the end of Fritz's "Conquest or Settlement? The Early Iron Age in Israel," *BA* 50 (1987): pp. 84-100.

[20] Anatoly Khazanov, *Nomads and the Outside World*, pp. 202-27.

[21] "Israelite Origins and the 'Nomadic Ideal': Separating Fact from Fiction," *Mediterranean Peoples in Transition*, Fss. Trude Dothan (Jerusalem, 1998): p. 228.

[22] Contrast Robert B. Coote and Daniel R. Ord's notion that the Judean upper class of the Hebrew Bible are analogous to Bedouin sheiks ruling a peasantry *à la* Jordan (*The Bible's First History* [Philadelphia, 1989]. Coote and Ord believe nomads are the minority, but are culturally and politically dominant.

[23] Lawrence E. Stager, "Archaeology, Ecology, and Social History: Background Themes to the Song of Deborah," *VTSup* 49 (1987): pp. 221-34; "The Song of Deborah," *BAR* 15 (1989): pp. 50-64.

[24] David Noel Freedman, "Early Israelite Poetry and Historical Reconstructions," *Symposia* (Cambridge, MA, 1979): pp. 88-96.

*Houses from Tent-Prototypes: The Evolution of Architecture*

Some scholars believe the four-room house, which remains one of the most popular criteria in identifying an Israelite presence at various sites, evolved from tent prototypes.[25] However, the association between the four-room house and Israelite ethnicity has been diminished. While four-room houses do in fact cluster in highland areas with known Iron Age Israelite settlements, the discovery of four-room houses in Iron Age Transjordan as well as in contexts dated to the Late Bronze Age have diminished their credibility as an absolute index of Israelite ethnicity.[26] While the Late Bronze Age context of the four-room house has been used to discredit an evolution from a tent prototype, there were many

---

[25] For the four-room house as an Israelite feature and the dominant house-form in ancient Israel, see Yigal Shiloh, "The Four-room House, Its Situation and Function in the Israelite City," *IEJ* 20 (1970): p. 180; Ehud Netzer, "Domestic Architecture in the Iron Age," *The Architecture of Ancient Israel*, Aharon Kempinski and Ronny Reich, eds. (Jerusalem, 1992): pp. 193-201; John S. Holladay, Jr., "Four-Room House," *EANE* II (New York, 1997): pp. 337-42. Note the more recent correlation between the Iron Age central hill country and Transjordanian four-room houses and collar-rim jars in C. Chang-Ho, Jr., "A Note on the Iron Age Four-Room House in Palestine," *Or* 66 (1997): pp. 387-413. Note also the correlation between this architectural form and biblical notions of kinship in Lawrence E. Stager, "The Archaeology of the Family in Ancient Israel," *BASOR* 260 (1985): pp. 1-35. Those arguing for the evolution from a tent to the four-room house include: Aharon Kempinski, "Tel Masos," *Expedition* 20 (1978): pp. 29-37; Ze'ev Herzog, *Beer-Sheba II* (Tel Aviv, 1984): pp. 75-77; Israel Finkelstein, *The Archaeology of the Israelite Settlement*, p. 257; Kenneth W. Scharr, "The Architectural Traditions of Building 23A/13 at Tell Beit Mirsim," *SJOT* 2 (1991): pp. 75-91; Volkmar Fritz, "The Israelite 'Conquest' in the Light of Recent Excavations at Khirbet el-Meshâsh," *BASOR* 241 (1981): pp. 61-73. However, Fritz has now abandoned this theory (personal communication), due to the LB context.

[26] E.g., Tell el-ʿUmeiri has a four-room house dating to the LB II and early Iron I (Larry G. Herr, "The Iron Age at Tell el-ʿUmeiri," *Institute of Archaeology Newsletter* 15, 1 [Philadelphia, 1995]); a similar house from Bethel also dates to the 13th century B.C.E. (James L. Kelso, *The Excavations of Bethel*, AASOR 39 [Cambridge, 1968]: pl. 4a); similarly, a four-room house from the LB II exists at Tell el-Fukhar (Magnus Ottosson, "The Iron Age of Northern Jordan," *VTSup* 50 [1993]: pp. 97-99) and another LB II exemplar at Batashi. However, these finds do not invalidate the four-room house criterion. Biblical tradition places Jacob/Israel in Canaan from the onset of the patriarchal period, and many may have experienced neither bondage in Egypt nor an Exodus. It is unlikely that all of the Israelites left Canaan (on both sides of the Jordan River) in the 17th century B.C.E. for Egypt, and only returned after 1250 B.C.E. with the Exodus.

tent-dwellers in the area during the Late Bronze Age.[27] The issue here is not the architectural transfer from house to tent as a means of identifying ethnicity; rather, the move is linked to changes in economy, namely pastoralism becoming increasingly sedentarized.

There are indeed examples of features of impermanent structures being incorporated in permanent architecture. For example, the sedentarization of many Bedouin has led to domestic architecture in which the form and function parallel their former tent dwellings.[28] So too early Nabataean urban architecture is said to have evolved from tents and camps.[29] The architecture of Persian stone palaces of the 15th century C.E. is frequently modeled on the form of ornate tents.[30] In Mongolia, many buildings resemble yurts in stone.[31] Some have even argued that the use of the dome in architecture is an attempt to imitate a tent-roof, just as decorated tiles adorning various buildings' exteriors seem to mirror designs woven in fabric.[32] So, while there are cases in which aspects of permanent buildings are based on tent-prototypes, it remains unclear whether or not the four-room house evolved from a tent.

*Missing Tents in the Material Record: The Case From Qumran*

The problems associated with tents in the archaeological record are made apparent by the excavations at Qumran. Here the lack of stone buildings in relation to the large cemetery and the remains of tent-poles have created a controversy regarding the degree to which tents were used by the Essenes.

---

[27] C. Chang-Ho, Jr., "A Note on the Iron Age Four-Room House in Palestine," pp. 387-413, and verbally from Volkmar Fritz. On LB tent-dwellers, see above, pp. 40-44.

[28] Avshalom Shmueli, *Nomadism About to Cease* (Tel Aviv, 1980): pp. 80, 154-55; further references listed in Israel Finkelstein, *Living on the Fringe*, p. 46 n. 7.

[29] Avraham Negev, *Nabatean Archaeology Today* (New York, 1986): p. 105.

[30] Bernard O'Kane, "From Tents to Pavilions," *Ars Orientalis* 23 (1993): pp. 249-68.

[31] A personal communication from Anatoly Khazanov.

[32] See p. 40 n. 36.

Five wooden poles, two with forked endings, were discovered in Cave 17 along with pottery characteristic of Qumran.[33] The preservation of such poles is remarkable, as even in Qumran's dry climate, virtually all wooden artifacts have completely decayed.[34] All five poles measured about 1.5 meters in length, the longest being 1.75 meters. Since they were found in an uninhabitable rock-crevice, de Vaux is probably correct in surmising these were tent-poles stored within the cave. The associated pottery consists of a lamp, a bowl with a lid, a cooking pot, and a juglet--vessels likely to be utilized along with the tent on a journey.

Despite these limited remains, the use of tents by the inhabitants of Qumran has become a much-debated topic due mostly to an absence of evidence. The relatively few fixed structures at Qumran have caused some scholars to theorize that the population was quite small, between 30 to 50 people.[35] Others claim the population was larger, between 100 to 200; the community supposedly inhabited tents, not stone houses.[36] However, any speculations on the use of tent-homes by the Qumranites, other than their use on journeys, are just that—speculations. Tents by nature leave very little for the archaeological record, and the extent to which they were employed at settlements such as Qumran cannot be determined.

*Tent Homes and Nomadism in the Early Iron Age: New Evidence From the Jabal Hamrat Fidan Project Cemetery and Survey*

The interface of textual history with the archaeological record is more problematic in areas in which nomadism is assumed to have

---

[33] Roland de Vaux, "Exploration de la falaise de Qumrân," in Maurice Baillet, Jozef T. Milik, and Roland de Vaux, *DJD* 3 (1962): pp. 16-17; plate 7.3.

[34] E.g., many nails remain from decayed wooden coffins. See Solomon H. Steckoll, "Preliminary Excavation Report in the Qumran Cemetery," *Revue de Qumran* 6 (1968): pp. 323-44.

[35] E.g. Joseph Patrich, in "The Enigma of Qumran," *BAR* 24:1 (Jan/Feb 1998): p. 81.

[36] Magen Broshi and Hanan Eshel, "How and Where Did the Qumranites Live?" *The Provo International Conference on the Dead Sea Scrolls* (Leiden, 1997); "The Archaeological Remains on the Marl Terrace Around Qumran," *Qadmoniot* 114 (1997): pp. 129-33; cf. Joseph Patrich, "Was There an External Residential Area at Qumran?" *Qadmoniot* 115 (1998): pp. 66-67, and the response by Broshi and Eshel, p. 67.

played an even larger role than in formative Israel. Such is the case with ancient Edom. To date, there is a paucity of archaeological material from southern Jordan that predates the 7th century B.C.E., despite various historical sources from both Egypt and the Hebrew Bible describing Edom/Seir in the Iron I-IIB periods (1200-720 B.C.E.).[37] This is probably due to a combination of three factors: 1) the nature of nomadic societies, in which material possessions hinder mobility, 2) the need for more systematic archaeological field surveys and 3) the need for additional large-scale excavations at Iron Age sites in Edom. Nevertheless, two recent studies under the auspices of the Jabal Hamrat Fidan Regional Archaeology Project (UCSD – Bristol) have produced significant data concerning the late Iron I and Iron II periods in the area of Edom depicted in Plate 5.[38]

First, in 1997 the Jabal Hamrat Fidan Project under the direction of Thomas E. Levy and Russell B. Adams excavated 62 graves containing the skeletal remains of 87 individuals at a cemetery (WFD 40)[39] along the north bank of the Wadi Fidan.[40]

The cemetery is quite large, covering 17,600 m$^2$ with an estimated minimum of 3,500 individuals.[41] The grave form was standardized (Plate 6).

---

[37] See Kenneth A. Kitchen, "The Egyptian Evidence on Ancient Jordan," pp. 21-34; Piotr Bienkowski, "The Beginning of the Iron Age in Southern Jordan: A Framework," *Early Edom and Moab* (Sheffield, 1992): pp. 1-12; and John R. Bartlett, "Biblical Sources for the Early Iron Age in Jordan," *Early Edom and Moab* (Sheffield 1992): pp. 13-20. However, Bartlett dates Exodus 15 to the 10th century based on verse 17's reference to Yahweh's שבת, which he argues refers to the Temple in Jerusalem. The word שבת may refer to Yahweh's throne, (William H. C. Propp, *Exodus 1-18*, pp. 542-43) and despite Bartlett's hesitancy, there is nothing to preclude the word from referring to Yahweh's Tabernacle. David N. Freedman presents a solid argument for an early 12th century B.C.E. date for the Song of the Sea ("Early Israelite History in the Light of Early Israelite Poetry," *Unity and Diversity* [Baltimore, 1975]: pp. 3-35).

[38] For further discussion of the following data, see Michael M. Homan, Russell B. Adams, and Thomas E. Levy, "The Iron Age in the Jabal Hamrat Fidan (Jordan), *Wadi Faynan Conference Publication*, forthcoming.

[39] Previous publications used the abbreviation WF for both the Wadi Fidan and the Wadi Faynan, resulting in confusion; thus, WFD is now used for the Fidan, while WF is reserved for the Faynan.

[40] Initial publication in Thomas E. Levy, Russell B. Adams, and Rula Shafiq, "The Jebel Hamrat Fidan Project: Excavations at the Wadi Fidan 40 Cemetery, Jordan (1997)," *Levant* 31 (1999): pp. 299-314.

[41] Levy et al., "The Jabal Hamrat Fidan Project," p. 298.

Each grave was marked on the surface by a circle (typically 1.5-2 m in diameter) of dolorite stones. Just over one meter below the surface a series of large capstones were found sealed with a pisé substance. Beneath the capstones, the burial was interred within a stone-lined cist; 90% of the burials and cists were aligned on a north-south axis.[42] The preservation of these remains was excellent, and included in one case a lung fragment and a human hair dyed red.[43] The skeletons showed no immediate evidence of pathology. Calibrated radiometric dating suggests a date ranging from 1015-845 B.C.E., approximately at the transition from the Iron I to the Iron II period.[44] Many of the burials were wrapped in two layers before being interred, the innermost consisting of textile, the outer a goat-skin shroud, which covered the body from head to toe.[45] One burial's fecal remains contained the shells of insect pupate, which seems to suggest that the corpse remained unburied long enough for insects to plant their eggs. Material goods primarily consisted of an abundance of beads (N=1,317), though also found were metal jewelry and wooden bowls containing food offerings (one of which contained a gazelle bone with knife marks).[46] One grave (WFD 40: grave # 92) proved particularly interesting (Plate 7). Grave 92 contained the skeleton of an adult woman, who was buried along with five pomegranates,[47] two copper anklets, an iron bracelet, a metal earring fragment, and a spindle whirl. Among the several beads on her necklace was a scarab dating to the MB II (Hyksos) period, acquired it would seem through trade or as an heirloom.[48] Interestingly, there were no pottery finds associated with these

---

[42] There was an equal distribution of sexes and ages, though infant burials were interred just below the surface. For further details, see Levy et al., "The Jabal Hamrat Fidan Project," pp. 296-98.

[43] The hair, apparently dyed with henna, belonged to an adult woman. Though speculative, this may relate to the etiology of Edom in Gen 25:25, in which Edom is born "red all over like a hairy cloak."

[44] Levy et al., "The Jabal Hamrat Fidan Project," p. 303.

[45] Also note Isaac's ruse Gen 27:16, in which he impersonates Edom by placing goat-skins on his arms.

[46] Levy et al., "The Jabal Hamrat Fidan Project," p. 301.

[47] One of the pomegranates provided a seed by which the radiometric date was obtained.

[48] For a drawing and detailed description of the scarab and its inscription, see Levy et al., "The Jabal Hamrat Fidan Project," p. 301.

burials. This lack of pottery, along with the nature of the buried artifacts, coupled with the lack of early Iron Age settlements in the area,[49] seems to suggest the cemetery served a population of tent-dwelling nomads, who at times inhabited the areas within the Wadis Fidan and Faynan. That they raised goats is indicated by the leather shrouds found within several cists, and perhaps they were in the area to mine copper, or at least to guard the entrance to the mining center of Faynan.

The second line of evidence concering the late Iron I and Iron II periods in southern Jordan comes from the 1998 Jabal Hamrat Fidan archaeological survey. The survey recorded 125 sites, 24 of them dating from the Iron Age, in a small sample zone (c. 4 km²) along the banks of the Wadi Fidan within the 240 km² JHF research area (Plate 8).

The survey was pedestrian, and covered an area within 500 m of the drainage channel along a length of 4.5 km beginning at the wadi's mouth where it debouched into the Wadi Araba.[50]

Prior to the survey, only two sites were known to possess Iron Age occupations.[51] The large number of Iron Age sites recorded on the survey (N=24) were identified based primarily on diagnostic surface pottery from the Iron II-III periods.[52] As would be expected, the majority of sites were involved in some capacity with metallurgy, often containing hundreds of small smelting furnaces (WFD 52a, 58, 59, 64). However, among the 24 sites, only one was found to be a settlement with architecture (WFD 52), and it was rather small (0.14 hectares). This lack of

---

[49] It is possible that the WFD 40 cemetery interred the inhabitants of Khirbet al-Nahas, the nearest large-scale settlement located 4.5 km to the northeast, though the distance and rugged terrain make this unlikley.

[50] Thomas E. Levy, Russell B. Adams, et al., "Early Metallurgy, Interaction and Social Change: The Jabal Hamrat Fidan (Jordan) Research Design and 1998 Archaeological Survey: Preliminary Report," *Studies in the History and Archaeology of Jordan* VII, G. Biseh, ed. (in press). The remaining 5.5 km of the drainage channel located within the JHF research area will be surveyed in the summer of 2000.

[51] This includes the cemetery (WFD 40) and the site Glueck misidentified as Khirbet Hamrat Ifdan, now WFD 77 (See Russell B. Adams, "Romancing the Stones: New Light on Glueck's 1934 Survey of Eastern Palestine as a Result of Recent Work by the Wadi Fidan Project," *Early Edom and Moab* (Sheffield, 1992): pp. 177-86.

[52] Thomas E. Levy, Russell B. Adams, et al., "Early Metallurgy, Interaction and Social Change," pp. 19-20.

permanent settlements, along with the surface remains of a large campsite (1.00 hectare) identified along the ridge overlooking the Arabah (WFD 48; Plate 9), suggests a nomadic pastoral presence.

## Some Concluding Remarks on the Archaeology of Tents

The evidence from both the cemetery (WFD 40) and the 1998 survey suggests a large nomadic population of tent-dwelling pastoralists for this area of Edom during the Iron Age. This corroborates ethnohistorical sources from both Egypt, recording the presence of *Shasu* in Edom/Seir, and the Hebrew Bible, recording that the Edomites were ruled by chiefs (אלופים), and also inhabited tents in the early Iron Age.[53] As the archaeological discipline increasingly pays attention to campsites, the degree of interface between history and the material record become more productive.

The following chapter examines the use of tents by various ancient Near Eastern militaries. It will be shown that tents played a vital role in the campaigns of Israel and her neighbors, thus heightening the importance of tents in the ancient Near East.

---

[53] Exod 15:15 mentions Edomite אלופים. On Edomite tents, see p. 30 n. 1 above.

CHAPTER FIVE

MILITARY TENTS: AN ANCIENT TRADITION

> The military has a long history of using tents
> on campaigns. Throughout the ancient Near
> East, tents and similar portable architecture
> sheltered troops from the natural elements. The
> armies of ancient Israel were no exception. A
> detailed examination of the Hebrew Bible,
> along with the literary and archaeological
> records of Egypt, Assyria, Persia, Greece, and
> Rome, illuminates the importance of tents for
> ancient militaries.

That the Israelites and their neighbors used tents on military
campaigns might be expected. Throughout history, tents'
relatively low production costs and portability have ensured a
long and integral relationship with the military. By way of
example, U.S. factories had manufactured more than one million
tents by the end of 1942 to shelter American troops during the
Second World War.[1] This phenomenon is not limited to the 20th
century. Martial tents housed such notables as Napoleon, Henry
VIII, Suleiman the Magnificent, Genghis Khan, Charlemagne,
Muhammad, Vespasian, Julius Caesar, and Alexander the Great
among others, along with their troops.[2] One is nearly five times as

---

[1] Erna Risch, "United States Army in WWII: The Technical Services," *The
Quartermaster Corps: Organization, Supply, and Services* I (1953): p. 169. For
the use of tents in WWI, see for example Thomas E. Lawrence, *The Seven Pillars
of Wisdom* (Garden City, NY, 1926): p. 170.

[2] Napoleon's tent still resides in the collection of the Mobilier National.
Over 1,000 ornate tents provided the setting for the meeting of Henry VIII and
Francis I at the Field of Cloth of Gold in 1520 (N. Williams, "The Master of the
Royal Tents and His Records," *Journal of the Society of Archivists* 2 [October,
1960]: pp. 2-4). The Ottoman camp was estimated to contain 2,000 tents by P.
Rycaut, *The History of the Turkish Empire From the Year 1623 to the Year 1677*
(London, 1687). See also Godfrey Goodwin, *A History of Ottoman Architecture*
(London, 1961): pp. 107, 429. For Genghis Khan, see 'Ala-ad-Din 'Ata-Malik
Juvaini, *Genghis Khan: The History of the World Conqueror* (Seattle, 1958): p.
113. Einhard, *Vie de Charlemagne* (Paris, 1923), describes Charlemagne's tent.
Muhammad's use of tents is described in Muhammad F. Ghazi, "Remarques sur

likely to encounter the word "tent" in a Shakespearean play with a martial setting than in a non-martial setting, just as the noun κλισίη (hut) occurs more than five times as often in Homer's *Iliad* as in the *Odyssey*.[3] Searching the concordances of ancient Near Eastern literature produces analogous results: the preeminent context for tents in all of ancient literature is martial.[4]

The affinity between war and portable housing visible in other literature remains largely absent in the Hebrew Bible, however. This is primarily due to the text's disproportionate focus on the Tabernacle; references to secular tents in any context are dwarfed by comparison. This factor alone does not compensate for the relative silence involving martial tents, however. Of the 347 examples of the word "tent" (אֹהֶל) in the Hebrew Bible, only six are indisputably war tents.[5] Moreover, not one of the six refers to an Israelite military tent; rather, they are tents used by Israel's enemies, be they Aramean, Babylonian, or unspecified future invaders.[6]

---

l'armée chez les Arabes," (Ibla, 1960) and Reuben Levy, *The Social Structure of Islam* (Cambridge, 1957): pp. 407-27. For Vespasian and Titus at Masada in military tents, see Josephus, *Wars*, 3.79.82, and Yigael Yadin, *Masada* (London, 1966): pp. 219-25. See also Yann Le Bohec, *The Imperial Roman Army* (London, 1994): pp. 132-33 on the form of the imperial camp. Julius Caesar and the Roman Republic's use of tents is explored in Michel Feugère, *Les Armes des Romains* (Paris, 1993): pp. 50-53, and Adrian K. Goldsworthy, *The Roman Army at War* (Oxford, 1996): pp. 111-13, who cites Virgil, *Aeneid* 7.126-29, where setting up the camp is the first thing Aeneas does upon arrival in Italy. Alexander dies in a military tent according to Quintus Curtius Rufus, *The History of Alexander*, 10.5-6.

[3] *A Shakespearean Thesaurus* produced this figure. *Richard III*, for example, mentions tent(s) 12 times, *Troilus and Cressida* 34 times, and *Julius Caesar* 10 times. In contrast, tent(s) is entirely absent from *Romeo and Juliet* and the *Tempest*. Similarly, κλισίη occurs 83 times in the *Iliad*, 14 times in the *Odyssey*.

[4] For example, Akkadian *kuštāru* in *CAD* 8, p. 61 refers most often to the military tents of Mesopotamian kings and to the tents of enemies, as Egyptian *im³w* refers to tents of Egyptian kings and their enemies in Adolf Erman and Hermann Grapow, *Wörterbuch der aegyptischen Sprache* I (Leipzig, 1926): p. 81.

[5] I.e. where normally non-tent-dwelling people utilize tents on a military expedition. The word אֹהֶל is used for a military tent four times in 2 Kgs 7:7-10, once each in Jer 37:10 and Dan 11:45.

[6] Passages such as 1 Sam 17:54 (David's tent) and Josh 7:22 (Achan's tent) will be examined in detail below, p. 76.

However, the Israelite military certainly used temporary shelters. In fact, while not called אֹהֶל, military tents and huts provide the setting for many of the Hebrew Bible's most dramatic scenes: David placing the weapons and possibly the head of Goliath in a tent shortly after decapitating the Philistine champion (1 Sam 17:54); Uriah refusing David's order to return to the comforts of his house while fellow-soldiers sleep in huts (2 Sam 11:11); military tents standing erect in the Assyrian camp just outside of Jerusalem while Isaiah instructs Hezekiah on how best to avoid the fate of Lachish (2 Kings 18-19); and the systematic execution of Zedekiah's sons and his subsequent blinding likely in Nebuchadnezzar's tent (2 Kgs 25:7). This chapter will examine the relationship between portable housing and the military, not only in the Hebrew Bible, but throughout the ancient Near East.

## Egyptian Military Tents

The oldest known epigraphic reference to a tent pertains to an Egyptian campaign into Nubia in the Sixth Dynasty (c. 2200 B.C.E.). The context is a letter from Pepi II to his official Harkhuf, who served as Governor of Upper Egypt.[7] Pepi II, at the onset of his reign, has discovered that Harkhuf on a campaign to southern Nubia has captured a dwarf renowned for his skill at dancing. The young king orders the prize captive to be brought to Egypt immediately, and commands Harkhuf to ensure the dwarf's safety. Pepi further instructs,

> When [the dwarf] sleeps at night appoint excellent people, who shall sleep beside him in his tent (ḥn); inspect ten times a night. My majesty desires to see this dwarf more than the gifts of Sinai and of Punt.[8]

---

[7] The letter from Pepi to Harkhuf is carved on the facade of Harkhuf's tomb. For description and translation, see James H. Breasted, *Ancient Records of Egypt* I (Chicago, 1906): pp. 150-154; 159-161; Edward Wente, *Letters from Ancient Egypt* (Atlanta, 1990): p. 21.

[8] James H. Breasted, *Ancient Records of Egypt* I, p. 161; Edward Wente, *Letters from Ancient Egypt*, p. 21.

Thus, literature's first reference to a tent is in the context of an Egyptian military campaign; the association between tents and the military has a history of nearly five millennia.

References to military tents also exist in the Middle Kingdom story of Sinuhe. During Sinuhe's exile in Syria, he lives in a tent, where he is challenged by a Retenu warrior.[9] Having slain the local champion, Sinuhe says, "I took what was in his tent (*im*) and stripped his encampment."[10]

We find the most frequent references to military tents in New Kingdom annals, when the end of Hatshepsut's reign sparked a revolution of Egyptian vassals in Southeast Asia. Thutmose III (reigned 1479-1425 B.C.E. [high chronology]) initiated the first of 17 campaigns to reassert Egyptian dominance, and it is no coincidence that the pharaoh most renowned for campaigning should claim the most references to tents in all of Egyptian literature. The records of Thutmose III's initial expedition provide unprecedented detail in regard to both the campaign itself and to the battle at Megiddo against allied forces headed by the King of Qedesh. Frequent references to tents illustrate their use in both the Egyptian and Asian camps. Thutmose III inhabits a tent throughout the campaign, which is said to be heavily guarded.[11] Immediately following the initial battle, Egyptian forces capture the King of Qedesh's son in his tent.[12] Moreover, seven prized tent-poles wrought with silver are among the booty secured by Egyptian forces.[13] The acquisition of these poles ultimately distracts Thutmose's army from destroying their enemy, who fall back behind the walls of Megiddo, necessitating a seven-month siege to terminate the anti-Egyptian coalition. Years later, similarly ornate tent-poles are again listed among the treasures

---

[9] Sinuhe, 109-110. See James K. Hoffmeier, "Tents in Egypt and the Ancient Near East," *SSEA Newsletter* VII.3 (1977): p. 23.

[10] *ANET*, p. 20. See also James K. Hoffmeier, "Tents in Egypt and the Ancient Near East," p. 23.

[11] James H. Breasted, *Ancient Records of Egypt* II, pp. 182, 192. Miriam Lichtheim, *Ancient Egyptian Literature* II (Berkeley, 1976): pp. 31-32. Note the formula for the onset of a new day: "Awakening in [life] in the royal tent at the town of Aruna."

[12] James H. Breasted, *ARE* II, p. 185.

[13] James H. Breasted, *ARE* II, p. 187. Miriam Lichtheim, *Ancient Egyptian Literature* II (Berkeley, 1976): pp. 33-34.

gained by marching up the Mediterranean coast, this time during Thutmose III's ninth campaign. However, instead of silver, these poles are wrought with bronze, and set with costly stones.[14] Such an ornate tent-pole is depicted in relief on a stele dating to the reign of Horemheb (r. 1323-1295 B.C.E.; Plate 11a). Here an abundance of food and drink, as well as furniture, is prepared in the martial tent of some high-ranking official.

Further evidence of the use of tents by ancient Near Eastern militaries can be seen in the 19th and 20th dynasties, during the reigns of Merneptah (r. 1213-1203 B.C.E.) and Rameses III (r. 1184-1153 B.C.E.). Merneptah's inscription at Karnak describes his victory over the Libyans. Here we read that the tents used by the Libyan forces are covered with leather.[15] Later, Merneptah brags about the extent of his victory, boasting that he set fire to the Libyan camp and their leather tents.[16] Merneptah's successor Rameses III follows in the long tradition of looting enemy tents. Rameses III defeats both Edomite and *Shasu* camps, claiming " I plundered the tents of their people."[17]

The link between tents and the Egyptian military is most clearly seen in the epigraphic and pictorial records of the Battle of Qedesh.[18] Like his predecessor Thutmose III, Rameses II inhabits a tent throughout the campaign.[19] In fact, it is within his royal tent that Rameses first discovers to his horror that he has been duped by his enemy. Egyptian records state that the pharaoh is meeting with his princes when he receives word that his is not the only army in the vicinity, and that the Egyptian camp is soon to be attacked.[20] Within this tent, Rameses quickly puts on his armor and joins the fight.[21] The initial panic is subsequently overcome,

---

[14] James H. Breasted, *ARE* II, p. 205.

[15] James H. Breasted, *ARE* III, p. 241.

[16] James H. Breasted, *ARE* III, p. 251.

[17] James H. Breasted, *ARE* IV, p. 201, from Papyrus Harris.

[18] For detailed information on the written and pictorial records of the battle, see Raymond O. Faulkner, "The Battle of Kadesh," *Mitteilungen des deutschen archäologischen Instituts Abteilung Kairo* 16 (1958): pp. 93-111; G. A. Gaballa, *Narrative in Egyptian Art* (Mainz, 1976): pp. 113-19.

[19] James H. Breasted, *ARE* III, p. 143.

[20] James H. Breasted, *ARE* III, pp. 147-48.

[21] Raymond O. Faulkner, "The Battle of Kadesh," p. 101; James H. Breasted, *ARE* III, pp. 147-48. The record does not remark on where the armor is stored, only that Rameses is in his tent when he hurriedly dresses with his war-gear.

and the Egyptian military survives one of history's most infamous military ruses. The profound impression made by the battle is evident from the fact that not only are the events of Qedesh captured for posterity epigraphically in ten different places, but they are artistically depicted on the walls of many Egyptian monuments. Scenes of the battle exist at Abydos, Karnak, Luxor, the Ramesseum, and Abu Simbel, while depictions of the Egyptian camp adorn walls at Abu Simbel, Luxor, and twice at the Ramesseum.[22]

These painted reliefs contain the first depictions of a military tent known to date. The Egyptian camp is represented in a similar fashion on all three reliefs: leather shields are set up side-by-side along the 2:1 rectangular camp perimeter.[23] The pharaoh's tent is by far the largest structure on all the reliefs, and the entrance is in the camp's center.

The tent itself is divided into two sections. Subjects would enter the pharaoh's tent and be received in a 2:1 long room structure, which immediately led to the pharaoh's square chamber. The relief at Abu-Simbel (Plate 10) differs from the other two in that the viewer is allowed access to events taking place inside the royal tent's reception room. The relief shows five individuals prostrating themselves before the pharaoh's cartouche, which is elevated and flanked by wings of two representations of Horus. The striking similarities the pharaoh's tent and the Egyptian camp share with the Israelite Tabernacle and courtyard will be analyzed below.[24]

Other Egyptian martial tents can be seen in reliefs documenting the Battle of Qedesh. Immediately below Rameses's tent stand three tents reserved for his princes. These, along with the pharaoh's tent, are surrounded by a wall separating the pharaoh's family from the rest of the camp. The number of remaining tents

---

[22] The battle's magnitude can also be seen in the Beth-Shean Stela, Year 18, which mentions the clash, and a Hittite version discussed by Gerhard Fecht, "Ramses II und die Schlacht bei Qadesch," *Göttinger Miszellen* 80 (1984): pp. 41-50. For a bibliography of written and pictorial records, see Michael G. Hasel, *Domination and Resistance* (Leiden, 1998): pp. 154-55; and G. A. Gaballa, *Narrative in Egyptian Art*, p. 114.

[23] For pictures of the reliefs from Luxor and the Ramesseum, see Plates 47-48.

[24] See pp. 111-16.

represented on the reliefs varies: four at Luxor, five at Abu Simbel, and at least seven at the Ramesseum.[25] These tents all share the same form, consisting of two vertical walls and a curved roof (Figure 3). The exact form and composition of these tents remain enigmatic. It is unknown whether cloth, leather, vegetation, or a combination were used to cover the tents. Similarly, there is no uniform function for these tents, as might be expected. Some appear to stable horses, some are used for food preparation, still others to house people.

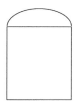

Figure 3 - Common Shape of Egyptian Tents at Qedesh

The number of tents falls well short of the number of troops depicted on the reliefs. This may suggest that tents were reserved for high-ranking officials, and we might speculate that shelter for the common soldiers, if used at all, was left up to the individual to forage and construct. Yet, this remains uncertain, and it must be concluded that both the Egyptian pictures and texts remain silent on the question of what housed the common soldier on military campaigns.

One other Egyptian relief warrants mention, as it provides a better insight into the form of Egyptian military tents. It too dates to the reign of Rameses II, and depicts his four sons battling the enemy before the Hittite fortified city of Zapur (Plate 11b).

Here the walls are not vertical as are those representing the camp at Qedesh. Rather, they slant upward, again culminating in a curved roof. Each has a rather large opening, through which can be seen a large support pole. These tents in many ways resemble the Native American Tipi, except the support poles of the Egyptian tent do not extend beyond the fabric roof.[26]

---

[25] The relief at the Ramesseum is cut off in the upper right corner; seven represents the lowest possible count.

[26] The shape of these tents lends support to a theory of Frank M. Cross, Jr., that Ugaritic *dd* designates a breast-shaped tent (F. M. Cross, Jr., *CMHE*, p. 55

## Assyrian Military Tents

Assyria's suppression of the revolt spearheaded by Hezekiah in 701 B.C.E. is one of the most widely documented campaigns in ancient Near Eastern history. Sennacherib's invasion, brutal destruction of several fortified cities, and ultimate withdrawal prior to Jerusalem's full capitulation are attested in both Israelite and Assyrian written sources.[27] The credibility of these accounts has received archaeological confirmation, as dozens of sites reveal a massive destruction level dated to the close of the eighth century B.C.E.[28] Moreover, at Nineveh were excavated several large reliefs documenting Sennacherib's campaign, including pictures of Assyrian military tent-camps (Plates 12-14).

Sennacherib's camps, unlike those of the Egyptians, are oval in shape.[29] Of like form are the camps of Sennacherib's predecessor Sargon II (Plate 15) and his successor Ashurbanipal (Plate 16).[30] A large central road runs through the camp's elongated axis. The form of the tents invariably falls into one of two categories.

The first category involves simple forked frame tents, with a tall central pole flanked by two slanted supports (Plate 17).

These tents are always shown in cross section, allowing the viewer to witness events transpiring behind the tent's walls. Inside the tent, a soldier returns home and is given a drink by one servant, while the other servant prepares the bed. From the tent-frames often hang a horn, water container, and cooking implements. Bed preparation, cooking, and eating are the three

---

n. 43).

[27] See 2 Kings 18-19, Isaiah 36-39. The Assyrian account comes from the Prism of Sennacherib, and is translated in *ANET*, pp. 287-88. Compare also Herodotus's version of Σαναχαριβον in *Histories*, 2.141. For a comparison of the Assyrian and biblical accounts, see Mordechai Cogan and Hayim Tadmor, *II Kings*, AB 11 (Garden City, 1988): pp. 246-51.

[28] See Mordechai Cogan and Hayim Tadmor, *II Kings*, pp. 223-51. Note especially Lachish and Ekron, both with massive destruction levels dated to 701 B.C.E. Concerning Lachish, see Olga Tufnell, *Lachish III: The Iron Age* (Oxford, 1953); for Ekron—see Seymour Gitin and Trude Dothan, "The Rise and Fall of Ekron of the Philistines," *BA* 50 (1987): pp. 197-222.

[29] Note also the likelihood that Israelite camps were oval in shape, based on the Hebrew word for camp, מַחֲנֶה, derived from the root חנה, meaning "bent," "curved," or "round."

[30] For further depictions of Assyrian oval camps, see David Ussishkin, *The Conquest of Lachish by Sennacherib* (Tel Aviv, 1982): p. 93, and John M. Russell, *Sennacherib's Palace*, fig. 34.

dominant activities occurring inside these tents. The form of these fork-framed tents may have been borrowed from the Arabs, as the palace of Ashurbanipal contains a relief showing identically constituted Arab tents engulfed in flames (Plate 18).

The form of the second type of Assyrian military tent remains enigmatic. These are always shown from the outside; the viewer is never offered a glimpse behind the curtains (Plate 14).

They appear more elaborate than the fork-framed tents. One side is always higher than the other, often with a midsection that has no roof, through which people converse at times. Albrecht Alt has claimed that the common soldiers camped in the fork-framed tents, with the sides open to allow the penetration of breezes, while the other structure, which Alt identifies as a booth, is reserved for royalty.[31]

The Assyrians, like the Egyptians, participated in looting the richly decorated structures of enemy forces. Merodach-Baladan erected his royal tent and fortified camp, only to have it taken by the forces of Sargon II.[32] The golden tent (*kul-tar ḫurāṣi*) of Nur-Adad meets a similar fate.[33]

## Canaanite Military Tents

Two passages in the Ugaritic corpus suggest the use of tents on military expeditions by Late Bronze Canaanite armies. The first comes from the Legend of Aqhat, where, following her brother's murder at the hands of Yatpan, Pughat seeks revenge. She dons the array of a warrior and then sets out to track down the soldier Yatpan. By nightfall, "Pughat arrives at the tents" (*mġy[t] pġt lahlm*).[34] However, it is not clear to whom the tents belong. Either

---

[31] Albrecht Alt, "Zelte und Hütten," *Kleine Schriften zur Geschichte des Volkes Israel* III (München, 1959): pp. 233-242. Similarly, Nigel Stillman and Nigel Tallis, *Armies of the Ancient Near East* (Worthington, Sussex, 1984): pp. 202-03, claim that the reliefs show two types of tent: the king's tent which opens only on the roof, and the officers' tents which are open-faced to catch the wind.

[32] Hugo Winckler, *Die Keilschrifttexte Sargons* (Leipzig, 1889): pp. 34:129; Arthur G. Lie, *The Inscriptions of Sargon II* (Paris, 1929): p. 413.

[33] *KAH* II 84:71. See *CAD* VIII (1971): p. 601 for further references. See also Israel Eph'al, *The Ancient Arabs* (Leiden, 1982): pp. 151-53.

[34] *CAT* 1.19.IV.49-50; *ANET*, 155.

they belong to the encampment of Yatpan, or else Pughat has brought them with her as part of her own military retinue. The second passage comes from the Kirta epic, where Kirta prepares for his journey to secure a bride by sacrificing a lamb and a bird in a tent (ḥmt).[35] Thus it seems Kirta will be traveling with a tent when he besieges his bride's city.

Diodorus of Sicily reports on the much later use of portable housing by Punic soldiers. A Carthaginian military camp contains a sacred tent and altar, reminiscent of the Tabernacle, as well as several other σκηναί, although they more strongly resemble "booths," as they catch fire due to their reed and straw construction.[36] Tents are also used by Phoenicians in nautical expeditions, as shown by Skylax's *Periplus*.[37]

*Military Tents from Greece, Persia, and Rome*

For pre-Classical Greece, huts, rather than tents, appear to be the main shelter of armies. Homer recounts in the *Iliad* that the Achaian forces encamp in "booths" (κλίσαι) before Troy's walls. These structures are inhabited by the Greek nobility; the text is characteristically silent regarding the common troops' dwellings.[38] Nevertheless, a great deal of information regarding the form of these booths can be found in a detailed description of Achilleus's κλισίη:

> But when they came to the lofty κλισίην of Peleus' son, which the Myrmidons had built for their king, hewing beams of pine, and they had roofed it from above with shaggy reeds gathered from the meadows; and around it they made for him, their king, a great courtyard with poles set close together, and the gate . . .
>
> *Iliad* XXIV:448-453

---

[35] *CAT* 1.14.III.159-62.

[36] 20.65.1. Note the same motif from Assyrian annals, in which the god Ashur drives back Assyria's enemies by burning their camps. See *ANET*, pp. 274-301, and Alan R. Millard, "Mesopotamia and the Bible," *Aram* 1:1 (1989): p. 27.

[37] Skylax, 112. See John P. Brown, "Peace Symbolism in Ancient Military Vocabulary," *VT* 21 (1971): p. 22.

[38] Achilleus inhabits a κλισίη in the *Iliad* IX:107, 663; XXIV:448; Agamemnon in IX:226 and 669, where the word appears in the plural. Patroklos has his wounds tended in his κλισίη in XII:1. While the dwellings of the common troops are not specified, they are said to inhabit a camp (στρατός); see X:66.

There is no evidence in Homer that a κλισίη is ever covered with fabric or animal skins, which would render it a tent in the proper sense of the word.

Homer's silence regarding true military tents is not the only factor suggesting their absence in pre-Classical Greece. The Greek word for tent, σκηνή, does not appear in literature until immediately after the Persian invasion.[39] The term is first employed by Aeschylus in 472 B.C.E., when the chorus in *The Persians* exclaims their surprise that many famous Persian soldiers did not return in Xerxes's mobile tents (σκηναῖς τροχηλάτοισιν).[40] Aeschylus seems to have in mind something more akin to a covered wagon, which offered shade to the nobility, than a standard tent. In any event, it is clear that a tent of some form was attributed to the Persian army; its impact may be judged from the frequent references to Persian tents in later Greek literature. In fact, Athenians claimed that Pericles' odeion below the Acropolis was modelled after Xerxes' tent.[41]

Much more information concerning the Persian use of military tents can be gleaned from Herodotus and Xenophon. Herodotus reports that Xerxes reviews his naval forces in a Sidonian ship equipped with a golden tent (σκηνή χρυσέη).[42] Herodotus also says that the Persian army sleeps in the open air, while Xerxes inhabits a tent.[43] Xenophon, however, records that all Persian soldiers inhabit tents, alongside their officers, a procedure that Xenophon claims builds camaraderie and military uniformity.[44] Xenophon also provides data on the formation of Persian encampments: the camp radiates outward from Cyrus the Great's tent, which was placed in the middle of camp facing east.[45]

---

[39] The etymology of σκηνή is much debated, but may relate to Semitic *škn*. See above, p. 11 n. 23.

[40] Aeschylus, *Persians*, 1000. See Oscar Broneer, "The Tent of Xerxes and the Greek Theater," *University of CA Publications in Classical Archaeology* I:12 (1944): pp. 305-12.

[41] As pointed out by Mark Munn. See Plutarch, *Life of Pericles*, 13.5. John Travlos, *Pictorial Dictionary of Ancient Athens* (New York, 1980): p. 387, claims that only the odeion's exterior is a tent imitation, though Plutarch suggests the interior as well is modelled after Xerxes' tent.

[42] Herodotus, *Histories*, VII:100.

[43] *Ibid.*, VII:119.

[44] Xenophon, *Cyropaedia*, II.i.25-28; IV.ii.11.

[45] *Ibid.*, VIII.v.3. The central placement is for protection, as the remaining

According to Xenophon, Cyrus's military tent is quite large, capable of entertaining 100 people.[46] Cyrus's tent not only serves for lodging and dining, but Xenophon records the trial of a Persian traitor in the monarch's tent. There the traitor is interrogated and condemned, although he is executed in another man's tent.[47] The royal guard naturally camps in Cyrus's immediate proximity; to the left of Cyrus's tent are placed the tents of the cooks and pack animals, while the bakers and horses are placed on the right.[48]

Herodotus reports that the Persian troops have the task of dismantling, transporting, and reassembling Xerxes's tent when they arrive at a new camp.[49] Xenophon claims that the Persian military tents are covered with animal skins.[50]

The splendor of the Persian military tents can be seen in the events that transpire immediately following the destruction of Athens in 480 B.C.E. The Persians under Mardonius fall back to their walled encampment. When Athenian soldiers ultimately penetrate these fortifications, the first thing they do is plunder the tent of Mardonius, which contains a spectacular bronze manger.[51] Moreover, the spoils of the Persian camp include tents adorned with gold and silver.[52] Similarly, when a Persian-allied Armenian camp falls to the Greeks, Xenophon lists as war-booty the Armenian tents.[53]

Some insight into Persian military tents is offered by one of the world's oldest cookbooks, *The Deipnosophistae* by Athenaeus,

---

tents provide a buffer should the camp be attacked. The orientation toward the rising sun is intriguing, given parallels to the Tabernacle and other tents of the Middle East (see p. 113), and the fact that the official religion of Persia would soon become light-worship.

[46] Xenophon, *Cyropaedia*, II.i.30; II.iii.21-22.

[47] Xenophon, *Anabasis*, I.vi.5-11.

[48] Xenophon, *Cyropaedia*, VIII.v.2-5, 8-14. The significance of this arrangement is unknown. The proximity of culinary tents to the king's is confirmed by Assyrian reliefs. The separation of horses from other pack animals seems arbitrary, and perhaps Xenophon is reinforcing his theme of Persian military precision.

[49] Herodotus, *Histories*, VII:119.

[50] Xenophon, *Anabasis*, I.v.10. See also II.iv.28, where inflated skins are employed to cross the Tigris river.

[51] Herodotus, *Histories*, IX:70.

[52] *Ibid.*, IX:80.

[53] Xenophon, *Anabasis*, IV.iv.21.

where we find a detailed description of the Persian royal tents at Susa appropriated by Alexander. In fact, Alexander later dies within this royal military tent.[54] Eventually these lavishly ornamented tents serve as the prototype for a very elaborate tent pitched by Ptolemy II in Alexandria. *Deipnosophistae* V.196-97 describes a massive pavilion used for entertaining, which strongly resembles a circus-tent: eighteen columns, each 50 cubits tall, are said to support a structure capable of housing 130 couches. The tent was composed of fine red linen on the inside, animal skins between the columns, and an outer layer of myrtle and laurel boughs.

Roman military camps are described at great length by the historian Polybius, who provides clear evidence that all Roman soldiers, not just the upper echelons, inhabited tents while campaigning.[55] Unlike Egyptian and Persian camps, which apparently had a consistent eastern orientation, the orientation of Roman camps varied with the topography.[56] Polybius describes the Roman camp's construction as initiated by the raising of the general's tent, the *praetorium*, and then the rest of the camp radiates from this fixed point (Plate 19a).[57] The Roman camp's perimeter is generally square in shape.[58] The rigid uniformity

---

[54] Quintus Curtius Rufus, *History of Alexander*, 10.5-6.

[55] Polybius, VI.32. See also Michel Feugère, *Les armes des Romains* (Paris, 1993): pp. 50-53. Note that the common infantryman's tent was known as a *papilio*, as the entrance flaps resembled the wings of a butterfly; it slept eight.

[56] Polybius, VI.27. Water and defensibility were the two primary concerns for camp choice. See Yann Le Bohec, *The Imperial Roman Army* (London, 1994): pp. 131-32.

[57] Polybius, VI.27-42. The average camp's construction has been estimated to have taken at least three hours; see Jacques Harmand, *L'Armée et le soldat à Rome de 107 à 50 avant nôtre ère* (Paris, 1967): p. 132, n. 240. The Roman camp is erected in much the same manner as the Israelite camp in Exod 40:17-33: first the Tabernacle is set up, and then the rest of the camp is constructed in relation to the Tabernacle's position. See below, chapter 8, pp. 129-85, for further details.

[58] Polybius, VI.31-32. These square camps became rectangular when two consuls joined forces. Not all authors describe the single camp as square in shape, however. Pseudo-Hyginus, XXI, writes of a rectangular camp with 2:3 proportions, although 200 years after Polybius, Josephus still speaks of a Roman military camp as square (*Jewish War*, III.5.1 [76-78]; 9.7 [477]; 10.1 [462]).

with which the Romans encamped and marched created fear in their enemies.[59]

In fact, Livy reports that upon Philip of Macedon's first glimpse of the Roman camp,

> he admired its whole arrangement and each section given its own place, with the rows of tents and also the evenly spaced streets between, and that he remarked that no one could believe that the camp belonged to barbarians.[60]

Remains of such a camp exist at the foot of Masada, in which the stone foundation of hundreds of contubernium "mess units" once served as the foundation for tents that sheltered eight to nine soldiers (Plate 19b).[61]

The impact of Roman military tents in the Near East may also be found in the New Testament, as Paul is described as a "tentmaker" (σκηνοποιος) in Acts 18:3, which most likely means Paul manufactured leather tents for the Roman military.[62] The drama in Paul's conversion to Christianity is perhaps increased by his supplying the Roman military with housing, a less direct form of persecuting Christians.

### The Israelites' Enemies and Their Tents in the Hebrew Bible

The above epigraphic and pictorial records indicate that when the armed forces of the ancient Near East and Mediterranean campaigned, whether Egyptian, Hittite, Assyrian, Babylonian, Persian, Greek, or Roman, they campaigned with tents. Despite this familiar association, the word "tent" (אֹהֶל) is employed in a clear martial context only six times in the Hebrew Bible. Nevertheless, this probably reflects, not the nonuse of tents, but

---

[59] Adrian K. Goldsworthy, *The Roman Army at War* (Oxford, 1996): p. 113, states that uniformity of the military camp and the organized march "was part of this attempt to intimidate the enemy into submission . . . The marching camp, although itself a defensive structure, was in a very real sense an instrument of the offensive."

[60] Livy, XXXI.34.8.

[61] Yigael Yadin, *Masada* (London, 1966): p. 219.

[62] Wilhelm Michaelis, "σκηνοποιος," *Theological Dictionary of the New Testament* VII (Grand Rapids, MI, 1977): pp. 393-94; Ernst Haenchen, *The Acts of the Apostles* (Philadelphia, 1971): p. 534, n. 3.

rather the biblical authors' relative uninterest in the techniques of warfare.[63]

2 Kgs 7:8-10 uses אֹהֶל four times to refer to the tents that Ben-Hadad of Syria used during his campaign against Samaria. When four famished lepers venture outside their besieged city in hopes of receiving food from the Syrians, they surprisingly discover the Aramaean camp void of people, thanks to divine intervention. The narrative continues:

> And these lepers came to the edge of the camp, and they came to one tent, and ate and drank; and they took up from there silver and gold and clothing and went and hid them. And they returned and went into another tent, and carried from there and went and hid them.[64]
>
> (2 Kgs 7:8)

Like the Egyptians and Greeks and doubtless all armies, the Israelites engage in the looting of martial tents. This passage mentions only the tents of the most elevated officials; nothing is said of the common soldiers' shelters.

Another passage in the Hebrew Bible featuring אֹהֶל in a military context is Jer 37:10. The prophet warns the besieged inhabitants of Jerusalem not to set their hopes on a rescuing Egyptian army, "because even if you had struck the entire army of the Chaldeans who fight against you, and there remained among them wounded men, they would rise up, each man in his tent, and burn this city with fire." This passage implies a large number of tents, perhaps an indication that each Babylonian soldier was protected by a tent. Another interpretation is that the Babylonian army travelled with hospital tents, or that the wounded lay down in their beds under tents (Plates 12, 13, 17).

The other occurrence is in Dan 11:45. The eschatological monarch, while battling foreign kingdoms, "shall pitch his

---

[63] By way of comparison, the Hebrew word for "helmet" כּוֹבַע is found only ten times and the word for "sling" קֶלַע eight times in the Hebrew Bible; yet both undoubtedly saw extensive use by the Israelite military. "Helmet" is found in 1 Sam 17:5, 38; Isa 59:17; Jer 46:4; Ezek 23:24; 27:10; 38:5; Ps 60:7; 108:8; 2 Chr 26:14. "Sling" is found in Judg 20:16; 1 Sam 17:40, 50; 1 Sam 25:29 (2x); Jer 10:18; 1 Chr 12:2; Prov 26:8.

[64] Compare the story in Josephus, *Antiquities*, IX:77-80.

palatial tents (וְיִטַּע אָהֳלֵי אַפַּדְנוֹ)" between the sea and the holy mountain during the end-time battles.

### King David's Military Tent

Other biblical passages may use the word אֹהֶל to refer to a war tent. According to 1 Sam 17:54: "David took the head of the Philistine [Goliath] and brought it to Jerusalem; and he put his weapons in his tent." This passage is filled with difficulties: Jerusalem is not captured for another 18 chapters; it is not clear whether the stored weapons belong to Goliath, David, or both; and the head's final destination is vague. We get the impression that the soldier's military tent was maintained in a constant state of readiness, equipped with the implements of warfare. Rameses II, too, keeps his armor in his tent, and Diodorus of Sicily records that Punic soldiers keep their armor and valuables inside their tents.[65] Josh 7:22 may be another example: Achan stores the booty from Jericho in his tent—although it is Achan's home, and not a war-tent *per se*. David's tent in 1 Sam 17:54 might also be the Tabernacle, just as the Philistines, after their victory on Mt. Gilboa, place Saul's armor and possibly his head in the temple of Ashtaroth (1 Sam 31:10).[66] Similar imagery is portrayed on an Assyrian wall relief, in which the heads of Elamite enemies are stored in a tent (Plate 20).

### Two Tents, Two Heroines, and Two Dead Generals: The Cases of Jael and Judith

Two of the most famous killings in the Hebrew Bible and Apocrypha occur in tents. The first is in Judges 4-5, where Jael kills Sisera. Even though a tent peg is the murder weapon, Jael's tent is not a military tent; rather, she and the rest of the Kenites are described as permanent tent-dwellers.[67] In the Apocryphal story of Judith, however, the heroine murders Holofernes inside his own

---

[65] For Rameses, see Raymond O. Faulkner, "The Battle of Kadesh," p. 101. Diodorus, XX.65.

[66] Note also Judith 13, in which Holofernes' severed head and his canopy are used to motivate Israelite troops.

[67] The Kenites are described as tent-dwellers in Judg 5:24. See also Baruch Halpern, "Kenites," *ABD* IV, pp. 17-22.

military tent.[68] The symbolism of both stories, in which a woman overcomes a war-experienced general, is enhanced by this background of martial tents.

## Israelite and Opposing Militaries Camping in Tents, and Issues of Sanitation

Although the noun אֹהֶל rarely appears, the Hebrew Bible frequently uses the root חנה "camp" apropos of the militaries of Israel and her neighbors.[69] Passages such as 2 Kgs 19:35 speak of the Assyrian camp (מַחֲנֵה), and the palace reliefs from Nineveh show that tents are a major feature in these camps.[70] Furthermore, the root חנה is used eight times in 2 Kings 7 for the Syrian camp ("tent" appears four times).

Other passages record the unclean environs of the military camp. Yahweh laments in Amos 4:10 that the people did not return to Him after "I made the stink of your camp go up into your nose." Related is a law in Deut 23:12-14, which instructs that one defecate "outside the camp"--although the explicit justification is characteristically religious:

> You shall have a place outside the camp and you shall go out to it; and you shall have a stick with your tools; and when you sit down outside, you shall dig a hole with it, and turn back and cover up your excrement. Because Yahweh your God walks in the midst of your camp, to save you and to give up your enemies before you, therefore your camp must be holy, that He may not see anything indecent among you, and turn away from you.

## Israelite and Syrian Militaries Campaigning in Booths

Three passages use סֻכּוֹת "booths" in reference to military shelters.[71] Uriah complains to David in 2 Sam 11:11 that he

---

[68] Judith 13.

[69] Israelite armies encamp in Josh 4:19; 5:10; 6:11, 14; 10:31, 34; Judg 20:19; 1 Sam 4:1, 3, 5-7, 11:11; 2 Sam 12:28; Jer 50:29, etc. Other armies encamp in Josh 10:5; Judg 6:4; 1 Sam 4:1; 13:5;
2 Kgs 7:16; 25:1; Jer 52:4, etc.

[70] For a discussion of the camp's location at Jerusalem, see David Ussishkin, "The 'Camp of the Assyrians' in Jerusalem," *IEJ* 29 (1979): pp. 137-42.

[71] See Michael M. Homan, "Booths or Succoth?: A Response to Yigael

cannot go home, while "the Ark and Israel and Judah are dwelling בַּסֻּכּוֹת." This provides the clearest evidence for the use of portable shelters by the Israelite military. Enemy forces also use booths in 1 Kgs 20:12, 16, where Ben-Hadad and thirty-two allied kings are carousing בַּסֻּכּוֹת while besieging Samaria.

## Some Concluding Remarks on Military Tents in the Hebrew Bible

The above survey indicates the use of tents in the military campaigns of ancient Israel and her neighbors. The extent to which tents were distributed to the lower-ranking soldiers is unknown, though it seems likely that most would sleep in a shelter of some sort. Indeed, Uriah reports in 2 Sam 11:11 that not just the elite, but "Israel and Judah are dwelling בַּסֻּכּוֹת. "

The following chapter explores yet another function of tents in the Hebrew Bible and the ancient Near East: as settings for activities of a sexual nature.

---

Yadin," *JBL* 118 (1999): pp. 691-97, which challenges Yadin's reading of סֻכּוֹת as the Transjordanian city (Yigael Yadin, "Some Aspects of the Strategy of Ahab and David," *Bib* 36 [1955]: pp. 332-51. For a less detailed argument, see also Yadin, *The Art of Warfare in Biblical Lands* (New York, 1963): pp. 274-75.

# CHAPTER SIX

# LOVE TENTS: SEX AND MARRIAGE UNDER
# TENT-RELATED SHELTERS

> While the Hebrew Bible is mostly silent
> regarding wedding rituals, several passages
> explicitly record the use of tents both in the
> ceremony and later as a chamber in which the
> marriage is consummated. Similar tents can be
> found throughout the ancient Near East.
> Furthermore, many lurid tales of sex and lust
> are set within tents in the Hebrew Bible.

When Rudolph Valentino's characters repeatedly conquered the
trepidation of otherwise virtuous girls in the early days of cinema,
more often than not the seduction occurred in a tent.[1] This
romantic aspect of tents was not invented in Hollywood, for a long
history links tent-related architecture to the erotic. This chapter
will explore the employment of tents in both ancient Israelite
marriage ceremonies and the consummation of nuptials, as well as
tent settings for biblical tales of luridness, seduction, and
exhibitionistic intercourse.

## Tents in Israelite Marriage Ceremonies

The Hebrew Bible is silent concerning the exact procedure by
which couples married in ancient Israel.[2] Nevertheless, various
passages attest to the use of tents in both the wedding ceremony
and the subsequent consummation. Solomon journeys with his
wedding procession inside a litter called מִטָּתוֹ "his bed" and

---

[1] Tents were prominent in such films as *The Sheik* (1921), *Blood and Sand*
(1922), *The Young Rajah* (1922), and Valentino's final film, *The Son of the
Sheik* (1926). For a more general discussion of the Western world's
preoccupation with Arab sexuality and procreativity, see Edward W. Said,
*Orientalism* (New York, 1979): p. 311.

[2] See for example Victor P. Hamilton, "Marriage (OT and ANE)," *ABD* IV, p.
560: "Ancient Israel never produced a marriage manual . . . the laws pertaining to
marriage in the legal codes . . . are few and scattered."

אַפִּרְיוֹן "palanquin" in Cant 3:7, 9.[3] The lavishly decorated litter is covered by dyed cloth and supported by silver poles.[4] Possibly related is Ps 45:14, where a wedding procession enigmatically includes a bride "inside" (פְּנִימָה), perhaps "inside" a litter similar to Solomon's.[5]

Then there is the nuptial tent itself. Ps 19:5-6 states that Yahweh has pitched a tent (אֹהֶל) for the sun, which comes forth like a bridegroom leaving his tent (חֻפָּתוֹ).[6] This is the biblical precedent for the use of the marriage canopy (חֻפָּה) in Jewish wedding ceremonies, a practice widely attested since the Rabbinic period.[7] Psalm 19 does not specify what the bridegroom is doing in the tent. But another passage suggests that the bridegroom is leaving his חֻפָּה following the marriage's consummation. Joel 2:16 prophesies that the Day of Yahweh is dire enough to necessitate total attendance at the assembly with none exempted: "Let the bridegroom exit his room (חֶדְרוֹ), and the bride her tent (חֻפָּתָהּ)."

*Marriage Tents: The Extra-Biblical Evidence*

Ps 19:5-6 and Joel 2:16 perhaps relate to a postbiblical practice of inhabiting a wedding tent for one week following the ceremony. In Rabbinic works, as well as various practices in the Islamic world, a bride returns to work following her seven days in the

---

[3] On the much-debated meaning and etymology of אַפִּרְיוֹן, see Marvin H. Pope, *The Song of Songs,* AB 7c (Garden City, NY, 1977): pp. 441-43.

[4] Cant 3:7-10.

[5] As suggested by Christoph Schroeder, "'A Love Song:' Psalm 45 in the Light of Ancient Near Eastern Marriage Texts," *CBQ* 58 (1996): p. 429, although he points out that many commentators replace פְּנִימָה with "coral beads" (פְּנִינִים) to parallel the following clause's "golden robes."

[6] See Samuel Krauss, "Der richtige Sinn von 'Schrecken in der Nacht,'" *Orient and Occident,* Moses Gaster 80th Anniversary Volume (London, 1936): pp. 323-30, who amasses biblical and anthropological data pertaining to the groom's danger on his wedding night. Thus the חֻפָּה protects the couple until dawn. This theory clarifies passages such as John 3:29, where the groom's friends are glad to hear his voice, and Cant 3:7, where Solomon's marriage litter is protected from "Night Fear" by 60 armed men.

[7] See Adolf Büchler, "The Induction of the Bride and the Bridegroom into the חופה in the First and the Second Centuries in Palestine," *Livre d'hommage à la mémoire du Samuel Poznański* (Leipzig, 1927): pp. 82-132. The affinity between marriages and חֻפּוֹת grows so strong in postbiblical Judaism that often the word חֻפָּה refers to the wedding itself, and not just the tent. See Avot 5:21.

חֻפָּה.[8] This bridal tent is routinely pitched near the dwelling of the groom's parents.[9] Similarly, Rebekah and Isaac consummate their marriage in his mother's tent.[10] Moreover, the Arabic phrase for the consummation of a marriage: "he built over her" (*bana 'alaiha*), is explained by the husband's role of making and furnishing a new tent for his bride.[11] Apparently related to a weeklong occupancy of the חֻפָּה is the week Jacob must live with Leah before he can marry Rachel; moreover, Samson's wedding is followed by a seven-day feast.[12]

An association between tents and weddings can also be found at Ugarit, although the correlation is not conclusive. Kirta's wedding is followed by the lines:

*tbrk · ilm · tity*
*tity · ilm · lahlhm*
*dr · il · lmšknthm*
The gods bless, they go
The gods go to their tents
The circle of El to their tabernacles.[13]

---

[8] Pesikta de-Rab Kahana 149b. See for further discussion Adolf Büchler, "The Induction of the Bride and the Bridegroom into the חופה in the First and the Second Centuries in Palestine," pp. 120-32. For a list of Islamic parallels ranging from Muhammad's era to the early 20th century, see W. Robertson Smith, *Kinship and Marriage in Early Arabia* (London, 1903): pp. 198-216. In Morocco, the marriage tent is still customary; see Edward Westermarck, *Ritual and Belief in Morocco* (New York, 1968) vol. 2, p. 9.

[9] W. Robertson Smith, *Kinship and Marriage in Early Arabia*, pp. 198-216. This parallels marriage practices in the Late Bronze Age; see Carlo Zaccagnini, "On Late Bronze Age Marriages," *Studi in onore di Edda Bresciani* (Pisa, 1985): pp. 593-605. See also Christoph Schroeder, "'A Love Song': Psalm 45 in the Light of Ancient Near Eastern Marriage Texts," p. 424, who discusses similar rituals.

[10] Gen 24:67. After the marriage, the woman may maintain her own tent. Thus, in Judg 4:22, the tent in which Sisera seeks refuge in belongs to Jael, not her husband Heber. Similarly, Sarah is said to have her own tent in Gen 18:6-10; 24:67; as do Leah, Rachel, and their servants in Gen 31:33.

[11] See W. Robertson Smith, *Kinship and Marriage*, p. 198.

[12] Gen 29:27-28 and Judg 14:12, 17. Tobit 8:20, however, prolongs a wedding feast for 14 days.

[13] *CAT* 1.15.III.17-19. See Adrianus van Selms, *Marriage and Family Life in Ugaritic Literature* (London, 1954): p. 41.

While tents are mentioned in a marital context, it is not clear if they played a role in the actual ceremony. More likely, the phrase expresses the disbanding of the divine assembly, an issue to be explored in the final chapter.[14]

From Egypt, an Aramaic text in Demotic script variously dated from the fourth to the second centuries B.C.E. describes a bridal chamber to be used in a sacred marriage, although the portions necessary to determine whether the structure is tent-related are missing.[15] Also relevant is a story concerning Alexander the Great that suggests a similar custom in Persia. After defeating Darius, Alexander orders the construction of 92 bridal tents for the marriages of Persian women to himself and his forces. Alexander's tent is supported by golden pillars, the others by silver, and the lavish wedding celebration is reported to have lasted for many days.[16]

*Four Lascivious Stories With a Tent Setting: Ham, Jael, Judith, and Pughat*

Tents not only provide the setting for weddings, but many additional acts of a lurid nature take place under their shelter in the Hebrew Bible and Ugaritic literature. For example, Ham witnesses his father's nakedness in a tent following Noah's drunkenness, an act some interpreters have read as indicative of homosexual rape.[17] Similarly in the tale of Jael and Sisera (Judges 4), although nothing in their relationship is explicitly sexual, various readers have found much in the way of sexual symbolism.[18] Also, Holofernes's military tent is the locale of four successive days of attempted seduction in the Apocryphal story of

---

[14] See below, chapter 9, pp. 187-92.

[15] Papyrus Amherst 63 is translated by Richard C. Steiner in *The Context of Scripture* (Leiden, 1997): p. 99. Note the damaged relevant portions in XI.1-3. For the papyrus as a whole, see Raymond A. Bowman, "An Aramaic Religious Text in Demotic Script," *JNES* 3 (1944): pp. 219-31; Stanislav Segert, "Preliminary Notes on the Structure of the Aramaic Poems in the Papyrus Amherst 63," *UF* 18 (1986): pp. 271-99.

[16] Athenaeus, *Deipnosophistae* XII.538d.

[17] Gen 9:20-27.

[18] Susan Ackerman, *Warrior, Dancer, Seductress, Queen: Women in Judges and Biblical Israel* (New York: Doubleday, 1998): pp. 90-117; Lillian R. Klein, "A Spectrum of Female Characters in the Book of Judges," *A Feminist Companion to Judges*, ed. Athalya Brenner (Sheffield, 1993): pp. 29-30.

Judith. Holofernes's efforts to win his desired's favor are less successful than Valentino's, as Judith cuts off his head within his tent.[19] Moreover, the canopy that covered Holofernes's bed is used, along with his severed head, as a trophy by which to inspire the Israelite forces.[20] Again, since the context is military, the presence of a tent is natural, and yet we find a pattern of seduction and violence under tent-related shelter. The tent connotes intimacy and security, and therefore makes the most horrid backdrop for crimes of sex. While not recorded in known ancient Near Eastern texts, it is likely that much sex took place with captives in military tents.

Similar in nature to the above three tales in the Hebrew Bible is the Ugaritic Epic of Aqhat, in which the heroine Pughat avenges her slain brother inside a tent. Pughat hospitably offers the soldier Yatpan wine, and then, although the tablet breaks off, it seems clear that she stabs Yatpan with a blade she had been concealing.[21]

### The Many Lusts of the Tent-Girl Sisters in Ezekiel 23

Further evidence of the sexual connotation of tents in the Hebrew Bible can be seen in the metaphorical sisters of Ezekiel 23, both of whose names allude to tents. Samaria is represented by Oholah "her tent," and Judah by her sister Oholibah "my tent is in her." According to Ezekiel, both girls are notorious for their sexual activities, notably with Egyptians (v. 3, 8, 19, 21), Assyrians (v. 5-7, 23), and Babylonians (17, 23). While tents elsewhere serve as metaphors for Israel and Judah, the sexual nature of the crimes in Ezekiel's metaphor is heightened by the mention of tents.[22] The Tent of Israel, which should be God's presence, is instead a shelter concealing fornication.

---

[19] Judith 13.

[20] Jud 13:15.

[21] Epic of Aqhat *CAT* 1.19-20. See Ronald S. Hendel, *The Epic of the Patriarch: The Jacob Cycle and the Narrative Traditions of Canaan and Israel*, HSM 42 (Atlanta, 1987): pp. 89-94; Susan Ackerman, *Warrior, Dancer, Seductress, Queen: Women in Judges and Biblical Israel*, pp. 198-200.

[22] On the use of tents as a metaphor for Israel and Judah, see above, pp. 7-9.

## The Love Tabernacle: Taboo Sex in Yahweh's Tent

Two specific sexual acts inside tents are among the most heinous breaches of ritual law in the Hebrew Bible. In Num 25:8, the priest Phinehas, grandson of Aaron, pursues an Israelite man and a Midianite woman into a tent and there executes the couple.[23] The couple's engagement in sexual intercourse at the time of their death is inferred from the description of Phinehas' spear piercing "the man and the woman to her belly."[24] Here the tent is called הַקֻּבָּה, a hapax legomenon with two possible explanations. Most likely it refers to the Tabernacle or a specific part of it, just as Arabic *qubba* refers to a tent shrine.[25] Furthermore, Num 25:6 says that all Israel were "weeping at the opening of the tent of the appointed time." The seriousness of the sin likewise suggests a Tabernacle setting, as the couple merits one of the harshest penalties in the Hebrew Bible, a plague killing 24,000.[26]

Alternatively, however, the story in Numbers 25 might be less dramatic; הַקֻּבָּה may simply refer to the couple's marriage tent. The costly plague would then have arisen from the intermarriage of Israelite men and foreign women, whether from Midian (P) or Moab (JE). If so, the couple executed in Num 25:8 are but one of many practicing international marriage. Later P texts make it clear that Midianite women, not just Kozbi, bear responsibility for the plague. Thus in Num 31:16, Moses reprimands the officers for not killing the Midianite women, claiming they caused the Israelite men "to act treacherously against Yahweh in the matter of Peor, so the plague came among the congregation of Yahweh." Phinehas's anger could result solely from frustration at the ever-increasing practice of intermarriage.

Eli's two sons also sin through sexual escapades within the Tabernacle at Shiloh. 1 Sam 2:22 records that Eli's sons "lay with the women assembled at the door of the tent of the appointed

---

[23] The couple remain anonymous until Num 25:14-15, which reveals that the man's name is Zimri, the woman's Cozbi. Both names have sexual overtones. "Zimri" refers to masculine strength, while Cozbi is related either to the Arabic goddess al-Kuṭba, or perhaps more likely to Akkadian *kuzbu* "voluptuousness," an attribute of Ishtar.

[24] Num 25:8. However, the Syriac replaces "to her belly" (אֶל-קֳבָתָהּ) with "in the qubbah" (בַּקֻּבָּה).

[25] See below, pp. 90-93.

[26] Num 25:9. Note too that Phinehas's action stays the plague.

time." While they are not killed immediately like the couple in Numbers 25, the text records that the sons failed to listen to their father's warnings concerning this grave sin, "because Yahweh desired to kill them" (v. 25). Evidence of the defiling power of sexual intercourse can be found in laws such as Lev 15:18, which prescribes a ritual bath and an interval to cleanse impurities for both the man and the woman following intercourse.[27] Consequently, sexual intercourse inside Yahweh's terrestrial tent-home ranks among the greatest taboos.

Also of interest is the postbiblical interpretation of the Tabernacle as the nuptial tent for the marriage of Yahweh to the people of Israel. This most clearly appears in Pesikta de-Rab Kahana 1:5, which midrashically reads "bride" (כַּלָּה) for the MT's "finished" (כַּלּוֹת) in Num 7:1, interpreting Moses as a bride before the Tabernacle.[28] Perhaps related to the standard week spent in a marriage חֻפָּה is the seven-day festival sponsored by Solomon upon the consecration of the Temple, although seven-day (de)consecrations are common.[29] The חֻפָּה metaphor of the Tabernacle and Temple arises out of the wedding imagery for God's relationship to Israel.[30]

## David's Concubines, A Rooftop Tent, and Absalom's Claim on the Throne

The clearest case in which a tent is used for a sexual purpose is in 2 Sam 16:20-22. Absalom and forces sympathetic to his claim on the throne force David out of Jerusalem. David's former adviser

---

[27] Both Num 25:6-9 and Lev 15:18 are P texts. Other authors record similar beliefs; e.g.: Exod 19:15 (JE) prepares Israel for their initial meeting with Yahweh by ordering them to abstain from sex for three days. Also, 1 Sam 21:5-6 reserves "holy bread" for men abstaining from sex, and Uriah's response to David in 2 Sam 11:11-13 shows that sex is forbidden to soldiers in Holy War, which requires the presence of the Ark.

[28] Howard Eilberg-Schwartz's *God's Phallus* ([Boston, 1994]: pp. 142-46; 166-67) discusses the feminization of Moses (and Israel) vis-à-vis God in biblical and Jewish literature.

[29] Solomon's feast following the consecration of the Temple similarly lasts seven days in 1 Kgs 8:65-66 and 2 Chr 7:8-9. Nevertheless, many changes of status last seven days (profane/sacred, unclean/clean, single/married, layman/priest).

[30] Wedding imagery is found in Isa 61:10; 62:5; Ezekiel 16, and Hos 2:16-18.

Ahithophel, now allied with Absalom, recommends a bold public declaration of the succession of kingship that transcends the traditional anointing ceremony and trumpet blast. He suggests that Absalom pitch "the tent" (הָאֹהֶל) on the palace rooftop and lie with the ten concubines David left behind to care for the Jerusalem palace.[31] The definite article prefacing אֹהֶל suggests a specific tent, likely akin to the marriage חֻפָּה.[32]

Absalom's sexual relations with David's harem fulfills Nathan's prophecy following David's sin against Uriah:

> Behold, I will raise up evil against you out of your own house; and I will take your wives before your eyes, and give them to your neighbor, and he shall lie with your wives in the sight of this sun. For you did it secretly; but I will do this thing before all Israel, and before the sun.
>
> (2 Sam 12:11-12)[33]

Intercourse with the previous king's harem as a claim of regal succession is paralleled in 2 Sam 3:7, where Ishbosheth questions Abner's relationship with Saul's concubine; 2 Sam 12:8, where attributes of kingship include the wives of the former king; and 1 Kgs 2:17-25, where Adonijah's request for David's consort Abishag is interpreted by Solomon as a claim on the throne.[34]

Absalom's rooftop tent partakes of the public and the private: while his actions are partially masked by a linen wall, presumably for decency's sake, nonetheless little is left to the voyeur's imagination: it is basically "before all Israel, and before the sun."

---

[31] See 2 Sam 15:16.

[32] Alternatively, the definite article may suggest the tent was in fact the "tent of the appointed time."

[33] Baruch Halpern observes this is the same roof from which David saw Bathsheba, *The First Historians* (University Park, 1996): pp. 51-52.

[34] Ken Stone, "Sexual Practice and the Structure of Prestige: The Case of the Disputed Concubines," *SBL Seminar Papers* (1993): pp. 554-73; François Langlamet, "Absalom et les concubines de son père," *RB* 84 (1977): pp. 161-209. Jacob similarly rebukes Reuben for sexual relations with Rachel's handmaid Bilhah (Gen 35:22; 49:3-4). Note also the Ugaritic king Arḫalba, who in the absence of a child to succeed the throne, wills his wife to his brother, and threatens divine retribution if another man takes her (*PRU* 3:16.144). This also recalls levirate marriage customs. Ultimately, it is a matter of primate social structure: the dominant male mates with all the females until he is displaced.

Proofs of sexual relations are elsewhere publicly displayed in the Hebrew Bible. A law recorded in Deut 22:15 seems to indicate that a cloth stained with hymeneal blood was evidence of a girl's premarital chastity.[35] The consummation of marriage before an audience finds widespread extra-biblical parallels.[36] Absalom's bold claim necessitated a bold forum. None could doubt the action and its significance.

The following two chapters explore the use of tents in religious contexts. Chapter seven investigates the many tent shrines mentioned in literature and archaeology throughout the Near East, while chapter eight specifically examines the history, form, and fate of the Hebrew Bible's most famous tent: the Tabernacle.

---

[35] David R. Mace, *Hebrew Marriage* (London, 1953): pp. 230-32; Raphael Patai, *Sex and Family in the Bible and the Middle East* (Garden City, New York, 1959): pp. 66-70. Awareness of the imprecision of this "proof" of virginity can be seen in the Mishnah (Ketuboth, 1.3), which discusses a case where a girl's hymen is ruptured accidentally. Virginity as a sought-after quality in a bride is especially apparent in Lev 21:13, which says priests can marry only virgins.

[36] See Edward Westermarck, *The History of Human Marriage*, I, pp. 435-39; II, pp. 445-48, 504, 586. Leo Africanus' 16th-century report from Morocco tells of bloodstained sheets displayed by the groom immediately following intercourse (p. 325). Similar accounts are in Joseph P. Tournefort, *Voyage in the Levant* II (London, 1718): p. 69; Johann L. Burckhardt, *Arab Proverbs* (London, 1830): p. 117; *Bedouins* I (London, 1831): p. 266; Johann G. Wetzstein in A. Bastian's *Zeitschrift für Ethnologie* (1873): pp. 290 ff.; and F. A. Klein, "Mitteilungen über Leben, Sitten und Gebräuche der Fellachen in Palästina," *ZDPV* 6 (1883): pp. 81-101. Further parallels are listed in H. Clay Trumbull, *The Threshold Covenant* (New York, 1896): pp. 243-52, and Shelagh Weir and Widad Kawar, "Costumes and Wedding Customs in Bayt Dajan," *PEQ* 107 (1975): p. 50, who discuss a white undergarment (*bayt al-shām*) worn by a Palestinian bride on the wedding night, the blood stains on which are then publicly displayed.

# CHAPTER SEVEN

# TABERNACLE PARALLELS: NEAR EASTERN PORTABLE SHRINES ACROSS THE AGES

Archaeological and literary data from the Near East attest to the existence of tent shrines, as well as many other portable sanctuaries more properly classified as booths or tented wagons. These range chronologically from the earliest historical periods to the modern era. Two of these shrines, one displayed on battle reliefs of Rameses II and one buried with Tutankhamon, parallel the descriptions of the Tabernacle's form and function to a degree implying a direct line of tradition. These two Egyptian tents date to the Late Bronze period, as does Ugaritic literature recording a similar tent dwelling for El. Finally, the many differences between the Jerusalem Temple and the Tabernacle refute the theory that the Priestly sacred tent is merely a fictitious copy of the Temple.

## History of Research

Scholarly faith in the Tabernacle's historicity declined with the advent of Higher Criticism. The elaborate tent shrine described in the priestly stratum became the focal point for Wellhausen's claim that a portable sanctuary was fraudulently invented to lend credence to a period of desert wanderings, thus justifying P's contemporary postexilic demands. Moreover, while Wellhausen conceded that a tent-covering of sorts might have played a role in early Israelite religion as a shelter for the Ark, he wrote that the priestly Tabernacle "ist in Wahrheit nicht das Urbild, sondern die Kopie des jerusalemischen Tempels."[1] Subsequent scholars, intending to bolster the Tabernacle's historicity, sought other Near Eastern tent shrines, ancient and otherwise. Parallels from the Islamic world dominated early endeavors, but while these camel-

---

[1] Julius Wellhausen, *Prolegomena zur Geschichte Israels* 6th edition (Berlin, 1905): p. 37. Current scholarly opinion essentially remains that of Wellhausen. See p. 2-3, n. 12.

borne tent litters and palladia testified to a long history of Semitic tent shrines, they better mirrored the Ark in function. In 1947, however, Frank M. Cross, Jr., published a seminal article on the Tabernacle in which he drew on various tent shrines from Phoenicia, Ugarit, Egypt, and Mesopotamia to argue the Tabernacle's reality.[2] Studies on biblical and ancient Near Eastern tents since Cross's article typically are limited to a specific material culture or a class of tent.[3] The intention of the present chapter is to examine the many portable shrines known to scholarship, both individually and collectively. In the process, the Tabernacle's historicity will be made more probable. Moreover, Wellhausen's solution to the shared characteristics of the Jerusalem Temple and the Tabernacle will be reversed: the priestly tent will be shown to have precedence.

*Bedouin and Pre-Islamic Tent Shrines: The ʿutfah, the maḥmal, and the qubba*

Prior to Cross's article, scholars seeking parallels to the Tabernacle focused almost exclusively on Bedouin palladia and sacred litters known as the ʿutfah, the maḥmal, and their apparent ancestor, the qubba.[4] The ʿutfah, the most famous of which is the markab of the Rwala tribe, consists of a wooden frame, decorated with ostrich feathers, at times covered with a tent (Plates 21a, 21b).

---

[2] Frank M. Cross, Jr., "The Tabernacle," pp. 45-68; "The Priestly Tabernacle," *The Biblical Archaeologist Reader I*, pp. 201-28.

[3] For a list and discussion of these studies, see p. 4, n. 18.

[4] These parallels were first pointed out by Robert W. Rogers in a letter to *The Academy*, March 31 (1883): pp. 221 ff. Numerous studies followed, most in the first half of the 20th century. Brenda Z. Seligman, "Sacred Litters Among the Semites," *Sudan Notes and Records* (1918): p. 269, and Richard Hartmann, "Zelt und Lade," *ZAW* 37 (1918): pp. 216-25, are of particular merit. The most thorough analysis of the qubba remains Henri Lammens, "Le culte des bétyles et les processions religieuses chez les arabes préislamites," initial publication in *Bulletin de l'Institut français d'archéologie orientale* 17 (1919), reprinted in *L'Arabie occidentale avant l'Hégire* (Beirut, 1928): pp. 101-79. For a comprehensive review of previous studies on the ʿutfah, maḥmal, and qubba, see Julian Morgenstern, "The Ark, the Ephod, and the 'Tent of Meeting,'" *HUCA* 17 (1942): pp. 153-266; *HUCA* 18 (1943): pp. 1-52. On the formerly extensive distribution of the ʿutfah, see Anne Blunt, *Bedouin Tribes of the Euphrates* II (London, 1879): p. 146, and Julian Morgenstern, "The Ark, the Ephod, and the 'Tent of Meeting,'" pp. 176, 191.

This frame is placed on the back of a camel, and is used primarily as a means of inciting fervor prior to military engagements. Sacrifices are made before it, the blood from which is sprinkled on its corners.[5] It is also valued as an oracular device.[6] Accounts of this structure include several stories that strongly recall the Ark's use as a palladium, and, like the Ark, horrible things are said to happen if the *'utfah* is captured by enemy tribes.[7]

Similar in nature to the *'utfah*, yet larger, is the *maḥmal*, a domed, camel-borne tent elaborately decorated; it typically houses Islamic religious texts (Plates 22, 23, 24a, 24b).[8] It is used occasionally as a palladium, but more often the *maḥmal* serves as a palanquin for tribal leaders on the Haj to Mecca, a practice already attested in the 13th century.[9]

Despite the similarities between the *'utfah* and the *maḥmal* on the one hand, and the Tabernacle and its cultic implements on the other, these biblical and Islamic tent shrines have been the victims of over-zealous parallelomania. Robert W. Rogers, for example, notes that both the Ark and the *maḥmal* bear silver-gilt knobs, are paraded circularly (the Ark seven times at Jericho, the *maḥmal* three times around an open space before the Cairo citadel), and may not be touched (Uzzah died because he grasped the Ark, a traveler confessed he had been overbold in holding the fringe of the *maḥmal*).[10] In the end, the most that can be said regarding the

---

[5] Brenda Z. Seligman, "Sacred Litters Among the Semites," p. 275, and Julian Morgenstern, "The Ark, the Ephod, and the 'Tent of Meeting,'" p. 158. Similarly, Lev 16:15 commands that blood be placed upon the Ark on the Day of Atonement.

[6] Julian Morgenstern, p. 158. Cf. Num 7:89.

[7] Julian Morgenstern, pp. 162-63, 178. Cf. 1 Samuel 4-7.

[8] What is contained within the *maḥmal* is disputed. Edward W. Lane, *The Manners and Customs of the Modern Egyptians* II (London, 1842): p. 202, says two copies of the Koran, while Johann L. Burckhardt, *Travels in Arabia* II (London, 1829): pp. 49-51, says a "small book of prayers and charms." Occasionally the *maḥmal* does not contain religious texts, but is empty. See Frants Buhl, "Maḥmal," *The Encyclopaedia of Islam* VI, New Edition (Leiden, 1986): p. 45.

[9] Frants Buhl, "Maḥmal," *The Encyclopaedia of Islam* VI, New Edition (Leiden, 1986): pp. 44-46.

[10] Robert W. Rogers, *The Academy*, (1883): pp. 221 ff. It is unknown what Rogers had in mind when he referred to the Ark's silver-gilt knobs. Rogers is not alone in parallelomania; see for example Carl R. Raswan, *The Black Tents of*

relationship between the *ʿutfah* and the *maḥmal* to the Tabernacle is that they provide extra-biblical evidence of a Semitic tent shrine serving in processions and battle.

The antecedent of these Islamic tents, the *qubba*, is again a miniature, camel-borne tent used as a palladium, oracular device, and procession leader.[11] While the differences between the massive biblical tent purported to require six carts and twelve oxen to transport it (Num 7:3) and a tent carried on the back of a single camel should not be underestimated, the *qubba*'s long and distinguished history manifests two elements that more closely link it to the Tabernacle. Like the Tabernacle, the *qubba* is covered by red leather; and more remarkable, the Tabernacle itself is referred to by this same word (הַקֻּבָּה) in Num 25:8.[12] Early Islamic sources report that Muhammad and his contemporaries traveled and fought bearing a *qubba*.[13] Interestingly, an early representation of the Arabian *qubba* exists in a carving from the temple of Bel at Palmyra (Plate 25a). Here a camel can be seen carrying a red leather tent in procession.[14] From the tent's front an item protrudes, often identified as a betyl.[15] The *qubba*'s existence is also attested in Palmyrene texts.[16]

---

*Arabia* (Boston, 1935): pp. 75-78, who calls the *markab* "the Ark of Ishmael," and Julian Morgenstern, "The Book of the Covenant," *HUCA* 5 (1928): pp. 112-13, who links Deborah to the "battle-maidens" who occasionally rode in the *ʿutfah*. See also Julian Morgenstern's "The Ark, the Ephod, and the 'Tent of Meeting,'" *HUCA* 17 (1942-1943): pp. 177-79; 204-07. Cross accuses Morgenstern of excessively pushing the parallels in "The Priestly Tabernacle," p. 219. More recently, Menahem Haran addresses this same issue in "Otfe, Mahmal and Kubbe—Notes on the Study of the Origins of Biblical Cult Forms: The Problem of Arabic Parallels," in *D. Neiger Memorial Volume*, (Jerusalem, 1959): pp. 215-21 (Hebrew).

[11] For early Islamic accounts of the *qubba*, see Henri Lammens, *L'Arabie occidentale avant L'Hégire*, Herbert G. May, "The Ark—A Miniature Temple," *AJSL* 52 (1936): pp. 229-31, and Julian Morgenstern, "The Ark, the Ephod, and the '"Tent of Meeting,'" pp. 207-23.

[12] On the existence and meaning of red tents in Islam, see Henri Lammens, "Le culte des bétyles," p. 134. On the *qubba*'s reference to the Tabernacle, see above, p. 13.

[13] For a list of early Islamic sources, see Herbert G. May, "The Ark—A Miniature Temple," p. 230 n. 56.

[14] Henri Seyrig, Robert Amy, and Ernest Will, *Le Temple de Bel à Palmyra, Texte et Planches* (Paris, 1975): p. 88, pl. 42.1. For a color facsimile, see *Le Temple de Bel à Palmyra*, Album (1968): p. 143.

[15] Henri Seyrig, R. Amy, E. Will, *Le Temple de Bel à Palmyra*, p. 88.

Three other terracotta images from Syria, tentatively dated to the first century B.C.E., depict camel-borne litters often identified with the *qubba*, although this is less certain (Plates 25b, 26a, 26b).[17] In sum, while the *qubba* and its successors the *'utfah* and the *maḥmal* are more austere than the Tabernacle, they point to the long history of Near Eastern tent shrines, and show that for pastoral societies where tents provide an important means of shelter, tents often find representations in the religion.

### The Ka'ba and the Tabernacle

One further Islamic structure is surprisingly neglected by those seeking parallels to the Tabernacle. This is the Ka'ba, the most sacred shrine in Islam.

The Ka'ba consists of a large stone building covered by a black curtain called the *kiswa* (Plate 27). The *kiswa* serves no utilitarian purpose, and it seems to be a symbolic representation of tent-related architecture. In fact, early witnesses claim the Ka'ba was a roofless wooden shrine covered by a tent until it was rebuilt by Muhammad.[18] Various legends within Islam support this as well. One story maintains that Adam, upon being cast out of Paradise, came to Mecca. Thither, God sent from Paradise a tent of red jacinth stone (sic!) in which Adam lived.[19] While it now consists of

---

Consequently, if the *qubba* is in fact the forerunner of the *maḥmal*, then the aniconic Islamic tradition has replaced the original betyl with religious texts. Similarly within Judaism the focus of worship is no longer an אֲרוֹן with stone tablets, but an אֲרוֹן with scrolls.

[16] Hans-Jürgen Zobel, "אֲרוֹן," *TDOT* 1:367.

[17] Described in Franz Cumont, "La double Fortune des Sémites et les processions à dos de chameau, *Études Syriennes* (Paris, 1917): pp. 263-76. The tented cover of figures 31-32 may have originally been red as well. See Harald Ingholt, "Inscriptions and Sculptures from Palmyra I," *Berytus* 3 (1936): p. 86.

[18] The Ka'ba is supposed to rest directly beneath God's throne in heaven. God ordered his angels to create the shrine prior to the creation of humans, and it was later rebuilt by Abraham. In the time of Muhammad, the shrine was roofless, measuring approximately 9 cubits tall and 30 by 20 cubits in length and width, built around the well of Zamzam. Then in 608, when Muhammad was approximately 38, he rebuilt it. See Keppel A. C. Creswell, *Early Muslim Architecture*, revised ed. (London, 1989): p. 3; Robin Bidwell, *Travellers in Arabia* (New York, 1976): p. 117. For the Ka'ba's tent-related predecessor, see Toufic Fahd, *Le Panthéon de L'Arabie centrale à la veille de L'Hégire* (Paris, 1968): 204-05, and Julius Wellhausen, *Reste arabischen Heidentums* 2nd edition (Berlin, 1897): pp. 73-79.

[19] Arent J. Wensinck, "Ka'ba," *Encyclopaedia of Islam* II (Leiden, 1927): p.

black panels, during the reign of the Wahhabis, the *kiswa*, like the Tabernacle's outer covering, was red.[20] Lastly, like the Tabernacle's curtains, the *kiswa* possesses a special sanctity; when replaced annually, pieces of the former *kiswa* are sold by the doorkeepers as amulets.[21]

*Tents in Ugaritic and Hittite Mythology and the Tabernacle*

The Tabernacle's most solid literary parallel comes from the tablets of Ras Shamra (Ugarit), where El, the elderly head of the pantheon, explicitly dwells in a tent (*ahl*).[22] Moreover, El's dwelling is frequently called a tabernacle (*mškn*).[23] Two other designations, *dd* and *qrš*, can be found in the common formula for entering El's abode:

tgly · dd · il · wtbu
qrš · mlk · ab · šnm

They rolled back the tent flap of El's domed-tent[24] and went into

---

589. This legend also claims that God sent a white jacinth to be Adam's throne, which is now the sacred black stone.

[20] Arent J. Wensinck, revised by Jacques Jomier, "Ka'ba," *Encyclopaedia of Islam* IV, New Edition (Leiden, 1978): p. 319.

[21] Toufic Fahd, *Le Panthéon de L'Arabie centrale*, pp. 203-36.

[22] El's *ahl* is attested in *CAT* 1.15.III.18-19; perhaps also 1.19.IV.50-60, where El is associated with *ytpn*'s tent camp. On El's status as chief deity, see E. Theodore Mullen, Jr., *The Divine Council in Canaanite and Early Hebrew Literature*, HSM 24 (Missoula, 1980): pp. 139-147, and Conrad E. L'Heureux, *Rank Among the Canaanite Gods: El, Ba'al and the Rephaim*, HSM 21 (Missoula, 1979).

[23] See for example *CAT* 1.15.III.17-19, where *mškn* is parallel to *ahl*. Similarly, אֹהֶל and מִשְׁכָּן are frequently paired in the Hebrew Bible (e.g., Num 24:5; Isa 54:2; Jer 30:18).

[24] As suggested by Richard J. Clifford, "The Tent of El and the Israelite Tent of Meeting," p. 222, and *The Cosmic Mountain*, pp. 51-53. The meaning of *dd* is uncertain; however, the verb *gly* (uncovering or rolling back, cf. Hebrew גלה) fits a tent flap perfectly, as proposed by Conrad L'Heureux in Richard J. Clifford, "The Tent of El and the Israelite Tent of Meeting," *CBQ* 33 (1971): p. 222, and *The Cosmic Mountain in Canaan and the Old Testament* (Cambridge, 1972): p. 52. In *CAT* 19.IV.213-14, *dd* is parallel to *ahl*. The proposed domed-shaped tent for *dd* arises from the supposed Semitic cognates "mountain" (Akkadian *šadû*) and "breast" (Hebrew שׁד). Note also the breast-shaped Egyptian tents in figure 14 (see Frank M. Cross, Jr., *Canaanite Myth and Hebrew Epic*, p. 55 n. 43). However, Marvin H. Pope, "The Status of El at Ugarit," *UF* 19 (1987): pp. 219-30, remains unconvinced by Clifford, arguing that in *CAT* 1.19.IV.213-214 *dd* is parallel not to *ahl*, but rather to *bhlm* "in here." See also Pope, *El in the*

The tent frames[25] of the king, father of years.[26]

El's tent is further attested in a Hittite fragment from Boğazköy, which apparently records a Canaanite myth involving El (here Elkunirsa).[27] Lines 5-7 of the tablet read:

na-aš ŠA $^{ID}$ma-a-la ḫar-šum-na-aša-ar[-aš]
[na-aš A-NA] $^D$el-ku-ni-ir-ša ŠA $^D$a-še-er-tum $^{LÚ}$MU-DI-ŠU a-a[r-aš]
[na-aš-kán ŠA] $^D$el-ku-ni-ir-ša $^{GIŠ}$ZA.LAM.GAR-aš an-da pa-it

He [Ba‘al] came to the source of the Euphrates; he came to Elkunirsa, the husband of Asherah. He entered the tent (ku-uš-ta-rū) of Elkunirsa.[28]

---

*Ugaritic Texts*, p. 66. Less appealing is Edward Lipiński's translation of *ḏd* as "'horror' in the sense of a horrifying thing" based on Arabic *ḏawd* (defense, protection) and *ḏāda* (to drive away, repel, defend) ("El's Abode," pp. 65-66).

[25] El's *qrš* appears to be a case of metonymy. A relationship clearly exists between Ugaritic *qrš* and the Hebrew Bible's קֶרֶשׁ, despite Marvin Pope's hesitancy (*El in the Ugaritic Texts*, VTS 2 [Leiden, 1955]: pp. 67-68). Pope's proposed Semitic parallels such as Arabic *ḳarasa* (freeze, congeal) and Akkadian *qarāšu* (split) seem less attractive in comparison, although the latter may relate to the construction of tent-frames. For Arabic *ḳarasa* as a cognate, see André Parrot, *Le "Refrigerium" dans l'au delà* (Paris: 1937): p. 19, and Edward Lipiński, "El's Abode," *OLP* 2 (1971): p. 66. For a tent shrine at Mari which uses *qrš*, see pp. 179-81. Possibly, just like the Tabernacle's קֶרֶשׁ (Exod 26:19), the *qrš* of El's tent may rest on pedestals in *CAT* 1.3.IV.16-17, as claimed by Charles Virolleaud, *La déesse ‘Anat* (Paris, 1938), and followed by Umberto Cassuto, *Commentary on Exodus*, trans. from Hebrew by I. Abrahams (Jerusalem, 1967): p. 323. This text, however, is reconstructed.

[26] *CAT* 1.4.IV.23-24; 1.6.I.34-36; and 1.1.III.23-24 (with a 3rd person m.s. subject rather than 3rd pl.); partially reconstructed in *CAT* 1.5.VI.1-2; 1.17.VI.48-49. See also *CAT* 2.III.5 and 3.V.15-16.

[27] Heinrich Otten suggests Elkunirsa may be the Hittite spelling of West Semitic *ʾl qn ʾrṣ* (El, creator of earth) in "Ein kanaanäischer Mythus aus Boğazköy" *Mitteilungen des Instituts für Orientforschung* 1 (1953): pp. 138-39.

[28] Translation by Harry A. Hoffner, Jr., in "The Elkunirsa Myth Reconsidered," *RHA* 76 (1965): p. 8. Hoffner suggests that El's abode here corresponds to Ugaritic *qrš* rather than to *ahl*, but this is unlikely, given that Akkadian *kuštaru* is the most frequent designation for "tent." For convenient translations of the text, see *ANET*, 3rd edition, p. 519; Harry A. Hoffner, Jr., *Hittite Myths*, Second Edition (Atlanta, 1998): pp. 90-92. For text and commentary, see also Heinrich Otten, "Ein kanaanäischer Mythus aus Boğazköy," pp. 125-50.

In Hittite culture proper, the "Great Assembly" convened in a tent, and an altar was set up within the divine tent along with a stele.[29] Moreover, a tent stood at the Hittite temple's gate and is once said to have resided within "the house."[30]

Thus, while no evidence of a "Tabernacle" dedicated to El has been discovered at Ugarit, El clearly lives in a tent in the world of myth.[31] Nevertheless, in addition to the tent-related designations for El's abode, it is also called a *mṯb* (dwelling), a *mẓll* (shelter) and even a *bt* (house) and a *hkl* (temple).[32] These difficulties have led some scholars to see a confluence of two traditions: an archaic one where El dwells in a tent, and a newer stratum where El dwells in a permanent house.[33] This is unnecessary given the ambiguity of domicile designations previously discussed: in the Hebrew Bible, the Tabernacle and other tents are frequently designated בית and sometimes היכל. Moreover, intra-Ugaritic evidence points in the same direction: the Aqhat legend calls El's abode *bt* five times, and in the same passage it is designated *ḏd//qrš*.[34]

The appellations *mškn, ahl,* and the wooden *qrš* supports are not the only similarities between El's tent and the Tabernacle.

---

[29] *KUB* 35:I:14ff. See Moshe Weinfeld, "Institutions in the Priestly Source," *Proceedings of the Eighth World Congress of Jewish Studies*, V (Jerusalem, 1983): p. 104 nn. 5 and 42.

[30] *IBOT* III 148:II:61 ff. See Moshe Weinfeld, "Institutions in the Priestly Source," p. 104, who points out the ramifications of this Hittite tent in a house for Richard E. Friedman's theory that the Tabernacle stood in the Temple (see below, pp. 167-71).

[31] It is noteworthy, however, that permanent temples dedicated to Dagon and Baʿal have been found at Ugarit, but no shrine of El. Perhaps El possessed his own "tent of the appointed time."

[32] El's *mṯb* and *mẓll* are found in *CAT* 1.4.I.13-19; 1.4.IV.52-57 and *CAT* 3.V.47-48. *bt* is used of El's abode in *CAT* 1.17.I.32-33; II.4-5, 21-22; 1.114.12. The word *hkly* is used in the text of *CAT* 1.21.8, although it is not entirely clear who owns this temple. Some reconstruct *h]kl[k]* in *CAT* 1.3.V.21, where Anath seems to be ordering El not to rejoice. But this must be a tent in any case, as *ḏd//qrš* appears 12 lines earlier.

[33] See for example E. Theodore Mullen, Jr., *The Divine Council*, p. 139, who states that the Aqhat text (*CAT* 1.17) "obviously contains a mixing of traditions." Frank M. Cross, Jr., *Canaanite Myth and Hebrew Epic,* p. 43, sees "uneven layers of tradition." Richard J. Clifford, *The Cosmic Mountain*, p. 54, argues that within the Baʿal cycle (*CAT* 1.1-11), El lives in a tent, whereas in the Aqhat legend and *CAT* 1.21, the situation is more confused.

[34] *CAT* 1.17.VI.48-49. Another option would be that it is a tent within a palace, paralleling Richard E. Friedman's idea that the Tabernacle resided within the Jerusalem Temple (see pp. 167-71).

They are both elaborate in form and furnishings. Each is large and consists of more than one room, as in one passage El is said to reply from the "seventh room // eighth enclosure."[35] El's tent is furnished with fittings cast (*yṣq*) from gold and silver, as well as a throne (*kḥṯ*), footstool (*hdm*), couch (*nᶜl*), and table (*ṯlḥn*), all built by the divine craftsman Kothar.[36] Yahweh appoints Bezalel and Oholiab to construct similar furnishings for the Tabernacle.[37]

El's tent apparently hosts the divine assembly (*pḥr mᶜd*), where the gods of Ugarit gather and engage in politics.[38] Clearly there is a link between Ugaritic *mᶜd* and the Tabernacle's most common epithet, אֹהֶל מוֹעֵד "tent of assembly/appointed time."[39] Richard J.

---

[35] *CAT* 1.3.V.11, 26-27; see E. Theodore Mullen, *The Divine Council in Canaanite and Early Hebrew Literature*, p. 134.

[36] *CAT* 1.4.I.33-39. The text states they are built by *hyn*, an appellation of Kothar. See William F. Albright, "The Furniture of El in Canaanite Mythology," *BASOR* 91 (1943): pp. 39-44. Albright further suggests Ugaritic *nᶜl ʾil* be translated "litter of El," and the following line's *yblhm ḥrṣ* "two golden poles," mirroring the two gold-covered poles used to transport the Ark (Exod 25:13-15). Cf. Theodor H. Gaster, "The Furniture of El in Canaanite Mythology," *BASOR* 93 (1944): pp. 20-23, who argues against Albright, preferring the reading "shoes of El" for *nᶜl ʾil* and "pours over with gold" for *yblhm ḥrṣ*.

[37] Bezalel and Oholiab are commissioned in Exod 35:30-36:1; although they are humans, they receive a divine spirit. While Yahweh does not explicitly command in Exodus that a throne or footstool be built, Yahweh's common epithet "enthroned on the cherubim" (1 Sam 4:4; 2 Sam 6:2; 2 Kgs 19:15; Isa 37:16; Pss 80:1; 99:1; 1 Chr 13:6) makes it likely that the two golden cherubim on the mercy seat serve as a throne (Exod 25:18-22) from which Yahweh governs (Exod 25:22; Num 7:89). The Ark is called a footstool (הֲדֹם) in 1 Chr 28:2 (cf. Pss 99:5; 132:7), the same name used of El's furniture. Moreover, in all six of its occurrences in the Hebrew Bible, הֲדֹם refers to the footstool of Yahweh. Yahweh, like El, requires a table (שֻׁלְחָן) in the shrine (Exod 25:23-30), an element of Canaanite anthropomorphism which the Israelites apparently retained. There is, however, no bed in P's Tabernacle, although Samuel sleeps in the shrine at Shiloh—just where and upon what is unspecified (1 Sam 3:3).

[38] This expression (*pḥr mᶜd*) occurs five times in *CAT* 1.2.I.14-31. For a list of post-Ugaritic Canaanite evocations of the Divine assembly, see Richard J. Clifford, *The Cosmic Mountain in Canaan and the Old Testament*, pp. 45-46. On the Mesopotamian divine assembly, see Thorkild Jacobsen, "Primitive Democracy in Mesopotamia," *JNES* 2 (1943): pp. 159-72.

[39] Frank M. Cross, "The Priestly Tabernacle in the Light of Recent Research," p. 173; Richard J. Clifford, "The Tent of El and the Israelite Tent of Meeting," pp. 223-25; *The Cosmic Mountain*, pp. 43-48; E. Theodore Mullen, *The Divine Council in Canaanite and Early Hebrew Literature*, pp. 128-75. The earliest known use of the word *mᶜd* for a political assembly is in the Tale of Wenamun, where the prince of Byblos summons his *mwᶜd* to confront a foreigner. See John A. Wilson, "The Assembly of the Phoenician City," *JNES* 4

Clifford argues that the Priestly source retained the archaic title "tent of meeting"/"tent of the appointed time" for the Tabernacle, simply substituting Yahweh's meeting with Moses for the convocation of the entire Canaanite pantheon.[40] Like Yahweh's use of the Tabernacle as the setting for his decrees, so too El mandates from his tent.[41] El lives in a tent situated on a mountain, and it is on top of Sinai that Moses is shown Yahweh's celestial dwelling (תַּבְנִית).[42]

There is evidence from Ugarit that El is not alone in inhabiting a tent shrine. Following a divine assembly, all the gods retreat to their tents and tabernacles in *CAT* 1.15.III.17-19:

> *tbrk · ilm · tity*
> *tity · ilm · lahlhm*
> *dr · il · lmšknthm*

The gods bless (i.e., say farewell), they go
The gods go to their tents
The circle of El to their tabernacles.

---

(1945): p. 245; Hans Goedicke, *The Report of Wen Amun* (Baltimore, 1975): p. 123

[40] Richard J. Clifford, "The Tent of El and the Israelite Tent of Meeting," 225-27; *The Cosmic Mountain*, pp. 43-48. William H. C. Propp in a private communication points out another sign of archaism: it is always אֹהֶל מוֹעֵד, never אֹהֶל הַמּוֹעֵד with a definite article.

[41] The early notion of a tent of assembly as the source of Yahweh's decrees can be found in the JE texts Exod 33:7-11; Num 11:16-30; 12:4-10. E. Theodore Mullen, *The Divine Council in Canaanite and Early Hebrew Literature*, p. 171, points out that in these passages Yahweh's theophany occurs at the door of the tent of the appointed time, corresponding to El standing in his tent shrine to address Anath in *CAT* 1.3.V.26-27. For Yahweh governing from His tent in the Priestly source, see Exod 25:22; Num 7:89. El sends forth decrees from his tent in *CAT* 1.1.IV.13-20; 1.2.I.36-37, V.33-35; 1.6.I.43-65. For further discussion, see E. Theodore Mullen, *The Divine Council in Canaanite and Early Hebrew Literature*, pp. 139-50.

[42] For El's mountain abode, see *CAT* 1.1.III.23; 1.2.I.20, discussed by Richard J. Clifford, *The Cosmic Mountain in Canaan and the Old Testament*, pp. 34-57, Mark S. Smith, "Mt. *ll* in *KTU* 1.2.I.19-20," *UF* 18 (1986): p. 458, and Marvin H. Pope, *El in the Ugaritic Texts*, pp. 61-72. The celestial Tabernacle is revealed in Exod 25:9, 40. Note that Yahweh's abode is not the mountain top itself, but above it, as Yahweh comes down to Mt. Sinai, while Moses climbs up.

Elsewhere, Kothar departs for his tent (*ahl*), also called a tabernacle (*mškn*).[43] Further evidence for Ugaritic divine tent dwellings comes from Ba'al's complaint that he is without a house.[44] While no tent shrine is explicitly in Ba'al's custody, it can be assumed that he and his daughters live in El's tent prior to the construction of Baal's temple. Alternatively, and based on ethnographic parallels, El would have had his won tent or tents, and his daughters would have separate tents. Also, tents are not limited to the divine realm in Ugaritic literature: Anath's henchman *ytpn* presumably lives in a military camp consisting of several tents.[45] Lastly, Kirta prepares for a journey by sacrificing a lamb and a bird in a tent (*ḥmt*), mirroring the sacrifices conducted within and in front of the Tabernacle.[46]

*Portable Shrines of Phoenicia and Carthage: The Literary Evidence*

The association between El and his portable sanctuary discovered at Ugarit is perhaps furthered by Philo of Byblos, who translated into Greek a Phoenician history ascribed to Sanchuniathon.[47] Philo records that a portable shrine drawn by oxen (ναον ζυγοφορουμενον) carried the image of one of the first primordial humans, named Αγρου ʿΗρως "Hero of the Field" or Αγροτης "Rustic."[48] Philo goes on to say that this individual, especially among the inhabitants of Byblos, is venerated as the greatest of the gods. Most likely he is the Canaanite god El. El's

---

[43] *CAT* 1.17.V.32.

[44] For example see *CAT* 1.3.IV.1-9; 1.3.V.46-52; 1.4.I.10-19.

[45] *CAT* 1.19.IV.50-60.

[46] *CAT* 1.14.III.159-162. The meaning of Ugaritic *ḥmt* can be deduced from Arabic and Ethiopic *ḥymt*, both meaning "tent."

[47] Philo of Byblos's Phoenician History survives in fragments cited in the fourth-century C.E. work of Eusebius of Caesarea, *Praeparatio Evangelica*. For the Greek text and English translation with notes, see Robert A. Oden, Jr., and Harold W. Attridge, *Philo of Byblos: The Phoenician History*, CBQMS 9 (Washington, DC, 1981), and Albert I. Baumgarten, *The Phoenician History of Philo of Byblos: A Commentary* (Leiden, 1981). The date of Sanchuniathon's original history is disputed, with estimates ranging from the second millennium B.C.E. to the Persian period, as discussed by Oden and Attridge, pp. 6-9, and Baumgarten, pp. 42-51.

[48] Eusebius, *PE*, 1.10.12-13

relationship with Byblos is well established,[49] and Αγρου Ἡρως "Hero of the Field" might be a Greek form of the Semitic epithet אֵל שַׁדַּי, "God of the field."[50] Philo's second name for the deity, Αγροτης "rural," possibly mirrors the Ugaritic epithet *ḏldy mrʿt* (who controls the meadow), although this is far less certain.[51] In

---

[49] Philo himself states that El (=Kronos) founded Byblos, the world's first city (Eusebius, *PE* 1.10.20). For El's frequent appearance on Byblian coinage, see Z. Sawaya, "Cronos, Astarté: deux légendes phéniciennes inédites sur des monnaies de Byblos," *Bulletin de la Société Française de Numismatique* 53 (Mai, 1998): pp. 93-99.

[50] This correspondence has long been recognized. See Heinrich Ewald, "Abhandlungen über die phönikischen Ansichten von der Weltschöpfung und den geschichtlichen Wert Sanchuniathons," *Abhandlungen der königlichen Gesellschaft der Wissenschaften zu Göttingen* 5 (1851): pp. 1-68, and M. Ernest Renan, "Mémoire sur l'origine et le caractère véritable de l'histoire Phénicienne qui porte le nom de Sanchoniathon," *Mémoires de L'institut Impérial de France* 23 (1858): pp. 241-334, esp. 268. For שַׁדַּי = שׂדה/שׂדי (field), see Manfred Weippert, "Erwägungen zur Etymologie des Gottesnames *ʾĒl Šaddaj*," *ZDMG* 36 (1961): pp. 42-62. Associating שַׁדַּי with שׂדה/שׂדי long proved a barrier for many scholars, including William F. Albright, "The Names Shaddai and Abram," *JBL* 54 (1935), pp. 183-84, and Frank M. Cross, Jr., *Canaanite Myth and Hebrew Epic*, pp. 52-60, who prefer separate etymologies: *\*ṯdw* for שַׁדַּי (cf. Akkadian *šadû*=mountain), and *\*śdw* for שָׂדַי/שָׂדֶ(ה). Thus שַׁדַּי אֵל would best be translated "God of the mountain," or "El, the mountain one." David N. Freedman, "The Refrain in David's Lament Over Saul and Jonathan," *Ex Orbe Religionum* 21 (1972): p. 122, and more recently, William H. C. Propp, "On Hebrew *śāde(h)*, 'Highland,'" *VT* 37 (1987): pp. 230-36, have pointed out several instances in the Hebrew Bible where שָׂדַי/שָׂדֶ(ה) is best translated "highland." Moreover, Propp proves that Akkadian *šadûm* is in fact related to Hebrew שָׂדֶה, thereby damaging Weippert et al.'s connection of שַׁדַּי with שׂדה/שׂדי, assuming the regular development of the sibilant (i.e., we would expect שַׂדַּי אֵל rather than אֵל שַׁדַּי). Nevertheless, a relationship between שַׁדַּי and שׂדה/שׂדי may still exist if the sibilant developed irregularly in Hebrew. Philo could reflect the same confusion about the two roots, and in Phoenician especially there is only one *š/s*, not two as in Hebrew. Consequently, it remains possible to equate El's epithet *šadday* with Philo's "Hero of the Field."

[51] As suggested by L. R. Clapham, "Sanchuniathon: The First Two Cycles," Harvard University Dissertation (1969): pp. 117-19. Cf. R. du Mesnil du Buisson, *Études sur les dieux phéniciens hérités par l'Empire Romain* (Leiden, 1970): pp. 46-53, who identifies Philo's Αγρου Ἡρως or Αγροτης with Jupiter Heliopolitanus (=Baal) based primarily upon two Syrian representations of Jupiter Heliopolitanus flanked by two bulls. Baal's association with bulls permeates Canaanite mythology and iconography; nevertheless, Philo's statement that oxen transport the deity's image is no reason to prefer Baal over El, as the animals available to draw a portable shrine were limited. El, too, owns the epithet *ṯr* "Bull" (e.g. *CAT* 49.IV.34; VI.26-27). Furthermore, to equate Αγρου Ἡρως or Αγροτης with Jupiter Heliopolitanus, du Mesnil du Buisson (pp. 50-51) must take "Byblos" as meaning "all Phoenicia," because Jupiter

any case, Philo provides evidence that a portable shrine conveyed an image of a god, likely El, throughout Phoenicia.[52] The Tabernacle, while seemingly much larger than this Phoenician abode, also housed Israel's chief deity and was transported by oxen.[53]

A further parallel stems from the first century B.C.E. Greek historian Diodorus of Sicily. Diodorus appears to mention a tent shrine while describing a Carthaginian military campaign against Libya. He remarkably refers to a sacred tent (ἱεραν σκηνην) with a nearby altar in the center of the Carthaginian camp.[54] It seems that a sudden blast of wind brought fire from the altar onto the sacred tent, which was engulfed in flames and rapidly spread fire to the other tents in the camp. However, the parallel to the Tabernacle is not as perfect as some would have it. Most commentators fail to point out that Diodorus states that the tents burned rapidly because they were composed of reed (καλαμου) and straw (χορτου).[55] Diodorus's word for the structure, σκηνη, was used in this period for both tents and booths.[56] Consequently, it seems the shelter was a hut and not a true tent. Even so, Diodorus records that the Carthaginians, like the Israelites in the

---

Heliopolitanus's cult was not centralized at Byblos, but 100 kilometers east (p. 50). See also Albert I. Baumgarten, *The Phoenician History of Philo of Byblos,* p. 171, who rejects du Mesnil du Buisson's identification of Jupiter Heliopolitanus but maintains that Αγρου ʿHρως or Αγροτης represents Baal in some form, because of a Latin inscription from Timna mentioning *Beelseddi,* identified with Jupiter. Yet, this by no means rules El out as the likely candidate for Philo's deity. It only means that the epithet was used in a wider context than previously thought. For a critique of Baumgarten's use of Semitic sources and identification of deities, see Edward Lipiński, "The 'Phoenician History' of Philo of Byblos," *Bibliotheca Orientalis* 40 (1983): pp. 306-308.

[52] Philo's word for the sanctuary, ναον, also refers to portable shrines in Herodotus 2.63 and possibly in Diodorus of Sicily I.15.

[53] Num 7:3 and 1 Sam 6:7.

[54] XX.65.1

[55] See for example Frank M. Cross, Jr., "The Priestly Tabernacle," p. 218, who mentions the Carthaginian sacred tent without commenting on its construction.

[56] The early word for booth, κλισιη, seems to go out of use after Homer. Following the Persian period, σκηνη becomes an inclusive word for portable architecture, see note 42. Notice also Diodorus of Sicily XX.25, where σκηνη is used for a covering on a wagon.

desert, maintained a portable sanctuary with an altar nearby within their military camp.[57]

Further evidence for Phoenician portable sanctuaries is provided by *Concerning the Syrian Goddess*, a work attributed to the second century C.E. satirist Lucian of Samosata.[58] In describing the temple of the Syrian city Hierapolis (modern Manbij), Lucian mentions that it is a bipartite sanctuary oriented east.[59] This recalls both the Tabernacle and the Temple of Israel. He further describes a puzzling structure placed in the inner sanctuary between figures of Hadad and Atargatis.[60] The structure is called a σημηιον , which means a symbol or mark by which a thing is known. Lucian writes that the structure is taken on a journey twice annually in a religious procession to carry water from the Mediterranean back to the temple.[61]

*Portable Shrines in Phoenicia, Syria, and Judea: Pictorial Evidence*

In addition to the written testimony discussed above, further evidence of Phoenician portable shrines comes from various coins, the most famous from Sidon.[62] On ten different Sidonian coins we find a two-wheeled cart, with four poles supporting what appears to be a tent roof, at times with palm branches emanating from it (Plate 28).

Centered in the portable shrine is an oval object, at times flanked by horns and/or winged sphinxes. The identity of this

---

[57] Elaborate Phoenician tents, albeit secular, also turn up in the *Histories* of Herodotus (VII.100.2), who mentions that Xerxes reviewed his fleet in a "Sidonian ship and sat under a golden tent." Perhaps this is comparable to the ornate Phoenician ships described in Ezekiel 27, discussed below (pp. 146-47).

[58] On the Phoenician nature of the Hierapolitan cult described by Lucian, see Philip C. Schmitz, "Phoenician Religion," *ABD* V, pp. 357-363, and Robert A. Oden, Jr., *Studies in Lucian's De Syria Dea* (Missoula, 1977): pp. 146-49.

[59] *Concerning The Syrian Goddess*, 30-31. For the Greek with English translation see Harold W. Attridge and Robert A. Oden, Jr., *The Syrian Goddess* (Missoula, 1976).

[60] *Concerning the Syrian Goddess*, 33. Hadad is identified with Zeus, Atargatis with Hera. Atargatis seems to be a combination of Semitic ʿAstarte, ʿAnat, and ʾAšerah.

[61] *Concerning the Syrian Goddess*, 33.

[62] George F. Hill, *Catalogue of the Greek Coins of Phoenicia* (Bologna, 1965): pp. 175-86, plates 23.9-12, 17; 24.5-9.

object and the shrine's deity remains uncertain. Many argue that the shrine contains a betyl dedicated to Astarte.[63] Perhaps related is the fallen star consecrated by Astarte in Tyre, mentioned by Philo of Byblos,[64] and Astarte's prominence at Sidon is also well documented.[65] Yet, at times the oval object more strongly resembles an urn, seen most clearly in Plate 29a, where carrying bars replace the wheels.[66] If the object is an urn, then Lucian's enigmatic water-carrying σημήιον , as well as the laver wagons in 1 Kgs 7:27-39, are called to mind.[67]

Similar portable shrines with wheels transported deities such as Demeter and Hercules, as depicted on other coins (Plates 29b, 29c).[68] A Greek inscription likewise records that an image of

---

[63] George F. Hill, *Catalogue of the Greek Coins of Phoenicia*, pp. 175-86, Martin J. Price and Bluma L. Trell, *Coins and Their Cities* (London, 1977): p. 216, and Mathias Delcor, "Astarte," *Lexicon Iconographicum Mythologiae Classicae* III.1 (München, 1986): pp. 1077-85. The identification with Astarte is most fully treated by Henri Seyrig, "Antiquités syriennes: divinités de Sidon," *Syria* 36 (1959): pp. 48-56, who argues that this is a pictorial representation not of Astarte's shrine at Tyre, but rather of Astarte's shrine at Sidon, mentioned in Lucian's *Concerning The Syrian Goddess*, 4. Seyrig maintains the Astarte identity based on the occasional presence within the shrine of sphinxes, which he claims are always "les acolytes d'Astarté dans cette région" (p. 50). Yet there are several representations of male deities flanked by sphinxes, as pointed out by Eugene D. Stockton ("Phoenician Cult Stones," *Australian Journal of Biblical Archaeology* 2 [1974-1975]: pp. 8-9). Sébastien Ronzevalle disassociates the object from Astarte altogether, preferring solar deities, "Le prétendu char d'Astarté", *Mélanges de l'Université S. Joseph*, 16 (1932): pp. 51 ff.

[64] Eusebius, *PE* 1.10.10.31-32.

[65] Lucian mentions Astarte's shrine at Sidon in *Concerning the Syrian Goddess*, 4. For thorough documentation, see Robert A. Oden, Jr., *Studies in Lucian's De Syria Dea*, pp. 76-81.

[66] See Martin J. Price and Bluma L. Trell, *Coins and Their Cities*, fig. 40.

[67] Against Robert A. Oden, Jr., who argues from representations on a pair of coins that Lucian's σημήιον consists of a caduceus within a vaulted shrine (*Studies in Lucian's De Syria Dea*, pp. 109-55, figs. 1-2). For a connection between the object on Sidonian coinage and the temple laver-wagons, see Wolfgang Zwickel, "Die Kesselwagen im Salomonischen Tempel," *UF* 18 (1986): pp. 459-61.

[68] For a description of three coins from the reign of Marcus Aurelius depicting the procession of Heracles, see Félix De Saulcy, *Numismatique de la Terre Sainte* (Paris, 1874): pp. 387-92, and Charles Clermont-Ganneau, "L'Heracleion de Rabbat-Ammon Philadelphia et la déesse Asteria," *Recueil d'Archéologie Orientale* 7 (1905): pp. 147-55.

Hercules was paraded around the city in a four-pillared, canopied, horse-drawn cart at Philadelphia in the second century C.E.[69]

Early rabbinic sources suggest that the chests containing the sacred Torah scrolls were also portable.[70] Such a Torah ark seems to be depicted on a wall relief from the fourth century C.E. synagogue at Capernaum (Plate 30).[71] The structure is portrayed in three dimensions: the front consists of a double-door beneath a semicircular half rosette; the side is represented by five Ionic columns and a base with four wheels, only two of which are depicted. The structure is covered by a curved roof, composed of an indeterminate material. Consequently, it is not clear whether the wheels support a shrine of cloth, vegetation, or stone.[72] A similar Ark-wagon, this one clearly tented by red cloth, exists on the plaster-paintings of the Dura Europos synagogue (Plate 31).

Several other tented wagons have been found in the material record, often millennia earlier than the Phoenician, Syrian, and Jewish examples. One such item is the EB covered wagon from Tepe Gawra in Iraq (Plate 32a).[73]

---

[69] The inscription dates to the reign of the Roman emperor Marcus Aurelius. See Charles Clermont-Ganneau, "L'Heracleion de Rabbat-Ammon Philadelphie et la déesse Asteria," pp. 147-55.

[70] E.g., Mishna, Ta'anith 2:1, where the Torah ark is brought from the synagogue to the center of the city during droughts. Other passages include Tosefta, Megillah 3:21, where the ark is left in the street, and to a lesser extent b. Sotah 39.b, where the Torah scroll is removed from the synagogue, perhaps inside an ark.

[71] See Stanislao Loffreda, "Capernaum," NEAEHL 1:294. The interpretation of the Capernaum frieze as a Torah ark seems sound, based on non-wheeled parallels depicted on the Beit Alpha mosaic and a relief from the synagogue at Bukeia. For depictions and discussion of these Torah arks and their inherent portable nature, see Eleazar L. Sukenik, Ancient Synagogues in Palestine and Greece (London, 1934): pp. 33; 52-54; plate 5c, and "Did the Synagogue of Capernaum Have a Fixed Torah-Shrine?" Kedem 2 (1945): pp. 121-22 (Hebrew).

[72] The striking similarity between this Torah ark and the earlier-mentioned portable shrines on coins, especially one not shown here minted in Ephesus, seems to show deliberate imitation, as suggested by Stanley A. Cook, The Religion of Ancient Palestine in the Light of Archaeology (London, 1930): p. 215.

[73] Ephraim A. Speiser, "Preliminary Excavations at Tepe Gawra," AASOR 9 (1927-1928): pp. 34-35, figs. 97, 102. This parallel to Capernaum's Torah ark was also noted also by Stanley A. Cook, The Religion of Ancient Palestine in the Light of Archaeology, p. 215.

Here upon the four-wheeled cart stands either a booth or a tent, as the clay markings indicate a covering consisting of matting or fabric. This covered wagon, found in a context with a miniature bed, a two-wheeled chariot, and various animal figurines, was interpreted by the excavators as votive in nature.[74]

## Egyptian Funeral Tents

Additional information concerning Near Eastern tent shrines can be culled from the historical and material records of ancient Egypt, where tents play a large role in the funerary cult. The corpse was transported westward across the Nile in a tented boat and then placed in the "tent of purification," where bodies were washed and ritually purified in preparation for later mummification.[75] This tent of purification is typically called *ꜣibw* in Old Kingdom records, but it is also commonly referred to as "the god's tent" (*sḥ nṯr*) when used to embalm royalty.[76] The latter term came to replace *ꜣibw* after the Old Kingdom, and became incorporated into a common title of Anubis: "Presiding over the god's tent."[77] Further evidence for a tent of purification comes from the Book of the Dead, which orders that the embalming must take place in a tent of cloth (*sḥ ḥbs*).[78] Tomb paintings portray these tents as long, broad-room structures facing east, with many vertical poles supporting a long horizontal top-pole (Plate 32b).[79]

---

[74] Ephraim A. Speiser, "Preliminary Excavations at Tepe Gawra," pp. 34-35.

[75] For detailed studies of the "tent of purification," see Bernhard Grdseloff, *Das ägyptische Reinigungszelt* (Cairo, 1941); Selim Hassan, *Excavations at Gîza* IV (Cairo, 1943): pp. 69-102; Ahmed A. Youssef, "Notes on the Purification Tent," *ASAE* 64 (1981): pp. 155-57, and James K. Hoffmeier, "The Possible Origins of the Tent of Purification in the Egyptian Funerary Cult," *Studien zur altägyptischen Kultur* 9 (1981): pp. 167-77.

[76] Bernhard Grdseloff, *Das ägyptische Reinigungszelt*, pp. 39-40. Cf. Selim Hassan, *Excavations at Gîza* IV, p. 78, and James K. Hoffmeier, "Possible Origins," p. 168, and "Tents in Egypt and the Ancient Near East," p. 19, who claim the word *sḥ* sometimes signifies a hut, sometimes a tent. The practice of ritually purifying the dead in a tent goes back at least to the 4th dynasty (Hassan, pp. 69-102, and Hoffmeier, pp. 167-77).

[77] Hassan, p. 78, and Hoffmeier, p. 173.

[78] Spell 148. See James K. Hoffmeier, "Tents in Egypt and the Ancient Near East," p. 19.

[79] See also Aylard M. Blackman and Michael R. Apted, *The Rock Tombs of Meir* V (London, 1953): p. 52, pls. 42-43 for further pictures. On the difficulty

Holes for these tent-poles have been found before various necropolises.[80] Like the Tabernacle, these tents were ritually purified before use.[81] Within these tents, the corpse was eviscerated, anointed, embalmed, mummified, and the opening of the mouth ceremony was conducted.[82] These tents were elaborately decorated, and often dyed red (Plate 33).[83]

At times they were painted with stars, and their entrance was called "the doors of heaven."[84] In Egyptian mythology, Re was purified in the eastern sky and reborn with the sunrise, and some have argued that the tent of purification is modeled after the starry eastern sky.[85] If so, then the Egyptian tent of purification, like the Tabernacle, was a terrestrial replica, built from a model, of a heavenly prototype (see pp. 131-32).

Not only were tents used to prepare the deceased for burial, but Egyptian notables were at times buried with tents. At Deir el Bahari, among the royal mummies was discovered a leather funeral pall for Queen Isi em Kheb, mother-in-law to Jerusalem's besieger Shishak (Plates 34-35).[86] The tent is a mosaic composed of thousands of pieces of gazelle hide, each dyed pink, yellow, green, or blue.

Its function appears to have been as a covering on a funeral bark, as boat models often depict similar forms and patterns.[87] Isi

---

of reconstructing their form, see Étienne Drioton's review of Grdseloff in *ASAE* 40 (1940): p. 1009.

[80] One set of holes, each 30 cm in diameter, was uncovered in front of the valley temple of Khafre at Giza. Similar holes were found before the valley temple of Pepi II at Saqqara. For further discussion, see Selim Hassan, *Excavations at Gîza* IV, p. 90.

[81] Aylard M. Blackman and Michael R. Apted, *The Rock Tombs of Meir* V (London, 1953): p. 50.

[82] Warren R. Dawson, "Making a Mummy," *JEA* 13 (1927): pp. 40-49. Bernhard Grdseloff, *Das ägyptische Reinigungszelt*, p. 17.

[83] A red tent of purification depicted on a panel of the Ramesside coffin of Khonsou can be seen in Christiane Desroches-Noblecourt, *Ramsès le grand* (Paris, 1976): pp. 201-02. Notice that in a nearby tent, Khonsou and Tamaket watch Anubis prepare the former's corpse.

[84] Edward Brovarski, "The Doors of Heaven," *Or* 46 (1977): p. 110.

[85] James K. Hoffmeier, "The Possible Origins of the Tent of Purification in the Egyptian Funerary Cult," p. 176. On the solar aspects of the washing ceremony, see Selim Hassan, *Excavations at Gîza* IV, pp. 98-102.

[86] See H. Villiers Stuart, *The Funeral Tent of an Egyptian Queen* (London, 1882). The tent now stands on display in Cairo's Egyptian National Museum.

[87] See for example James E. Quibell, *The Ramesseum* (London, 1898): p. 9;

em Kheb's pall is composed of a central panel measuring 2.75 by 1.83 m, from which four flaps protrude. The entire fabric measures 6.86 by 5.94 m, and when erected, the tent would stand approximately 2 m tall (Plate 35).[88]

Unfortunately, the pall was discovered in a secondary context, and as the tomb was badly looted, no remains of the tent frame were discovered.

Also of interest is that among the four nested gold-plated catafalques covering Tutankhamon's sarcophagus was found a linen tent and wooden frame (Plates 36-39a; Figure 4).[89]

To date, little attention has been paid to this shrine, which lay between the outer two gold-plated catafalques. As the exterior shrine was roofless, the tent covering provided the outermost ceiling. The tent consisted of several panels of coarsely-woven brown linen sewn together and placed so the seams ran parallel to the entrance, comparable to the Tabernacle of Exodus.[90] These panels were decorated with gilt bronze rosettes. The fabric's poor state of preservation exemplifies the difficulty inherent in trying to find tents in the archaeological record.[91]

---

plate 14, where a blue, red, yellow, and green pavilion covers the bark of Osiris on a lintel dated to Rameses III.

[88] H. Villiers Stuart, *The Funeral Tent of an Egyptian Queen*, p. 6. Note also a decorated leather covering for a small wooden box (Heinrich Schäfer, "Lederbespannung eines Holzkästchens," *ZÄS* 31 [1893]: pp. 105-07).

[89] In Howard Carter, *The Tomb of Tut-ankh-amen* II (New York, 1927): pp. 33, 43-44, 197, pls. 4, 36a; 55-56. Studies of the tent and frame remain to be completed (Nicholas Reeves, *The Complete Tutankhamun* [London, 1990]: p. 101). For studies on the four catafalques, see Alexandre Piankoff, *The Shrines of Tut-ankh-amon*, Bollingen Series 40.2 (New York, 1955).

[90] No cotton was found in the material, which consisted of pure flax. Alexander Scott, "Notes on Objects from the Tomb of King Tut-ankh-amen," in Howard Carter's *The Tomb of Tut-ankh-amen*, pp. 272-74

[91] Alexander Scott, "Notes on Objects from the Tomb of King Tut-ankh-amen," pp. 272-74. Though Carter and his team took initial steps to preserve the fabric, it was irreversably damaged when it was left untreated and exposed while Carter shut down his operation to voice his dissasitisfaction with the new Egyptian Minister of Public Works, who had cancelled a planned visit of the tomb by the wives of those on the expedition. After the work stoppage came to an end, Carter blamed the Egyptian government for the tent-fabric's horrible condition, and stated "Well, anyway, it's your pall, not mine, and it's the only one in the world." See Nicholas Reeves, *The Complete Tutankamun*, p. 66; 101.

The tent's wooden frame consists of seven crossbars to support the fabric's weight, and a front-hinged panel to facilitate entrance. The frame measures 4.32 by 2.93 m, and is 2.78 m in height.[92]

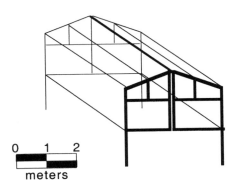

Figure 4 – Tutankhamon's Tent Frame (drawing)

This wooden frame, as well as the more elaborate gold-plated catafalques, provide some of the best parallels to the craftsmanship involved in creating the Tabernacle.[93]

A close parallel to Tutankhamon's tent and catafalques is depicted on a papyrus showing the tomb of Rameses IV (Plate 39b). Four catafalques encase the coffin, and just inside the outermost catafalque is a red line connecting four blocks in the corners.[94] The red line and the blocks are most likely a tent and its bases. The sacred nature of the catafalques can be seen in their

---

[92] Nicholas Reeves, *The Complete Tutankamun*, p. 101.

[93] For the depiction of similar portable catafalques, see Norman de G. Davies, *Two Rameside Tombs at Thebes* (New York, 1927): pp. 64-69, pls. 31b, 38, where a catafalque is being constructed of similar proportions to the Tabernacle. See also Theodore M. Davis, *The Tomb of Queen Tìyi* (London, 1910): p. 13, pls. 31-38, and Torgny Säve-Söderbergh, *Four Eighteenth Dynasty Tombs* (Oxford, 1957): p. 5, pls. 4-5. Tutankhamon's catafalques had inscriptions to facilitate their construction. See Alexandre Piankoff, *The Shrines of Tut-ankh-amon*.

[94] The lines of the proposed catafalques are depicted in yellow, seemingly representing gold overleaf. The tent's covering may have been red, as indicated by the red line. The tomb's dimensions suggest the tent is a cube measuring 10 cubits; see Howard Carter and Alan H. Gardiner, "The Tomb of Ramesses IV and the Turin Plan of a Royal Tomb," *JEA* 4 (1917): p. 133.

presence in Amon's barque (Plate 40a) and in Tutankhamon's funeral procession (40b).

Similar in nature to Tutankhamon's catafalque is a wooden shrine with gold overlay belonging to Akhenaten's mother Tiye (Plates 41a, 41b).[95] The shrine consists of several wooden planks linked together with mortises and tenons, composing a long-room rectangular catafalque.

## The Tent of Min

Further Egyptian evidence concerning tent shrines comes from the conical tent, referred to as a *šhnt*, associated with the Egyptian fertility god Min.[96] The structure consists of a tall central pole, surrounded by four support poles, which lean against the central pole significantly below the top (Plates 42, 43).[97]

The phallic form of Min's portable sanctuary does not resemble the Tabernacle.[98] However, it is interesting to note that various traditions attest both Min's role as a nomadic deity and

---

[95] The shrine was discovered in the enigmatic Theban Tomb 55 by Theodore M. Davis in 1907. Originally, Tomb 55 and the wooden shrine seem to have been constructed for Akhenaten's mother, Queen Tiye. However, this tomb also apparently contained the mummy and canopic jars of Kiya, a secondary wife of Akhenaten. The wooden shrine was partially dismantled and much of the gold overlay was removed presumably when workers constructing the tomb of Rameses IX (located just above Tomb 55) discovered the earlier burial. See Theodore M. Davis, *The Tomb of Queen Tiyi* (London, 1910), who maintains that all of the objects in the tomb belong to Tiye; contrast Nicholas Reeves, *The Complete Tutankhamun* (London 1990): pp. 20-21, who provides an excellent summary of the controversy.

[96] On the lack of a satisfactory etymology for *šhnt*, see Alexander Badawy, "Min, the Cosmic Fertility God of Egypt," *Mitteilungen des Instituts für Orientforschung* 7 (1959): pp. 163-179. On Min's tent, see Irmtraut Munro, *Das Zelt-Heiligtum des Min*, Münchner Ägyptologische Studien 41 (München, 1983). On Min's nature as a fertility god, see Hans Bonnet, "Min," *Reallexikon der ägyptischen Religionsgeschichte* (Berlin, 1952): pp. 461-67.

[97] The frame is depicted on the mortuary temple of Pepi II at Saqqara. The central pole in this relief appears to be over 10 meters in height. See Gustave Jequier, *Le monument funéraire de Pepi II* (Cairo, 1938): pl. 12. See also Pierre Lacau, "L'érection du mât devant Amon-Min," *Chronique D'Égypte* 55 (1953): pp. 13-22, and Irmtraut Munro, *Das Zelt-Heiligtum des Min*, pp. 54-59.

[98] Still, it is notable that the statue of Min was transported on a box-shaped carrying-stand covered by red cloth; see Marie-Francine Moens, "The Procession of the God Min to the *htjw*-Garden," *Studien zur altägyptischen Kultur* 12 (1985): p. 71.

his archaism, some sources claiming he was Egypt's first deity.[99]
Thus, as with Ugaritic El and Yahweh, the earliest Egyptian god
originally inhabited a tent sanctuary.

### Other Egyptian Tent Shrines

Tent shrines were also used by the Egyptian upper class. In the
Report of Wenamun (c. 1100 B.C.E.), an Egyptian official
records his business vicissitudes along the Mediterranean coast.
During his voyages, Wenamun takes along a statue referred to as
"Amon-on-the-Road." When he finally gets situated at Byblos,
Wenamun erects a tent ('imw) on the beach to house the idol.[100]
Thus, Egyptian officials on journeys seem to have brought their
religion along with them, in this case, a portable tent for an
idol.[101] Similarly, when Akhenaten visited the site where he
intended to build a new capital, the divine king stayed in an 'im,
possibly resembling the red tent pictured in Plate 44.[102]

---

[99] On Min as a deity for nomads, possibly originating in Punt, see Alexander
Badawy, "Min, the Cosmic Fertility God of Egypt," pp. 163-179; Claas J.
Bleeker, *Die Geburt eines Gottes* (Leiden 1956): pp. 34-40; Marie-Francine
Moens, "The Procession of the God Min to the *ḥtjw*-Garden," pp. 69-73; and G.
A. Wainwright, "Some Celestial Associations of Min," *JEA* 21 (1935): pp. 152-
170. On Min's archaism, see Moens, pp. 69-73; also Elise J. Baumgartel,
"Herodotus on Min," *Antiquity* 21 (1947): pp. 145-50, where she convincingly
claims that Herodotus's two mentions of Min (Μινα), the first king to unite
upper and lower Egypt, refer to a deity and not a human (*Histories* II, 4; 99).
Moreover, Herodotus later claims that Pan, the Greek deity most often associated
with Egyptian Min, is in fact the very first god (*Histories* II, 145-46). Thus, the
first deity and uniter of Egypt is believed to have inhabited a tent. The case for
Min's archaism is furthered by Walter B. Emery, *Excavations at Saqqara 1937-
1938: Ḥor-aha* (Cairo, 1937): pp. 4-7, pls. 14; 20-23, who lists occurrences of
the hieroglyph *mn* in the 1st dynasty. Both Narmer and Merneith use the title
"Min," and in the case of Merneith, the hieroglyph *mn* is actually enclosed in a
pavilion.
[100] Wenamun 1.47-48. For convenient translations, see *ANET* 26; Miriam
Lichtheim, "The Report of Wenamun," *The Context of Scripture*, ed. William W.
Hallo (Leiden, 1997): pp. 90-91. Hans Goedicke, *The Report of Wen Amun*
(Baltimore, 1975): p. 48, surprisingly objects to the traditional reading of
"tent," because "a 'tent' is not a religious structure and thus would be a rather
inappropriate place for performing a ritual act to a deity." However, from such
passages as Sinuhe 110 and 145, the word clearly means tent, and a tent setting
for religious acts is certainly credible.
[101] Phoenician traders also traveled with tents, as recorded in Skylax,
*Periplus* 112.
[102] As inscribed in the Amarna Boundary stele. See Norman de G. Davies,
*Rock Tombs of Amarna* V (London, 1908): pl. 26.

Much earlier than Akhenaton, a tent frame surrounding and covering a bed is depicted in relief within the tomb of Mehu (V^th Dynasty at Saqqara; Plate 45). This strongly resembles in form an actual tent frame encased with gold that was found among the furniture of Hetepheres, the mother of Kheops (Plate 46).[103]

Like the Tabernacle, Hetepheres's tent consists of gold-plated woodwork employing tenon-mortise joints and reinforced corner pieces. Also worth noting is the Leiden Magical papyrus, in which Hathor is invoked to enter a tent, but here the tent seems to belong to a noble woman giving birth.[104] Birth in ancient Egypt, like death, often took place in a tent.

## Tent Homes of Egyptian Gods

One other New Kingdom text illustrates the Egyptian use of tent shrines. In the "Contest of Horus and Seth," the Egyptian divine council of Thirty, here misnamed the Ennead, quarrels. Following some name-calling, the text reads "And they [gods] went to their tents (*'imw*). The great god [Re] slept in his pavilion (*sh*)."[105] So tents were inhabited by at least some of Egypt's pantheon.

## Rameses's Military Camp and the Tabernacle

Surprisingly, one of the most remarkable parallels to the Tabernacle and its court has been largely ignored: the military camp of Rameses II at Qedesh.[106] The four reliefs and corresponding writ-

---

[103] George A. Reisner, William S. Smith, *A History of the Giza Necropolis II: The Tomb of Hetep-heres* (Cambridge, 1955): pp. 23-27, pls. 5-10. For similar tent poles see Kenneth A. Kitchen, "The Tabernacle—A Bronze Age Artefact," *Eretz-Israel* 24 (Jerusalem, 1993): p. 120.

[104] Leiden Magical Papyrus I.348.33.1. See James K. Hoffmeier, "Tents in Egypt and the Ancient Near East," p. 17. For information on Egyptian birthing tents, see Emma Brunner-Traut, *Die altägyptischen Scherbenbilder* (Wiesbaden, 1956): pp. 67-69.

[105] This text's relevance to the Hebrew Bible's expression "To Your Tents, O Israel," will be explored below, pp. 265-71. For translations of the "Contest of Horus and Seth," see Miriam Lichtheim, *Ancient Egyptian Literature* (Berkeley, 1976): p. 216, and *ANET* p. 15. For the Egyptian texts, see Alan H. Gardiner, *Late Egyptian Stories* (Brussels, 1932): p. 41 (3,13).

[106] Their similar form has occasionally been pointed out, but never fully explored. Hugo Gressmann, *Mose und seine Zeit* (Göttingen, 1913): p. 241, uses the reliefs to illustrate P's preference for placing the tent in the middle of the camp. See also the short description in Gressmann, *Altorientalische Texte und Bilder zum Alten Testament* II, 2nd edition (Berlin, 1927): p. 58, fig. 550.

ten sources of the battle of Qedesh portray a 2:1 rectangular camp, the entrance of which is in the middle of the short wall (Plates 10, 47, 48).[107]

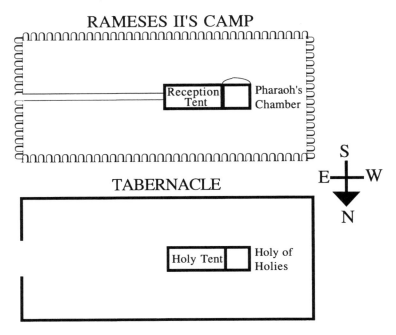

Figure 5 - Comparison of Rameses II's Military Tent (Abu Simbel) with the Tabernacle

Directly in the camp's middle lies the entrance to a 3:1 long-room tent, composed of a 2:1 reception tent leading to the square

---

Kenneth A. Kitchen explores the parallel in more detail but still briefly in "The Tabernacle—A Bronze Age Artefact," p. 121 n. 21. For more detail on the comparison, see Michael M. Homan, "The Divine Warrior in His Tent," *BR* 16.6 (2000): pp. 22-33.

[107] Rameses's camp is depicted on four temple reliefs at Luxor, Abu Simbel, and in duplicate at the Ramesseum. The primary written source, known as the "Report," is inscribed alongside the temple-reliefs, as is the epic referred to as the "Poem." On the battle of Qedesh and its sources, see James H. Breasted, *The Battle of Kadesh* (Chicago, 1903); C. Kuentz, *Bataille de Qadech* (Cairo, 1928); Raymond O. Faulkner, "The Battle of Kadesh," *Mitteilungen des deutschen archäologischen Instituts Abteilung Kairo* 16 (1968): pp. 93-111; and Hans J. Polotzky, "The Battles of Megiddo and Kadesh," *The Military History of the Land of Israel in Biblical Times*, ed. J. Liver (Israel, 1973): pp. 17-26 (Hebrew).

throne tent of the pharaoh (Plate 49).[108] Furthermore, we learn
from the Abu Simbel relief that the height of Rameses's tent
corresponds to its width. All of this matches the description of the
Tabernacle and its camp in Exodus 25-27 (Figure 5). Moreover,
Rameses's tent is oriented eastward.[109] The pharaoh's golden
throne is flanked by falcon wings, just as the ark is flanked by
winged cherubim.[110] The campaigning Egyptian army is divided
into four units, as Israel encamps and marches by four standards
according to Numbers 2.[111] In sum, the military tent and camp of

---

[108] Cf. James K. Hoffmeier, "Tents in Egypt and the Ancient Near East," pp.
18, 20, who views the reception tent as an awning supported by two poles,
protruding from the main square tent supported by five poles. That the Abu
Simbel relief (Plates 10 and 49) depicts events inside the reception tent,
however, need not mean that the tent's sides were left uncovered. Hoffmeier is
attempting to correlate Egyptian military tents and the Asiatic tents encountered
by Thutmoses III, whose troops carry off seven tent posts overlaid with silver,
two of which he claims supported an awning. However, the Abu Simbel relief
also shows the inside of Rameses's main tent-chamber, which even Hoffmeier
concedes was covered on all sides. In other words, we are dealing with an artistic
convention.

[109] The eastern orientation is known from a short inscription in the upper
right-hand corner of the Ramesseum relief, which clearly states that the pursued
princes arrive on the west end of camp, the camp's backside. See James H.
Breasted, *The Battle of Kadesh*, pp. 35, 43, and Alan H. Gardiner, *The Kadesh
Inscriptions of Ramses II* (Oxford, 1960): pp. 36-37. The frequent expression
"waking in life in the tent of the pharaoh" signals the beginning of a new day,
as Rameses, the son of the solar deity, wakes with the sunrise. See Anthony J.
Spalinger, "Some Notes on the Battle of Megiddo and Reflections on Egyptian
Military Writing," *MDIK* (1975): p. 222. All of this disproves Julius
Wellhausen, *Prolegomena zur Geschichte Israels*, p. 37, who, following Graf,
argued that the Tabernacle's eastern orientation meant that it was a fixed
building, not a tent. On the eastward orientation of temples, see Th. A. Busink,
*Der Tempel von Jerusalem* I (Leiden, 1970): pp. 252-56. On the consistency of
the orientation of other tents, see Roger L. Cribb, "Mobile Villagers: The
Structure and Organisation of Nomadic Pastoral Campsites in the Near East,"
*Ethnoarchaeological Approaches to Mobile Campsites* (Ann Arbor, MI, 1991):
p. 380.

[110] Rameses is described as sitting on his golden throne in the Qedesh Record
11:7-8; 14. The cartouche of the pharaoh flanked by falcon wings, or the wings
of Nekhbet, is a common Egyptian theme. For parallels, see Howard Carter, *The
Tomb of Tutankhamen* II, pl. 49; Alexandre Piankoff, *The Shrines of Tut-ankh-
amon*, pls. 19, 21, 24 , 50; and Henri Stierlin and Christiane Ziegler, *Tanis*
(Seuil, 1987): pls. 16-17, 22, 85, 92, 104. Cf. also an Arslan Tash ivory on
which two deities cover the sun god with their wings (Plate 64).

[111] Raymond O. Faulkner, "The Battle of Kadesh," p. 93. On the form of the
Israelite camp in Numbers 2, see above, pp. 32-34, and Figure 2.

Rameses II at Qedesh constitute the best parallel to the Tabernacle known to date.[112]

The significance of the parallel is great. Here is a tent shrine for the living Egyptian god from the same time and area in which the events in P purport to take place. The rectangular shape shared by Rameses's camp and the Tabernacle is extraordinary; most military camps are elliptical.[113] Admittedly, these are our only pictorial representations of an Egyptian military camp. Certainly P is not basing the Tabernacle's disposition on an Egyptian model knowingly. Rather, P is reconstructing based on historical records in his possession that pictorially or verbally describe an earlier Israelite tent-shrine.[114]

The Egyptian military's influence on the Hebrew Bible has been shown in the similar records of Joshua 1-11 and the Annals of Thutmoses III.[115] The influence was by no means uni-

---

[112] On the accuracy of the reliefs, see G. A. Gaballa, *Narrative in Egyptian Art* (Mainz, 1976): pp. 113-19, who notes that "the traditional theme of a pharaoh dominating and overshadowing the scene was sacrificed for the sake of an overwhelming and impressive representation of the battle as a whole." For further possible examples of Egyptian influence on Israelite public architecture, see Paolo Matthiae, "Some Notes About Solomon's Palace and Ramesside Architectural Culture," *Vicino Oriente* 1 (1997): pp. 117-30; Kenneth A. Kitchen, "Two Notes on the Subsidiary Rooms of Solomon's Temple," *Eretz-Israel* 20 (1989): pp. 107-12; Th. A. Busink, *Der Tempel von Jerusalem*, pp. 566-70; Ronald J. Williams, "A People Come Out of Egypt," *VT Sup* 28 (1975): pp. 234-39.

[113] See above, p. 62. Even later Abassid military camps were typically ovoid in shape. See Mas'udi, *The Meadows of Gold: The Abassids* (London, 1989): p. 315.

[114] Thutmoses III, for example, also inhabits a tent on his several military campaigns (see above, p. 60). The shape of the camp is unknown, but a brief description begins with the camp being set up, goes to the pharaoh's tent, and then to the pharaoh himself (*Urk* IV, 655.15-656.13). Seven centuries after Thutmoses III, Xenophon, *Cyropaedia*, VIII.v.3, describes the Persian military camp, where Cyrus's tent is placed in the middle and oriented eastward (see above, pp. 71-73). The Roman army used both rectangular and square camps, with the general's *praetorium* in the center (see Plate 19a). See Yann H. Bohec, *The Imperial Roman Army* (London, 1994): pp. 131-133, pls. 27, 33. For a picture of a rectangular Bedouin camp of about 19 tents, see Gustaf Dalman, *Arbeit und Sitte in Palästina*, vol. 6, pl. 12.

[115] James K. Hoffmeier, "The Structure of Joshua 1-11 and the Annals of Thutmose III," *Faith, Tradition and History*, Alan R. Millard, James K. Hoffmeier, David W. Baker, eds. (Winona Lake, IN, 1994): pp. 165-79.

directional, as the Egyptian lexicon contains various military titles of Semitic origin, including *mhr*, *mškb*, and *n'r*.[116]

The close correspondence between the Tabernacle and Rameses's camp heightens Yahweh's role as a warrior god.[117] The verbal descriptions of Yahweh as divine warrior have been well documented.[118] Suffice it to say that Yahweh fights for Israel in Exodus 14-15, owns the tools for war in Deut 32:41-42, and is even called a man of war (אִישׁ מִלְחָמָה) in Exod 15:3 and a warrior (גִּבּוֹר מִלְחָמָה) in Ps 24:8. Yahweh alone defeats the entire enemy army, much as Rameses boasts to have done at the battle of Qedesh.

Other elements of the Israelite desert sanctuary mirror what little is known about ancient military camps. The pillar of fire and cloud by which Yahweh guides the Israelites may have a military basis, as Alexander the Great notified his troops when to move camp by placing a signal of smoke by day and fire by night upon a pole.[119] The Priestly source regularly calls the Israelite tribes in

---

[116] Alan R. Schulman, *Mhr* and *Mškb*, Two Egyptian Military Titles of Semitic Origin," *Zeitschrift für ägyptische Sprache und Altertumskunde* 92 (1966): pp. 123-32. Alan H. Gardiner, *The Kadesh Inscriptions of Ramses II*, p. 37, discusses the Egyptian euse of the Canaanite term נַעֲרִים for Egyptian soldiers in the Kadesh inscription. For Egyptian loanwords in the Tabernacle pericope, see Joshua M. Grintz, "Ancient Terms in the Priestly Laws," *Leshonenu* 39 (1975): pp. 5-20, 163-80.

[117] Similarly, Ugaritic divine tents may have a military aura. El is not the decrepit old god of passivity; he too is a warrior. See Patrick D. Miller, "El the Warrior," *HTR* 60 (1967): pp. 411-31, and Frank M. Cross, Jr., *Canaanite Myth and Hebrew Epic*, p. 40.

[118] See Frank M. Cross, Jr., *Canaanite Myth and Hebrew Epic*, pp. 91-111; Patrick D. Miller, Jr., "El the Warrior," *HTR* 60 (1967): pp. 411-31; *The Divine Warrior in Early Israel*, HSM 5 (Cambridge, MA, 1973); and for a full treatment of Yahweh's military role in the Exodus, Millard C. Lind, *Yahweh is a Warrior* (Scottsdale, PA, 1980): pp. 46-64.

[119] Quintus Curtius, *History of Alexander* 5.2.7. This parallel, along with cognate signaling methods used by Islamic armies, was noted by 19th century scholars, including August Knobel, *Die Bücher Exodus und Leviticus* (Leipzig, 1857): p. 134. André Dupont-Sommer later dismissed the parallel due to the unspectacular nature of such a utilitarian practice, "Nubes tenebrosa et illuminans noctem," *RHR* 125 (1942-43): p. 10. More recent commentaries ignore the parallel of Alexander's camp altogether, tending to explain the cloud/fire pillar by natural phenomena such as a volcano (Martin Noth, *Exodus* OTL (Philadelphia, 1962): p. 109), a desert whirlwind, or sacrificial smoke (Alan Cole, *Exodus* Tyndale OT Commentary [Leicester, 1973]: p. 118). The notable exception is William Propp, *Exodus 1-18*, p. 489. On fire and cloud

the wilderness צבאות "armies,"[120] a term normally used for
Yahweh's army of stars (e.g. 1 Kgs 22:19; Neh 9:6; Ps
103:21)—P is demythologizing here. Moreover, implements of
the Israelite camp such as trumpets and standards, and the way in
which the camp is disassembled and carried, all correspond to
ancient Near Eastern military practice.[121] Lastly, the connection
between Israelite religion, tents, and the military is seen in David's
placing his armor, and Goliath's severed head, in his tent (1 Sam
17:54), just as Rameses II stores his armor in a tent.[122] Soon
thereafter we discover that Goliath's sword is kept in linen behind
the ephod, presumably within the Tabernacle.[123]

## Mesopotamian Tent Shrines and 10 Big Qersū from Mari

Mesopotamia also provides evidence concerning tent shrines and
portable sanctuaries. One example comes from the "Curse of
Agade," a lament at the destruction of the city of Nippur and its
main temple Ekur. Enlil, the chief of the pantheon and god of
Nippur, does not take this lying down. He constructs a reed
sanctuary (TUR.TUR) which includes a holy of holies (itima).[124]
But this structure is temporary until his temple can be rebuilt; the
fact that he resides in a reed sanctuary is seen as wholly
negative.[125] Tent shrines may appear in pictorial reliefs, the most

---

battle theophanies by ancient Near Eastern deities, see Moshe Weinfeld, "Divine
Intervention in War in Ancient Israel and in the Ancient Near East," *History,
Historiography, and Interpretation* (Jerusalem, 1983): pp.131-36.

[120] E.g., Num 1:3; 10:15-16, etc.

[121] Num 10:1-10 describes the trumpets, expressly said to be used to summon
the congregation, for breaking camp, and for war. For pictorial representations
of similar trumpets, see Hans Hickmann, *La trompette dans l'Égypte ancienne*
(Cairo, 1946): figs. 4, 15, and 21. The Roman Army set up camp by first
erecting the *praetorium* and then radiating outward (Polybius, VI.VI.27-42).

[122] This is the armor Rameses races to put on once he hears of the enemy
breach. See James H. Breasted *ARE* III, pp. 147-48. Note earlier discussion of
valuables and booty stored in tents, p. 76.

[123] 1 Sam 21:9. Also note the placement of Saul's armor in a Philistine
temple (1 Sam 31:10).

[124] Curse of Akkad, 194, 209. Thorkild Jacobsen renders *itima* as "holy of
holies" in *The Harps that Once . . .* (New Haven, 1987): p. 371. Cf. Jerrold S.
Cooper, *The Curse of Agade* (Baltimore, 1983): p. 253, who prefers
"bedchamber." For a convenient translation, see *ANET* pp. 646-51.

[125] See Victor (Avigdor) Hurowitz, "Temporary Temples," *kinattūtu ša dārâti,
Raphael Kutscher Memorial Volume* (Tel Aviv, 1993): p. 39.

famous example showing an enthroned sun deity covered by a tent (Plate 50a).[126] The sun disk seems to be transported by an anthropomorphized form of the solar tent. This pavilion parallels the base and foundation of a canopied structre discovered just inside the ciety gate at Tel Dan in Israel (Plate 50b).[127]

Stronger parallels to the Tabernacle come from the 18th century B.C.E. cuneiform tablets from Mari, where several texts mention tents (ḫurpatum).[128] One of these is said to be supported with10 qé-er-su, a word etymologically linked to the qrš of El's tent at Ugarit and the Tabernacle's קְרָשִׁים.[129] The qersū at Mari are large, each requiring two men for transport.[130] The ritual association of the qersū is strengthened in another Mari text:

u$_4$-um gi-im-ki-im
qé-er-su-ú
iš-ša-ak-ka-nu
ANŠE di-da-ak
DINGER[meš] ù e-nu-t[um]
i-na li-ib-ʳbi qé-erˈ-si
uṣ-ṣ°-ú DINGIR-lum a-na bi-ti-šu
LUGAL a-n[a] É.[GAL- š]u i-la-ak

"On the day of gimkum, qersū are set up. A donkey is killed. The gods and their paraphernalia depart from the qersū. [Each] deity goes to his temple, and the king goes to his palace."

(FM III.4.ii.7-14)[131]

---

[126] Walter Andrae (ed. B. Hrouda) Das wiedererstandene Assur, 2nd ed. (Munich, 1977): pp. 153 ff., fig. 29.

[127] Avraham Biran, Biblical Dan (Jerusalem, 1994): pp. 238-41.

[128] Mari's close association with tent-dwelling pastoralists has been well documented. See Victor H. Matthews, Pastoral Nomadism in the Mari Kingdom (ASORDS 3; Cambridge, MA, 1978).

[129] M. 6873. J. –M. Durand and M. Guichard, "Les rituels de Mari, in Florilegium Marianum III, D. Charpin and J. –M. Durand, eds., (Paris, 1997): pp. 65-66. On the irregular phonetic correspondance, see Daniel E. Fleming, "Mari's Large Public Tent and the Priestly Sanctuary," VT 50.4 (2000): 484-98. The Tabernacle's קְרָשִׁים are examined below, pp. 137-47.

[130] Daniel E. Fleming, "Mari's Large Public Tent," 484-98.

[131] Originally transliterated in Florilegium Marianum III; expanded in Daniel E. Fleming, "Mari's Large Public Tent," 484-98.

The *qersū* at Mari are erected for a donkey sacrifice, after which
the gods depart from these same *qersū*.[132] Also of interest is the
verb *šakānum*, here used to setting up the *qersū*,   and used
nominally at Ugarit for El's tent (*mškn*) and in the Priestly
Tabernacle's most frequent appelation: מִשְׁכָּן.[133]

## A Midianite Tent Shrine in the Negev

The only certain material remains of an ancient Semitic tent
shrine come from Timna, a frequently-used site for the extraction
and production of copper in the Negev Desert (Plate 51a).[134]
Here Egyptian miners beginning in the 19th dynasty (1320-1200
B.C.E.) constructed an open-roofed shrine to the goddess Hathor
by carving a niche into the sandstone cliff and constructing three
walls around it.[135] Abandoned for a century, the Hathor shrine
was reused and slightly expanded in the 20th dynasty.[136] Then,
the Egyptian presence at Timna suddenly disappeared in the 12th
century B.C.E., due at least in part to an extensive earthquake that
destroyed much of the site.[137] However, shortly after the Egyptian

---

[132] *Florilegium Marianum* III 4 ii 7-14. Daniel E. Fleming, "Mari's Large
Public Tent," 484-98.

[133] On Ugarit's *mškn*, see pp. 94-99; on the use of מִשְׁכָּן for the Tabernacle,
see pp. 11-12.

[134] Copper mining at Timna began possibly as early as the Chalcolithic
period and continues to the present day. See Beno Rothenberg, *Timna* (London,
1972): pp. 18, 24-62.

[135] Beno Rothenberg's *terminus ante quem* for the Egyptian temple comes
from an inscription bearing the name of King Seti I (1313-1292 B.C.E.), the
founder of the 19th dynasty (*Timna*, p. 130). Rothenberg's theory that the
initial shrine was open-roofed (*Timna*, pp. 131-32) arises from the absence of
roofing material at the site, as well as the natural protection offered by the large
cliff comprising the northwestern wall. This sandstone cliff belongs to the so-
called "King Solomon's Pillars," a name popularized following Nelson Glueck's
identification of the site, *The Other Side of the Jordan* (Cambridge, MA, 1970):
pp. 59; 91-94. However, Beno Rothenberg's excavations have revealed no
remains from the 10th century, and in fact the site was unoccupied from the
second half of the 12th century until the Roman Period. See Beno Rothenberg,
"Les mines du roi Salomon," *Bible et Terre Sainte* 25 (Jan 1960): pp. 4-10.
Moreover, 1 Kgs 7:64 states that the majority of Solomon's copper implements
were cast far to the north in the Jordan Valley.

[136] The expansion consisted of extending the side walls from seven to nine
meters. Beno Rothenberg, *Timna*, p. 131-32.

[137] This seems to have occurred during the reign of Rameses V (1160-1156
B.C.E.). While the names of every Egyptian king of the 19th and 20th dynasties
were found at Timna, Rameses V, the final king of the 20th dynasty, was the

withdrawal, the temple was briefly reoccupied by Midianite miners, who significantly altered the previous shrine.[138]

An aniconic tradition is suggested in that hieroglyphic inscriptions were effaced and votive offerings were removed from the temple.[139] Stone sculptures of Hathor, which had apparently occupied the central niche, were removed from the shrine and replaced by a single copper serpent.[140] A row of מַצֵּבוֹת was erected along the southwestern wall. It was behind this row of standing stones, as well as along the facing wall, that masses of textile were uncovered. The thick fabric consisted of a well-woven mixture of flax and wool. It was dyed varying shades of red and yellow, and had beads woven into the fabric.[141] The material's function as a tent covering for the shrine was confirmed when two stone-lined pole holes were discovered piercing into the earlier Egyptian floor (Plate 51b).[142] In addition, several wood fragments were discovered in the Timna temple, mostly acacia.[143] The tent

---

latest discovered (Beno Rothenberg, *Timna*, p. 163; for a discussion of the earthquake, see pp. 149, 201).

[138] Beno Rothenberg identifies this people as Midianite based on the large concentration of Midianite pottery, which increases dramatically in the 13-12th centuries B.C.E.; see Beno Rothenbeg and Jonathan T. Glass, "The Midianite Pottery," *Midian, Moab, and Edom*, John Sawyer and David Clines, eds. (Sheffield, 1983): pp. 65-124. Rothenberg further theorizes that Midianite workmen were employed by the Egyptian mining campaigns at Timna; following the Egyptian withdrawal from the area, the workmen returned to the mine for a brief period and appropriated the temple (Rothenberg, *Timna*, pp. 151-163). See also Rothenberg, "מקדש הכורים בבקעת תמנע," ישראל-עם וארץ Series 19 (Tel-Aviv, 1983-84): pp. 85-122.

[139] Beno Rothenberg, *Timna*, p. 151.

[140] The serpent measures 12 cm in length, has a gilded head, and calls to mind the Hebrew Bible's נְחֻשְׁתָּן built in Num 21:8-9 and destroyed in 2 Kgs 18:4. See Beno Rothenberg, *Timna*, pp. 152, 173, 183. One of the Hathor stelae was effaced, overturned, and reused as a מַצֵּבָה (Rothenberg, *Timna*, p. 150).

[141] Beno Rothenberg, *Timna*, p. 151. For a thorough study of the tent fabric and other Timna materials, see Avigail Sheffer and Amalia Tidhar, "Textiles and Textile Impressions on Pottery," *The Egyptian Mining Temple at Timna*, ed. B. Rothenberg (London, 1988): pp. 224-32, pls. 133-34. They suggest that the red dye, most likely from the roots of *Rubia Tinctorium*, increased the rate of disintegration.

[142] Beno Rothenberg, *Timna*, p. 151.

[143] Ella Werker, "Wood," *The Egyptian Mining Temple at Timna*, ed. B. Rothenberg (London, 1988): pp. 232-35.

shrine was short-lived, however, as the site was permanently abandoned in the second half of the 12th century.[144]

The Midianite tent shrine provides many parallels to the Tabernacle and other cultic implements as described in the Hebrew Bible. There was a red tent, likely supported by acacia wood poles, covering a sacred area featuring מַצֵּבוֹת. All around were found a large number of animal bones, mostly goat.[145]

### Semitic Names, Sacred Tents, and a New Etymology for Aaron

There are five names in the Hebrew Bible incorporating the root אהל, expressing the connection between tents and the sacred. Oholiab (אָהֳלִיאָב) means "the (divine) father is my tent," befitting Oholiab's occupation of building the Tabernacle and its cultic implements.[146] The wife of Esau and an Edomite chief share the name Oholibamah (אָהֳלִיבָמָה), "tent of the high place."[147] Also, without a theophoric element are the names of two metaphorical sisters in Ezekiel: Oholah "tent-woman" representing Samaria, and Oholibah "my tent is in her" representing Jerusalem.[148] Lastly, Ohel (אֹהֶל) "tent" is the name of Zerubbabel's son.[149]

Extra-biblical evidence adds a few parallels. A bulla from the City of David includes the personal name אהל.[150] Nearby on Mt. Zion, a seal was discovered in a burial cave with the name חמיאהל

---

[144] Beno Rothenberg, *Timna*, p. 152.

[145] On the general use of מַצֵּבוֹת, see Dale W. Manor, "Massebah," *ABD* IV, p. 602. The most notable מַצֵּבוֹת in the Israelite material record come from the 10th century shrine to Yahweh at Arad. See Yohanan Aharoni, "Arad: Its Inscriptions and Temple," *BA* 31 (1968): pp. 2-32. The animal bones are recorded in Beno Rothenberg, *Timna*, p. 176. Na'avah Panitz-Cohen called to my attention a pink fabric fragment discovered during the 1990 season at Tel Beth Shean Area S, possibly used for a tent-related covering. The stratum dates to the 11th century B.C.E.

[146] Jeaneane D. Fowler, *Theophoric Personal Names in Ancient Hebrew*, JSOT SS 49 (Sheffield: JSOT, 1988): pp. 80-81, 162, and Martin Noth, *Die israelitischen Personennamen* (Stuttgart, 1928): p. 158. Cf. the etymology of Oholiab's supervisor Bezalel: "in the shade/protection of El." For references to Oholiab, see Exod 31:6; 35:34; 36:1-2; 38:23.

[147] Gen 36:2, 5, 14, 18, 25, 41; 1 Chr 1:52.

[148] Ezekiel 23.

[149] 1 Chr 3:20.

[150] Yigal Shiloh, "A Group of Hebrew Bullae from the City of David," *IEJ* 36 (1986): p. 29, no. 29.

"My (divine) father-in-law is a tent."[151] Four Phoenician names likewise show that tents played a large role in religion: ʾhl "tent," ʾhlmlk "the (divine) king is a tent" or "the tent of the (divine) king," grʾhl "tent dweller," and ʾhlbʿl "Baal is a tent/Baal's tent."[152] Further afield, relevant Sabaean names likewise have been found: ʾhlʾl "El is a tent/El's tent" and ʾhl ʿttr "ʿAthtar is a tent/ʿAthtar's tent."[153] Finally, Lihyanic ʾhlbn "son is a tent" illustrates the widespread nature of names incorporating tents.[154]

The biblical name Aaron (אַהֲרֹן) may also ultimately be derived from Semitic אהל.[155] Past attempts to solve the question of Aaron's etymology have been unconvincing. Scholars seeking solutions from Semitic roots have fared poorly, finding only a rare Syriac cognate (ʾhrʾ) which means "libidinous/lascivious."[156] Others link Aaron's name to the sacred ark (הָאָרֹן), claiming the definite article ה through metathesis became the second root letter,[157] or that אהר derives from אור" shine," much like נהר from נור "shine."[158] Scholars have done slightly better with Egyptian etymologies, as this would fit other Levitical names from Egypt such as Moses, Phinehas, and Hophni.[159] Among proposed

---

[151] David Davies and Amos Kloner, "A Burial Cave of the Late Israelite Period on the Slopes of Mt. Zion," *Qadmoniot* 41 (1978): pp. 18-19 (Hebrew).

[152] For ʾhl see Joseph Naveh, "Phoenician Ostraca from Tel Dor," in *Solving Riddles and Untying Knots*, Fs. J. C. Greenfield; Z. Zevit, S. Gitin, M. Sokoloff, eds. (Winona Lake, IN, 1995): pp. 461-62. For the others, see Frank L. Benz, *Personal Names in the Phoenician and Punic Inscriptions* (Rome, 1972): pp. 60, 262.

[153] Joseph Halévy, *Inscriptions sabéennes* (1872): 46.2; *CIH* 434.1, 547.1. See also Gonzaque Ryckmans, *Les noms propres sud-sémitiques, tome I: Répertoire analytique* (Bibliothèque du Muséon 2; Louvain, 1934): pp. 27-28.

[154] Berhard Moritz, "Edomitische Genealogien," *ZAW* 44 (1926): p. 87.

[155] See Michael M. Homan, "A Tensile Etymology for Aaron: ʾahărōn < ʾahălōn," *BN* 95 (1998): pp. 21-22.

[156] Wilhelm Gesenius, *Thesaurus Philologicus Criticus Linguae Hebraeae et Chaldaeae Veteris Testamenti* (Leipzig, 1829): p. 33.

[157] Eduard Meyer, *Die Israeliten und ihre Nachbarstämme* (Halle, 1906): pp. 93-94. Some argue that a title "sons of the ark" (בְּנֵי הָאָרֹן) became "sons of Aaron" (בְּנֵי אַהֲרֹן), resulting in the personification of Aaron. See William H. Bennett, *Exodus*, Century Bible (London, 1908): p. 63.

[158] William H. C. Propp, *Exodus 1-18*, p. 213.

[159] Hence, John R. Spencer writes, "The meaning of the name 'Aaron' is uncertain, although it is perhaps derived from Egyptian," in "Aaron," *ABD* I, p. 1. For the Egyptian derivation of many Hebrew Bible names, see Martin Noth, *Die israelitischen Personennamen*, pp. 63-64.

Egyptian etymologies are "Great is the name" ('3 rn) or
"Horus" (ḥwr).[160] In the absence of an easy etymology, we are
driven to the farfetched.

An explanation that better fits Aaron's occupation as
maintainer of the Tabernacle is that his name is simply an
Egyptianized form of Semitic אהל with an adjectival or diminutive
suffix -ōn; hence, אַהֲרֹן would mean "tent-man."[161] The Egyptian
language, in the absence of an "l" sound, replaced foreign "l"
with "r". Thus the name Israel is represented as ysr'ir on the
Merneptah stele, and Ptolemy is rendered ptwrmys on the Rosetta
stone. There are multiple recordings of 'hr for "tent" in Egyptian
records beginning in the New Kingdom.[162] Furthermore, among
the many Egyptian names of Semitic derivation exists an 18th or
19th dynasty stable master named 'aharaya, which means either
"Yahweh is a tent," or simply "tent."[163] Finally, we find the
name 'hln (tent-man) on a Thamudic rock inscription.[164]
Strengths of this etymology are a name corresponding to Aaron's
duties and an Egyptian derivation similar to his fellow Levites.
Also, the name Aaron, like Moses, was not adopted into the
Hebrew onomasticon until postbiblical times, suggesting foreign
origins. However, we must admit that there are no other examples

---

[160] For the "great is the name" etymology, see I. Hösl, *Zur orientalischen
Namenkunde: Maria - Moses - Aaron. Eine philologische Studie* (Leiden, 1952):
p. 85. However, the disappearance of an ʿayin in transcription is not probable.
For a review of other even less likely Egyptian candidates, including "Horus"
(this necessitates an unplausible conversion of a ḥēt into a ḥēḥ), see Manfred
Görg, "Aaron—von einem Titel zum Namen?" *BN* 32 (1986): pp. 11-17, who
derives the name Aaron from an Egyptian title meaning "Overseer."

[161] On the adjectival use, see Gesenius, *Hebrew Grammar*, 2nd English
edition (Oxford, 1910); on the diminutive, see Jacob Barth, *Nominalbildung in
den semitischen Sprachen*, [Leipzig, 1894]: pp. 348-49). Hebrew comparisons
include אִישׁוֹן (little-man), שְׁפִיפֹן (adder), שַׂהֲרֹן (new-moon), and צַוָּרֹן (necklace).

[162] James E. Hoch, *Semitic Words in Egyptian Texts of the New Kingdom and
Third Intermediate Period* (Princeton, 1994): p. 31.

[163] The -ya suffix may bear no independent meaning, as shown by the many
Eblaite -ya names. On the Egyptian name 'aharaya, see Thomas Schneider,
*Asiatische Personennamen in ägyptischen Quellen des Neuen Reiches* OBO 114
(Freiburg, 1992): pp. 105-06. For the interchange of אֶהְלָן and אהלי, compare
Hebrew שִׁמְשׁוֹן/שִׁמְשׁוֹן, both from שֶׁמֶשׁ "sun." For other examples of Egyptian names
from Semitic origins, see Raphael Giveon, *The Impact of Egypt on Canaan*,
OBO 20 (Göttingen, 1978): pp. 15-21.

[164] Antonin Joseph Jaussen, *Mission archéologique en Arabie* II (Paris,
1914): p. 583. The inscription was found near ʾel-Hebou ʾesh-Šarky near Teima.

in the Hebrew Bible where a Semitic word, altered by a foreign language, reentered the original language as a borrowing.

## Making Tents in the Temple? Further Evidence for Tent Shrines

Among the many reforms attributed to Josiah is the enigmatic statement in 2 Kgs 23:7: "He tore down the ritual houses (?) which were in the house of Yahweh, where the women were weaving (אֲרֻגוֹת) there houses (בָּתִּים) for Asherah." While we have seen the ambiguity of "house" in Hebrew, the root ארג is used only in the manufacturing of things tensile.[165] The passage suggests that prior to Josiah's reforms, the Temple was being used as a production center for tent shrines.

## Tent-like Temples: Jerusalem, Tayinat, Ain Dara, and Arad

The Iron Age temples in Jerusalem, Tayinat, Ain Dara, and Arad constitute the last remaining parallels to the Tabernacle to be explored here. Much has been written on the similarities between the Solomonic Temple described in 1 Kings 6-7 and P's Tabernacle. The identical 3:1 ratio of length to width, the eastern orientation of a long-room structure, and the retention of the Tabernacle cultic implements including the Ark, Menorah, altars of incense and burnt offerings, table of showbread, and the laver, all indicate that, at least for P's reconstruction of early Israelite history, when the cult center ceased being mobile, much of the religion was perpetuated in Solomon's newly founded Temple.[166] These shared features were among the main pieces of evidence used by Wellhausen to argue the Priestly Tabernacle's fraudulence.[167]

The many differences between the two structures have frequently gone unnoticed, however. The most obvious is that one is a portable tent and the other a permanent temple. Moreover, the Temple's height of 30 cubits is three times that of the Tabernacle, while the length and width are twice the Tabernacle's.[168]

---

[165] Note Exod 28:32; Isa 19:9 and אֶרֶג "loom."

[166] See Menahem Haran, "Shiloh and Jerusalem," *JBL* 81 (1962): pp. 14-24.

[167] Julius Wellhausen, *Prolegomena zur Geschichte Israels*, p. 45.

[168] As pointed out by Richard E. Friedman, "Tabernacle," *ABD* VI, p. 296; "The Tabernacle in the Temple," *BA* 43 (1980): p. 241; and *Who Wrote the Bible?* (New York, 1989): pp. 182-87. This refutes Wellhausen's claim that the

Additional features, such as the Temple's extra rooms, porch, molten sea, basins, and stands have no precedent in the Tabernacle. The twin pillars at the Temple's entrance, which figure prominently in Solomon's and Ezekiel's Temples, are absent in the Tabernacle.[169] Also the Temple has a total of ten lampstands (five north and five south) according to 1 Kgs 7:49, whereas the Tabernacle has only one. All of these features show the two structures to be not so similar after all. If P modeled the Tabernacle on the Temple, why did he do such a poor job of copying?

Complicating the question is the fact that the exact forms of both the Tabernacle and the Temple are uncertain.

---

Priestly Tabernacle is a half-size Temple. Victor (Avigdor) Hurowitz, "The Form and Fate of the Tabernacle: Reflections on a Recent Proposal," *JQR* 86 (1995): p. 139, claims that the 2:1 ration from Temple to Tabernacle still works if one counts, not the 30 cubit height of the Temple, but the 20 cubit height of the Temple's holy of holies. Yet, the holy of holies' length and width are irrelevant in the supposed 2:1 ratio, which is based on the entire Temple.

[169] 1 Kgs 7:15-22; Ezek 40:49.

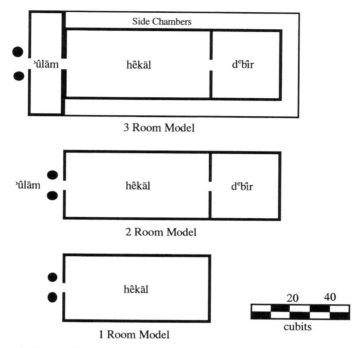

Figure 6 - Three-, Two-, and One-Room Floor Plans of Solomon's Temple

Most interpret the structure described in 1 Kings 6 as tripartite, consisting of the אוּלָם (porch), the הֵיכָל (room), and the דְּבִיר (holy of holies).[170] This three-part division of a long room temple finds a close correspondence in a 9th century B.C.E. temple at Tell Tayinat in northern Syria (Plate 52).[171] Here too we find an eastern orientation, twin pillars at the entrance, and an adjacent *bīt ḫilani* palace, all mirroring the description of Solomon's building endeavors. However, while the parallels of Tayinat's temple to the

---

[170] This tripartite model is followed by William F. Albright, *Archaeology and the Religion of Israel* (Baltimore, 1942): pp. 142-155, G. Ernest Wright, "The Stevens Reconstruction of the Solomonic Temple," *BA* 18 (1955): pp. 41-44, Yigael Yadin, "The Fourth Season of Excavations at Hazor, *BA* 22 (1959): pp. 2-8, Kurt Möhlenbrink, *Der Tempel Salomos* (Stuttgart, 1932), and André Parrot, *Le temple de Jérusalem* (Neuchâtel, 1954).

[171] Calvin W. McEvan, "The Syrian Expedition of the Oriental Institute of the University of Chicago," *AJA* 41 (1937): pp. 8-9; Th. A. Busink, *Der Tempel von Jerusalem* I, pp. 558-62. David Ussishkin, "Solomon and the Tayinat Temples," *IEJ* 16 (1966): 104-10.

Jerusalem Temple are remarkable, there is little in common with the Tabernacle aside from the long room layout and orientation.

Another structure with several parallels to Solomon's Temple is the Iron Age temple at Ain Dara, excavated in the early 1980's (Plate 53).[172] It is a tripartite long-room structure with twin columns in the portico, and it is surrounded by side-chambers, as is the Jerusalem Temple (1 Kgs 6:5). However, it shares little in form with the Tabernacle.

Others have separated the אוּלָם from the temple proper (see Figure 6's two-room model), yielding a bipartite plan for Solomon's Temple which does match the most common reconstructions of the Tabernacle.[173] Yet, the variations in size, dimensions, the twin pillars, and side rooms continue to distinguish the two structures.

More extreme is the interpretation of the Temple as a one-room building, demoting the דְּבִיר from a separate room to furniture.[174] The מִגְדָּל temples at Shechem and Megiddo are arguably similar, as they are composed of one room with a central niche. Nevertheless, Ezekiel 40:49 clearly describes a wall between the הֵיכָל and the דְּבִיר, and a wooden cube measuring 20 cubits in all three dimensions is hardly "furniture."[175] Still, the 10th century B.C.E. temple at Arad consists of a single room sanctuary, and, next to Rameses II's camp and Tutankhamon's funeral tent, the Arad Temple more closely mirrors the Tabernacle than any structure known to date.[176]

---

[172] Ali Abu Assaf, *Der Tempel von 'Ain Dara* (Damaszener Forschungen 3; Mainz, 1990); John Monson, "The New 'Ain Dara Temple," *BAR* 26.3 (2000): 20-35, 67.

[173] See Yohanan Aharoni, "The Solomonic Temple, the Tabernacle and the Arad Sanctuary," *Orient and Occident* ed. Harry Hoffner (Neukirchen, 1973): pp. 1-2, 7, who separates the אוּלָם, creating a two-room structure with a third adyton demarcated by a curtain.

[174] Hermann Schult, "Der Debir im salomonischen Tempel," *ZDPV* 80 (1964): pp. 46-54, and Martin Noth, *Könige* (Neukirchen, 1968): pp. 105 ff., note 11.

[175] As pointed out by Arnulf Kuschke, "Der Tempel Salomons und der 'syrische Tempeltypus,'" *Das Ferne und Nahe Wort*, Fs. L. Rost (1967): pp. 124-32.

[176] See Yohanan Aharoni, "Arad: Its Inscription and Temple," *BA* 31 (1968): pp. 2-32; "The Solomonic Temple, the Tabernacle, and the Arad Sanctuary," pp. 1-8. The Arad temple seems to be a Yahwistic cult center, yet cf. Shmuel Yeivin, *American Academy for Jewish Research Proceedings* 34 (1966): pp. 152 ff., who

The Arad temple is oriented with the entrance east and the holy of holies west (Plate 54a). Just in front of the Arad temple's entrance was a stone altar measuring five cubits in both length and width, the exact size of the Tabernacle's altar.[177] Two מַצֵּבוֹת were found in the adyton (Plate 54b), and a stone basin was discovered nearby, similar in function to the Tabernacle's bronze laver.[178] The temple at Arad measures 20 by 6 meters, which corresponds to the reconstruction of the Tabernacle by Aharoni and Friedman, where the frames overlap.[179] Furthermore, Friedman's model of a one-room Tabernacle, where the פָּרֹכֶת is not a room divider but a canopy over the ark, matches Arad's one-room plan.[180] Yet, there exists one major difference between the Arad temple and the Tabernacle: Arad's temple is a broad-room structure.[181] Aharoni's theories that the Tabernacle at Shiloh was a broad-room tent, and that the Priestly author moved the entrance 90 degrees to fit the Temple, seem forced.[182] The Tabernacle, like its Egyptian parallels, was a long-room tent.

---

believes the Arad temple belonged to foreign mercenaries.

[177] Exod 27:1.

[178] Exod 30:18.

[179] First pointed out by Yohanan Aharoni, "Arad: Its Inscription and Temple," p. 25 and "The Solomonic Temple, the Tabernacle, and the Arad Sanctuary," p. 4, and expanded upon by Richard E. Friedman, "Tabernacle," *ABD* VI, pp. 292-300, "The Tabernacle in the Temple," 241-48. Note that the main chamber of the Solar Shrine at Lachish also has the same measurements, in Olga Tufnell, *Lachish* III (London, 1953): p. 121. This model of the Tabernacle, in which the frames overlap, will be explored below, pp. 247-54.

[180] Richard E. Friedman, "Tabernacle," *ABD* VI, p. 295, "The Tabernacle in the Temple," pp. 244-45. The similarities between the Arad sanctuary and the Tabernacle are excessively stressed by Jorge L. da Silva, who uses the shared features to date P's Tabernacle descriptions to the tenth century B.C.E. (*The Implications of the Arad Temple for the Question of Dating P* [Ann Arbor, 1992]).

[181] Th. A. Busink, *Der Tempel von Jerusalem,* 593-94.

[182] Yohanan Aharoni, "The Solomonic Temple, the Tabernacle and the Arad Sanctuary," p. 7, and a more tentative argument in "Arad: Its Inscriptions and Temple," p. 25. Aharoni is followed by Th. A. Busink, *Der Tempel von Jerusalem,* p. 595. Busink's evidence is scant, however, consisting of 1 Sam 1:9-10, where Hannah goes to Shiloh's tent and prays "before the Lord," and 1 Sam 3:3, which states that Samuel was lying down in Shiloh's "temple of Yahweh, where the Ark of God was." Aharoni and Busink infer that the Ark was not separated from the Tabernacle's main room. But these passages make sense also with a פָּרֹכֶת understood in the traditional way as a veil dividing between the two rooms, and furthermore they show at best only that the Shiloh Tabernacle

Thus, all attempts to render P's Tabernacle as a portable copy of the Temple, be it one-, two-, or three-roomed, are problematic. Syro-Palestinian temples thus far unearthed, with the exception of the Arad sanctuary, shed little light on the Priestly Tabernacle's form and authenticity. And, even the Arad sanctuary differs considerably from the Tabernacle, leaving the Tabernacle's form without an indisputable parallel in temple architecture.

The many parallels to the Tabernacle examined in this chapter support the historicity of an early tent shrine for ancient Israel. The following chapter explores the Tabernacle's historicity, form, and fate.

---

was a single room. They shed no light whatsoever on its being a broad-room structure.

# CHAPTER EIGHT

# THE TABERNACLE: HISTORICITY, FORM, FATE

The likelihood of the Tabernacle's existence was strengthened in the previous chapter by examining the many examples of tent shrines from the Near East. Now we turn to its manner of construction. It will be shown that the Tabernacle's קְרָשִׁים, if understood as thin boards rather than thick frames, make construction and transportation feasible. The many reconstructions of the Tabernacle will be summarized and evaluated, and the theory that the Tabernacle came to reside within the Temple will be explored. Finally, a new model is proposed for the Tabernacle, based on realistic form and craftsmanship of ancient Near Eastern tents and wooden shrines.

## The Actuality of the Tabernacle

The Tabernacle does not seem to be the "copy" of the Temple, as argued by Wellhausen.[1] The many differences between the two structures, as well as the tent shrine parallels accumulated in the previous chapter, all support the Hebrew Bible's claim that a tent sanctuary provided the focal-point for ancient Israel's cult prior to the construction of Solomon's Temple.[2] For any structural similarities shared between the Tabernacle and the Temple, it is likely that the Tabernacle has precedence. Moreover, the strongest parallels to P's Tabernacle, Rameses II's military camp at Qedesh and the funerary shrines of Tutankhamon and Tiye, all arise from Late Bronze Age Egypt, the correct context according to the Hebrew Bible for the Tabernacle's construction. Moreover, contemporary Ugaritic literature places a Late Bronze Canaanite senior deity and pantheon head in a tent.[3] Thus, a Late Bronze

---

[1] For Wellhausen's claim, see p. 89 n. 1.

[2] Contrast Martin Noth's claim about the Tabernacle: "There is no analogy to this astonishing construction anywhere in cultic history (*Exodus* [Philadelphia, 1962]: p. 211).

[3] The material remains from Ugarit testify to a strong connection with Egypt

II/Iron I Israelite tent sanctuary, heavily influenced by Egyptian techniques, would not be an anomaly. It might even be expected.

Much of the Tabernacle's cultic furniture and associated terminology place P's Tabernacle in a LB II Egyptian context as well. The Tabernacle's Menorah, distinct from the later lampstands of Solomon's Temple (1 Kgs 7:49) and Zechariah's vision (4:2), best belongs here based on terminology, artistic parallels, and craftsmanship.[4]

Other aspects of the Tabernacle also recall Egyptian practice, though not necessarily in the LB II. The table of showbread set with twelve loaves of bread (Lev 24:5-6) finds its best parallel in Egyptian tomb iconography, where the table for the deceased is set with loaves, often numbering twelve (Plate 55a).[5] The Tabernacle's covering of שׁשׁ "fine linen" is also of Egyptian derivation, at least etymologically (sšr[w]).[6] The best parallel to the form of the Tabernacle's altar, a horned structure composed of wood with a hollow inside, comes from a miniature model of a Middle Kingdom granary and butchery (Plate 55b).[7] Thus,

---

from the MB to LB, as mentioned in Marguerite Yon, "Ugarit," *ABD* VI, pp. 695-706. Although we do not know who constructed El's tent, it would likely be Kothar, who has strong Egyptian ties. Concerning Ugaritic El's tent, see pp. 94-99.

[4] Carol L. Meyers, *The Tabernacle Menorah*, ASOR Dissertation Series 2 (Missoula, MT, 1976): pp. 181-84, n. 74; "Lampstand," *ABD* IV, pp. 141-43.

[5] On these reliefs, the number of bread-loaves varies from six to eighteen, the average being twelve. Stephen Rosenberg, "The Tabernacle Archetype," *Journal of the Visual Arts* vol. 3, no. 4 (Winter 1960-61): p. 23. In a Mesopotamian ritual, 12 loaves of bread are placed on a table dedicated to Ishtar (*CAD* A/1 244 7'). Also, 12 loaves are depicted on a Beni Hasan tomb painting (Percy E. Newberry, *Beni Hasan* I [London, 1893]).

[6] Thomas O. Lambdin, "Egyptian Loan Words in the Old Testament," *JAOS* 73 (1953): pp. 145-55. שׁשׁ is one of four terms for linen in the Hebrew Bible, and its usage is consistently preexilic, being replaced by בוץ after the sixth century B.C.E. See Avi Hurvitz, "The use of šēš and bûṣ in the Bible and its Implications for the Date of P," *HTR* 60 (1967): pp. 117-21. On other words of Egyptian derivation used in the Tabernacle's description, see Joshua M. Grintz, "Ancient Terms in Priestly Laws," 5-20, 163-80.

[7] The model was found in Tomb 366 at Beni Hasan, and dates to the Middle Kingdom. Note that no parallels to the Tabernacle's horned altar (Exod 27:1-8) have been found in the Syro-Palestinian material record prior to the 10th century B.C.E. Five horned incense altars dating from the 10th century were found *in situ* at Megiddo, one at Lachish. Moreover, these horned altars are all stone; none is composed of metal-overlaid wood as in Exodus. For information on these and the corpus of c. 40 horned altars, as well as the debate surrounding their function,

whatever the date for the Priestly writings as a whole, the Tabernacle texts seem to be based on a structure that predates the author by at least six centuries.

Various rituals associated with the Tabernacle are also mirrored in Late Bronze texts. The practice of anointing priests with oil and blood (Exodus 29) finds strong parallels in LB cuneiform texts from Emar in northern Syria.[8] Likewise, the function of priests and Levites both guarding and maintaining the Tabernacle resembles the shared custody of Hittite temples, which are run by two classes of temple guards: the *karimnaleš* priests who sustain the inner temple, and the outer temple guards, the *ḫalliyataleš*.[9]

The Tabernacle's symbolism, and the process by which it is revealed and constructed, all reflect known building accounts of ancient Near Eastern temples. Yahweh showing Moses a model of the Tabernacle in heaven to serve as the celestial prototype fits perfectly into the genre of temple building. So too Gudea, king of Lagash (c. 2200 B.C.E.), is shown a model of the temple of Ningirsu in a dream before he begins construction.[10] Most often in the conception of ancient Near Eastern temples, various aspects of each temple's form reflect its corresponding god's personal domain and attributes. For example, the mythic temple of the

---

see Seymour Gitin, "Incense Altars from Ekron, Israel, and Judah," *Eretz-Israel* 20 (1989): pp. 52-67; "New Incense Altars from Ekron," *Eretz-Israel* 23 (1992) pp. 43-49. Cf. Menahem Haran, who holds to the biblical claim that incense was burned only at the Jerusalem Temple, and that the unearthed horned altars were used for grain offerings, in "Incense Altars—Are They?", *Proceedings of the 2nd International Congress on Biblical Archaeology*, June 1990 (Jerusalem, 1993): 237-47; and *Temples and Temple Service*, pp. 236-38.

[8] Daniel E. Fleming, "More Help From Syria: Introducing Emar to Biblical Studies," *BA* 58 (1995): pp. 126-147. Daniel Arnaud, *Emar VI* (Paris, 1986). See also Alan R. Millard, "Mesopotamia and the Bible," *Aram* 1:1 (1989): pp. 25-26, and "La prophétie et l'écriture: Israel, Aram, Assyrie," *RHR* 202 (1985): pp. 125-145.

[9] Jacob Milgrom, "The Shared Custody of the Tabernacle and a Hittite Analogy," *JAOS* 90 (1970): pp. 204-209.

[10] Thorkild Jacobsen, *The Treasures of Darkness* (New Haven, 1976): pp. 80-81; Henri Frankfort, *Kingship and the Gods* (Chicago, 1948): pp. 255-56. Note also a similar belief in Egypt, where Thoth plans the temple of Re at Heliopolis (Frankfort, pp. 269-71). For many further parallels, some closer in date to the Hebrew Bible, see Victor (Avigdor) Hurowitz, "The Priestly Account of Building the Tabernacle," *JAOS* 105 (1985): pp. 21-30; *I Have Built You an Exalted House: Temple Building in the Bible in Light of Mesopotamian and North-west Semitic Writings* (Sheffield, 1992).

Ugaritic storm deity Baal must have a window for lightning bolts, and the use of lapis-lazuli in the construction mirrors the sky's color.[11] Like Baal, Yahweh rides the clouds and lives in the heavens, and so too Yahweh's mythic home is adorned with lapis.[12] Yet Yahweh's manifestations transcend the storm, and so channels for lightning are not a prerequisite for His dwelling. The primary concern for Yahweh's early home seems to be mobility, a quality best exhibited by tents. Although the Tabernacle lacks the overt cosmic symbolism found in many ancient Near Eastern temples, phenomena in Yahweh's heavenly domain are repeatedly referred to with terminology associated with tents: the sun, the clouds, the firmament, and the heavens in general.[13]

The Priestly source's detailed description further implies that a real structure influenced P's Tabernacle account. Nearly 400 verses are allotted to the Tabernacle's form and furnishings, far more attention than comparable structures receive in the Hebrew Bible and other ancient Near Eastern writings.[14] Elsewhere P evinces little concern with man-made structures, as only three verses describe Noah's ark (Gen 6:14-16). The cumulative evidence suggests an actual prototype underlay P's Tabernacle.

---

[11] The use of lapis in Baal's house is recorded in *KTU* 1.4.V.18-19, 33-35. Note also that Mesopotamian Bel sits on a throne over lapis (*uqnû*) in Alasdair Livingstone, *Mystical and Mythological Explanatory Works of Assyrian and Babylonian Scholars* (Oxford, 1986): pp. 82-83. Cf. also 1 Enoch 14, in which the ceiling of the heavenly throne-room consists of stars and hailstones.

[12] Exod 24:10 claims Yahweh is enthroned on a throne of lapis lazuli.

[13] E.g., Ps 19:5-6 says that Yahweh has pitched a tent (אֹהֶל) for the sun, which comes forth like a bridegroom leaving his tent (חֻפָּתוֹ). Similarly, Isa 4:5 describes the heavens as a "tent of righteousness." See also the use of נטה in Jer 10:12; Job 26:7-9; Ezek 1:22. Pesikta Rabbati 31:6 contains more analogies between Yahweh's home and various heavenly phenomena; cf. also Hebrews 9:23, Josephus (*Antiquities of the Jews*, III:6) and especially Philo (*On the Life of Moses* II, 16-23).

[14] In contrast, only 70 verses describe Solomon's Temple and its furnishings (1 Kgs 6:2-10, 15-38; 7:15-51), and Solomon's house receives 12 verses (1 Kgs 7:1-12). Two structures receive considerable detail, but still less than the Tabernacle: Ezekiel's temple (Ezekiel 40-48) and the building recorded in Qumran's Temple Scroll. For accounts of ancient building, see Victor (Avigdor) Hurowitz, *Temple Building in the Bible in Light of Mesopotamian and North-West Semitic Writings* (Jerusalem, 1983): pp. 224-38 (Hebrew); *I Have Built You an Exalted House* (English).

*P's Motivation and the Model for the Tabernacle: A Synthesis*

The historical context of the priestly writer seems increasingly likely to be the early seventh century B.C.E., based primarily on the linguistic studies of Avi Hurvitz and Meir Paran showing P's language to be antiquated compared to Ezekiel's.[15] This chronological frame also provides an opportune time for P's message, given the renewed Assyrian threat and the religious turmoil under Hezekiah and Manasseh.[16] The influx of refugees from northern Israel into Judah, with their *written* histories often portraying unfavorably things dear to the author of P (e.g. Aaron), would have provided ample motive for the Priestly writer. Yet, the problem of motivation for the Tabernacle account in particular remains. Why would an Aaronid priest, now 200 years after the alleged Zadokite split,[17] write with such detail about the Tabernacle?

Thus, the Priestly writer was either a polemicist or a historian. There is no evidence that the author of P wished to do away with

---

[15] Avi Hurvitz, *A Linguistic Study of the Relationship between the Priestly Source and the Book of Ezekiel*, CahRB 20 (Rome, 1982); "The Language of the Priestly Source and its Historical Setting: The Case for an Early Date," *PWCJS* 8 (1981): pp. 83-94; Meir Paran, *Literary Features of the Priestly Code: Stylistic Patterns, Idioms and Structures*. Hebrew University Dissertation (1983); Ziony Zevit, "Converging Lines of Evidence Bearing on the Date of P," *ZAW* 94 (1982): pp. 502-09; Gary A. Rendsburg, "Late Biblical Hebrew and the Date of P," *JANES* 12 (1980): pp. 65-80; Risa Levitt-Kohn, *A New Heart and a New Soul* (University of California, San Diego dissertation, 1997): p. 118. See also Richard E. Friedman, *Who Wrote the Bible?*, and Jacob Milgrom, "Priestly ('P') Source," *ABD* V, pp. 454-61. The majority of scholarship, however, continues to date P to the exilic or postexilic eras (e.g. Frank Crüsemann, *The Torah : Theology and Social History of Old Testament Law* [Minneapolis, 1996]).

[16] Thus there is much merit to Menahem Haran's reconstruction of events, where the Priestly writer composes during the Assyrian threat under Hezekiah's reign, motivated by Manasseh's drastic restructuring of the Temple, in which the inner sanctum was rid of the Ark and the cherubim. I disagree, however, with Haran's claim that "one cannot avoid the conclusion that what is reflected in P's tabernacle is the Temple of Solomon in a stage that antedated those changes [Manasseh's alterations]" (Menahem Haran, "Behind the Scenes of History: Determining the Date of the Priestly Source," *JBL* 100 [1981]: 331; *Temples and Temple Service*, pp. 192-94, 277-84, 288).

[17] "Zadokite split" refers to events surrounding the succession to the throne of King David, c. 965 B.C.E. Zadok, a descendant of Aaron, sided with Solomon, while Abiathar, a descendant of Moses, sided with Adonijah. Subsequently, Solomon's victory restricted access to the highpriesthood to the descendants of Zadok. See Frank M. Cross, Jr., *CMHE*, pp. 208-15

the Temple and begin anew with a tent sanctuary.[18] More likely is
that the Tabernacle accounts show the author of P acting as a
responsible historian. Far from inventing the structure, he is using
written texts, composed several centuries earlier, which record in
detail an elaborate tent shrine. P's source would be records
describing an actual structure dating to the Late Bronze II/Iron I,
as accounts of monumental construction and associated rituals are
normally composed during their fabrication, not centuries later.[19]

Just as Cross argued in 1947, the author of P is using written
documentation to record an actual tent sanctuary.[20] However, for
Cross the prototype is not the early shrine located at Shiloh,
explicitly called אֹהֶל מוֹעֵד, but rather the tent David erects for the
Ark in 2 Sam 6:17.[21] Cross's main objection to the structure at
Shiloh is 1 Sam 1:9, where Eli is described as sitting in a chair by
the doorpost (מְזוּזַת) of the temple of Yahweh (הֵיכַל יהוה).[22] These
features negate the possibility of a tent, according to Cross.
However, due to the fluidity of domiciliary terminology previously discussed, these features are not as problematic as he
would have it.[23] In any case, the massive Tabernacle is a
compromise of sorts between the sedentary and the nomadic;
while it is portable in theory, transport is cumbersome and in fact
rarely happens.[24] So it might be expected that biblical authors,

---

[18] Contra Terence E. Fretheim, "The Priestly Document: Anti-Temple?," *VT*
18 (1968): pp. 313-29; I disagree with Fretheim's placement of P in the
Babylonian exile, as a member of a group opposed to rebuilding the Jerusalem
Temple.

[19] For examples, see Alan R. Millard, "Mesopotamia and the Bible," *Aram*
1:1 (1989): 25-26.

[20] Frank M. Cross, "The Priestly Tabernacle," pp. 213-14.

[21] Cross, "The Priestly Tabernacle," p. 213; *CMHE*, pp. 231-32 (n. 52), 322.
In addition to Cross, those favoring a Tabernacle modeled on the tent of David
include: Virgil W. Rabe, "The Identity of the Priestly Tabernacle," *JNES* 25
(1966): pp. 132-34, Th. A. Busink, "Les origines du temple de Salomon,"
*Jaarbericht Ex Oriente Lux* 17 (1963): p. 186, and *Der Tempel von Jerusalem*, p.
603. Wellhausen also argues that while the Priestly Tabernacle is fictitious, the
tent referred to in Nathan's prophecy (2 Samuel 7) was the tent of David
(*Prolegomena zur Geschichte Israels*, p. 45).

[22] Similarly, Shiloh's shrine is called בֵּית־הָאֱלֹהִים in Judg 18:31; בֵּית־יהוה in 1
Sam 1:7, 24; and הֵיכַל יהוה in 1 Sam 3:3.

[23] On the blended usage of terms pertaining to dwellings, see above pp. 16-
27.

[24] Note for example that of the 40 years attributed to wandering in the
wilderness, for c. 38 of them the Tabernacle remained at Qadesh-Barnea ac-

when writing about the Tabernacle, even more than with standard tents, adopt terminology typically reserved for houses. Also, Yahweh declines David's offer to build a temple due to the fact that from the Exodus until now, "I have been moving about in a tent and in a Tabernacle" (2 Sam 7:6), seemingly referring to Shiloh.[25] Elsewhere the Shiloh sanctuary is clearly tent-related, called "tent of the appointed time" (Josh 18:1; 19:51; 1 Sam 2:22), a "tent" and a "tabernacle" (Ps 78:60). Nothing is said of a temple at Shiloh or anywhere else. Thus, some, most notably Menahem Haran and Richard E. Friedman, have preferred the tent shrine located at Shiloh as the model for P's Tabernacle.[26] Given the strong Egyptian influence on the form, furnishings and orientation of the Tabernacle, it is not surprising that the Shiloh shrine is maintained by officials bearing Egyptian names: Hophni and Phinehas (1 Samuel 1-4).[27]

Cross further objects to Shiloh's shrine as the model because he argues it was destroyed after the Battle of Ebenezer.[28] Excavations at Shiloh have shown a massive Iron I destruction layer.[29] Later biblical passages may corroborate this destruction.

---

cording to the Priestly author's chronology. This is deduced from the fact that of the 40 years, one year elapsed from the Exodus to the erection of the Tabernacle (Exod 40:2). Leviticus transpires in one month (Num 1:1), and Israel leaves Sinai 19 days after the census (Num 10:11) and shortly arrive at Qadesh, from where the spies are sent out (Num 13:26). This leaves the march from Qadesh-Barnea to the plains of Moab (Numbers 20-36) at the end of the 40 years (although cf. Deut 2:14, which claims 38 years pass *after* the Israelites depart from Qadesh-Barnea). Later, the Tabernacle is attested only at four sites prior to arriving at Jerusalem: Gilgal (Josh 4:19; 5:10; 9:6; 10:6, 43), Shiloh (1 Sam 21:1-6), Gibeon (1 Chr 16:39; 21:29; 2 Chr 1:3, 13), and Nob (1 Sam 21:1-6).

[25] Cf.1 Chr 17:5, examined below, p. 136 n. 32.

[26] Menahem Haran, "Shiloh and Jerusalem," p. 21; *Temples and Temple Service*. Richard E. Friedman's view is that Shiloh, like Jerusalem, has a tent inside of a temple ("Tabernacle," *ABD* VI, pp. 294-95); see also Jan Dus, "Noch zum Brauch der 'Ladewanderung,'" *VT* 13 (1963): pp. 126-32.

[27] Phinehas derives from Egyptian *p3nḥsj* "the southerner" and Hophni from *ḥfn(r)* "tadpole." See John R. Spencer, "Phinehas," *ABD* V, pp. 346-47; "Hophni," *ABD* III, pp. 285-86. Yahweh's shared attributes with various solar deities, including Egyptian, are enhanced by the correlation between the Tabernacle and the Egyptian military camp. See Paul E. Dion, "YHWH as Storm-god and Sun-god," *ZAW* 103 (1991): pp. 43-71; Mark S. Smith, *The Early History of God*, pp. 115-24.

[28] Cross, "The Priestly Tabernacle," p. 213.

[29] See Israel Finkelstein, Shlomo Bunimovitz, and Zvi Lederman, *Shiloh: The Archaeology of a Biblical Site* (Tel Aviv, 1993): pp. 388-89. Note also the

For example, while standing in the Temple court, Jeremiah predicts that due to disobedience, Yahweh "will make this house like Shiloh, and will make this city a curse to all the nations of the earth" (Jer 26:6).[30] Also Ps 78:60-61 says that for sins of the same nature, Yahweh "forsook the Tabernacle of Shiloh, the tent (where) He dwelled among people, and He gave His strength into captivity, and His glory into the enemy's hand."

No biblical text, however, explicitly includes the Tabernacle in Shiloh's destruction. One might anticipate a more detailed account of the central sanctuary's violent end, if it was demolished by the Philistines.[31] Thus it is possible that the Tabernacles of Shiloh and Zion are one and the same, and perhaps the Tabernacle went with the Ark to the Philistines.

The tent David erects for the Ark may in fact be the very Tabernacle that stood at Gilgal, Shiloh, Gibeon, and Nob. The main obstacle to this synthesis is that the Chronicler envisions two tents existing simultaneously: David's tent in Jerusalem (1 Chr 16:1), and the Tabernacle at Gibeon (1 Chr 16:39).[32] This is easily accounted for, given the Chronicler's motivations and known sources.[33] There is much to suggest that David's tent and

---

presence of MB III and LB cultic objects and installations, verifying the site's sacred usage (pp. 377-83).

[30] Note also Jer 7:12, 14; 26:9.

[31] Cf. the destruction of the Jerusalem Temple in 2 Kings 25, 2 Chronicles 36, Jeremiah 52, etc.

[32] 2 Chr 1:3-4 also attests to the separation of these tent-sanctuaries. Note that Yahweh's dwelling "in a tent and in a tabernacle" (2 Sam 7:6) is altered in 1 Chr 17:5 to read "from tent to tent and from tabernacle." Richard E. Friedman sees this as evidence that according to the Chronicler, the Ark moved from the Tent of Shiloh to the Tent of David ("The Tabernacle in the Temple," pp. 245-46).

[33] Gibeon's early cultic status is apparent from its inclusion as a Levitical city (Josh 21:17). More problematic for the Chronicler is that Solomon's inaugural dream, and his subsequent sacrifice of 1000 burnt offerings, all occur at the high place of Gibeon rather than in Jerusalem (1 Kgs 3:4-5 [ = 2 Chr 1:5-13]). To maintain the legitimacy of the Zadokite priests in the early Israelite monarchy, as well as the centralization of the cult, Solomon cannot sacrifice on his own at some illegitimate Gibeonite shrine as recorded in Kings. On the contrary, in 2 Chronicles 1, he journeys with an assembly to the Tabernacle, and uses not just any altar, but the very altar constructed by Bezalel (2 Chr 1:5). To further legitimize this Gibeonite sanctuary, the Chronicler ensures that Zadok himself regularly sacrifices there (1 Chr 16:39). In short, the distinction in Chronicles between David's tent and the Tabernacle is a retrojection to make

the Tabernacle are one and the same. The tent David erects in 2 Sam 6:17 is prefaced by the definite article (הָאֹהֶל), suggesting it is something previously mentioned.[34] Furthermore, David does not build this tent from scratch. Rather he "spreads (it) out" נָטָה.[35] More importantly, when the Ark and the Tabernacle (אֹהֶל מוֹעֵד) are transported to Solomon's Temple, they come from the City of David (1 Kgs 8:4; 2 Chr 5:5). Thus, if David's tent is called אֹהֶל מוֹעֵד, the natural inference is that it really is the Tabernacle.

## The Tabernacle's Form

Despite P's unprecedented attention to the Tabernacle's detail, the precise form of the tent shrine remains enigmatic. The text contains several pieces of evidence that must be individually and collectively assessed, and several models of the Tabernacle have been proposed over the past 2,000 years. The following pages will explore the components (boards, bars, curtains, skins, veil/canopy, and veil) first individually, and then collectively, and evaluate five previously proposed models for the Tabernacle's form.

## Boards (קְרָשִׁים)

[15]And you shall make the boards (קְרָשִׁים) for the Tabernacle [from] standing planks of acacia (עֲצֵי שִׁטִּים עֹמְדִים). [16]Ten cubits is the length of the board and a cubit and a half-cubit the width of the one board. [17]Two arms (יָדוֹת) to the one board connecting each [arm] to its sister; thus you shall make for all the boards of the Tabernacle. [18]And you shall make the boards for the Tabernacle; 20 boards for the south side southward. [19]And 40 silver sockets (אֲדָנֵי) you shall make under the 20 boards; two sockets under the one board for its two arms and two sockets under the one board for its two arms. [20]And for the second side of the Tabernacle, the north side, 20 boards. [21]And 40 sockets of

---

licit a non-centralized shrine at Gibeon. For further discussion on the cult at Gibeon, see Joseph Blenkinsopp, *Gibeon and Israel* (Cambridge, 1972); Patrick M. Arnold, "Gibeon," *ABD* II, pp. 1010-12.

[34] Note, however, that the article might be grammatically necessary rather than optional, as it is an antecedent of a relative clause.

[35] Contrast the repeated use of the verb עשה "to make" during the construction of the Tabernacle (Exodus 35-40) and Solomon's Temple (1 Kings 6), as well as the verb הקים "to raise" for the Tabernacle as a whole in Exod 40:1, 17-18.

silver; two sockets under the one board and two sockets under the one
board. ²²And for the west side of the Tabernacle, you shall make six
boards. ²³And two boards you shall make for corners of the Tabernacle
in the sides. ²⁴And they shall be double from below and they shall be
double / joined (LXX and Samaritan תאמים, MT תמים) at the top to the
one ring; thus shall it be for the two of them, for the two corners they
shall be. ²⁵And shall be the eight boards and their 16 silver sockets;
two sockets under the one board and two sockets under the one board.

(Exod 26:15-25)

The priestly author's term for the Tabernacle's supporting
structures, קרש, is deliberately chosen, drawing on the terminology
of earlier Semitic tent shrines attested at Mari and Ugarit.[36] The
shape and arrangement of the Tabernacle's 48 קרשים are crucial
to reconstructing its overall form.

The identification of שטים with acacia is linguistically sound.[37]
Acacia wood is ideally suited for the frames, as it is durable,
strong, abundant, and relatively lightweight.[38] The text remains
vague, however, regarding three items: the thickness of the boards,
the shape and arrangement of the two corner pieces, and the final
positioning of the boards (i.e. whether they are placed side-by-
side or overlapping).[39]

Two of the boards' dimensions are known: they are 10 cubits
in height and 1 1/2 cubits in width. The text says nothing of their
thickness; later proposals range from a cubit to four fingers.[40]

---

[36] For the use of *qrš* in El's Ugaritic tent, see pp. 194-99. For large *qersū* at
Mari, and *qersū* in a ritual connotation, see pp. 116-18.

[37] Hebrew שטים seems to derive from Egyptian *šnd.t*, as argued by Thomas O.
Lambdin, "Egyptian Loan Words in the Old Testament," *JAOS* 73 (1953): p.
154. Cf. Arabic *sanṭ*. Other than referring to the wood of the Tabernacle and its
furnishings, שטים occurs in Isa 41:19 and in the place-names Shittim (Num
25:1), Abel-shittim (Num 33:49), Beth-shittah (Judg 7:22), and Nahal-ha-
shittah (Joel 4:18).

[38] On the wood's durability, note that the LXX refers to acacia as ξυλα
ασηπτα "imperishable wood."

[39] Here the LXX is no help, as it uses στυλοι "pillars." Jerome used *tabulae*,
whence Tindale got "boards." These *tabulae* were used in the construction of
Roman *tabernacula*, from which the word "Tabernacle" is derived.

[40] Scholars' variant estimates of the thickness of the קרש have been based on
one of two things: 1) producing a structure that parallels the Temple's 3:1 ratio
in length to width, or 2) producing a wooden exterior on which one of the two

Those favoring a thickness of one cubit for each board include the Babylonian Talmud as well as Rashi.[41] Yet, a major problem hinders this interpretation. The burden of such enormous objects would render transportation impractical if not impossible. The approximate weight for a solid acacia board measuring 10 x 1.5 x 1 cubits approaches one ton at 1,772 lbs/804 kg.[42] All 48 frames would weigh 85,056 lbs/38,592 kg.

Others more plausibly argue a 1/2 cubit thickness for the קְרָשִׁים.[43] Nevertheless, the same problem of weight exists, though to a lesser degree. Now the weight of each board is 886 lb/402 kg (48 frames=42,528 lbs/19,296 kg).

Here the anatomy of acacia trees becomes relevant. While there are approximately 750 species of the acacia tree, few can produce such massive lumber.[44] For boards measuring 10 x 1.5 x 1 cubits, a trunk diameter of 32.4 inches/81 cm is necessary. For half-cubit thick boards, the tree's diameter needs only to be 12.78 inches/31.95 cm (Figure 7).

---

curtains hangs uniformly. The advantages and disadvantages of the various models are examined below, pp. 159-85.

[41] Rashi, on Exod 26:17. In bShab 98a-b there is a debate between R. Judah, who suggests the frames are one cubit thick at their bottom, but taper to a finger-breadth at the top, and R. Nehemiah, who states they were one cubit all the way up. See also the medieval commentary on the Tabernacle, *Baraita de-Melekhet ha-Mishkan*, critical edition by Robert Kirschner (Cincinnati, 1992), p. 154, which argues for a thickness of one cubit.

[42] Each frame in this model consists of 50.625 cubic feet, given 18 inches per cubit. The weight is achieved using the formula of 35 pounds per square foot (Gerald E. Wickens, "A Study of Acacia albida," *Kew Bulletin* 23 [1969], p. 197). William Brown, *The Tabernacle* (Edinburgh, 1899): p. 275, arrives at the same estimate.

[43] Including Archibald R. S. Kennedy, "Tabernacle," *Hastings Dictionary* (1902): pp. 659-61.

[44] Kennedy points out the difficulty in finding such large trees, "Tabernacle," p. 659. On the many species of acacia, see Michael Zohary, *Flora Palaestina* 2 (Jerusalem, 1972): p. 26.

Trunk Diameter for Boards Measuring 1.5 x 1 and 1.5 x 0.5 Cubits

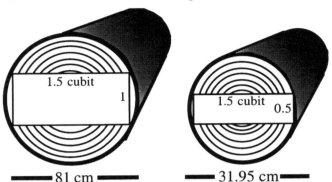

Figure 7 - Acacia Trunk Diameter for Tabernacle Boards

In both cases the tree must stand c. 20 ft/6 m tall to produce an adequate trunk height of 10 cubits. Only two species of acacia located in the Near East, *Acacia nilotica* and *Acacia albida*, could produce such massive boards.[45] *Acacia nilotica* is the larger of the two trees, but currently the nearest indigenous area is tropical Africa; its presence in the Sinai/Southwest Asia in antiquity remains unknown. Thus, *Acacia albida* is the more likely contender. These trees at times reach a height of 30 m and occasionally possess a trunk diameter of 2 m, giving ample space to create even one cubit thick boards.[46] Still, while tree physiology makes it possible to construct boards of this magnitude, their weight remains prohibitive.

To overcome this difficulty, most scholars follow a suggestion first put forward by Archibald R. S. Kennedy, that the קְרָשִׁים were not "boards," but rather "frames."[47]

---

[45] Ziony Zevit, "Timber for the Tabernacle: Text, Tradition, and Realia," *Eretz-Israel* 23 (1992): p. 140.

[46] Ziony Zevit, "Timber for the Tabernacle: Text, Tradition, and Realia," p. 140-42; Michael Zohary, *Flora Palaestina* 2, p. 27; Abraham Fahn and Ella Werker, *Wood Anatomy and Identification of Trees and Shrubs from Israel and Adjacent Regions* (Jerusalem, 1986): p. 116. Note also the description עֲצֵי שִׁטִּים עֹמְדִים, possibly meaning "tree of standing acacia," which would seems to rule out many indigenous species which resemble bushes rather than trees. If so, the author of P has in mind a tall, upright tree.

[47] Archibald R. S. Kennedy, "Tabernacle," pp. 659-61. The translation

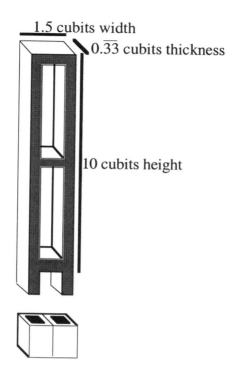

1.5 cubits width

0.3̄3 cubits thickness

10 cubits height

Figure 8 - Kennedy's Tabernacle Frame with its Bases

Kennedy's model no longer requires a large trunk diameter, although the tree's height must still range from 4.5 to 6 meters to produce 10 cubit upright beams assuming the vertical יְדוֹת are of a single piece of wood.[48] The two holes created by latticed frames would allow the Tabernacle's ornate covering to be seen; whereas in the solid קְרָשִׁים model, the fabric is obscured except on the

_____

"frames" is found in RSV; Richard E. Friedman, "Tabernacle," p. 295; Henry J. Grimmelsman, *The Book of Exodus* (Cincinnati, 1927): p. 176; Martin Noth, *Exodus*, p. 212; and Howard Hatton, "The Projections on the Frames of the Tabernacle," *The Bible Translator* 42.2 (1991): pp. 205-09. Ziony Zevit interestingly employs flora studies to conclude the superiority of Kennedy's model. However, he considers only the above proposed models of 1 and 1/2 cubit thicknesses for the frames. More plausible, given the weight difficulties, are thin boards (see below, pp. 144-45).

[48] Ziony Zevit ignores the possibility that the frames might be composed of more than a single piece of timber ("Timber for the Tabernacle," p. 141*).

ceiling. Kennedy further contends his model accounts for the text's silence regarding the thickness of the קְרָשִׁים, as he writes " a frame has, strictly speaking, no thickness,"[49] even though he later assumes 1/3 of a cubit thickness.[50] Kennedy places the 1 1/2 cubit frames side-by-side, creating a length for the Tabernacle of 30 cubits (each long-side has 20 frames) and a width of 10 cubits (six frames [9 cubits] plus 1/3 cubit for each of the long-sided frames' thicknesses and 1/6 of a cubit for the bars on each side [Plate 62]).

## The Arrangement of Kennedy's Tabernacle Frames

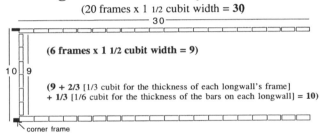

(20 frames x 1 1/2 cubit width = 30

(6 frames x 1 1/2 cubit width = 9)

(9 + 2/3 [1/3 cubit for the thickness of each longwall's frame] + 1/3 [1/6 cubit for the thickness of the bars on each longwall] = 10)

corner frame

Figure 9

As the Tabernacle's coverings are visible both inside and outside of the Tabernacle, the measurements of 30 x 10 x 10 cubits are the length, height, and width of the fabric as it hangs upon the frames, making the debate regarding whether the measurements apply to the interior or exterior of the frames irrelevant, according to Kennedy.[51]

Nevertheless, Kennedy's reconstruction involves several difficulties. First and foremost, these frames resemble no tent-frame construction known to antiquity or modernity. Also, the limited display of the ornate linen covering to which Kennedy objected is only slightly improved. It still remains invisible from outside the Tabernacle, and even within, the frames' one-third-

---

[49] Kennedy, p. 660.
[50] Kennedy, p. 661.
[51] Kennedy, p. 661.

cubit wide windows largely obstruct the view. Kennedy translates
Exodus 26:15-17:

> [15]And thou shalt make the frames for the dwelling of acacia wood,
> standing up, [17]two uprights for each frame, joined to each other by
> cross-rails -- [16]10 cubits the height and a cubit and a half the breadth
> of the single frame.
>
> (Kennedy, p. 660)

Kennedy claims verse 16 is parenthetical, and so he places it after
verse 17. Thus the יָדוֹת of verse 17 are components of verse 15's
קְרָשִׁים, not accessories.[52] Kennedy's translation of מְשֻׁלָּבֹת as
"joined to each other by cross rails" is cumbersome though
possible, as the root implies a connection of some sort.[53]
Occasionally in rabbinical sources, שְׁלַבִּין can be used for the rungs
of a ladder, though the root more often is used for bolts as well as
mortises and tenons.[54]

Lack of parallels to Kennedy's structure and textual difficulties
are not the only problems with interpreting קְרָשִׁים as "frames."
The main feature that attracts scholars to Kennedy's model is the
reduction in weight; yet, Kennedy's frames weigh approximately
444 lbs/200 kgs each, still excessive.[55]

Num 7:8 provides eight oxen along with four wagons to
transport the 48 boards of the Tabernacle, their 96 bases, and
other wooden and metal objects of lesser weight, including the 60

---

[52] Kennedy, p. 660.

[53] The root שלב connotes joining in 1 Kgs 7:28-29, the only biblical context
where שלב is used outside of the Tabernacle's קְרָשִׁים.

[54] For שְׁלַבִּין, see Marcus Jastrow, *A Dictionary of the Targumim, the Talmud
Babli and Yerushalmi, and the Midrashic Literature* (New York, 1992): p. 1577.

[55] The frames' weight was originally calculated by Ziony Zevit ("Timber for
the Tabernacle," *Eretz-Israel* 23 (1992): p. 141) to be 290 kgs. Zevit reaches
this figure by the following calculations: two uprights at 10 x .5 x .5 cubits at
35 lbs per cubic foot, equaling 590 lbs/268 kgs. Zevit then adds 50 lbs for the
two crossbars, totaling 640 lbs/290 kgs. However, Kennedy argued that the
frames were .33 cubits thick, not .5 as Zevit claims (Kennedy, p. 661). Thus the
weight of Kennedy's frames is reduced from 290 kgs to 200 kgs. Cf. Menahem
Haran, who criticizes Kennedy's theory *because* of this supposed weight-
reduction. Haran claims the קְרָשִׁים were meant to be heavy, as they are transported
in oxen-driven carts. See "The Priestly Image of the Tabernacle," *HUCA* 36
(1965): pp. 192, and *Temples and Temple Service*: pp. 150-51.

columns and bases for the courtyard, and the nine columns and bases for the Tabernacle's screen and פָּרֹכֶת.[56] The maximum weight that a pair of oxen can pull in a cart has been estimated at 4,400 lbs/2,000 kg.[57] The 96 silver bases of the קְרָשִׁים and the four silver bases of the פָּרֹכֶת are said to weigh 100 talents or 6,600 lbs/3000 kg.[58] This already fills the allotted weight for 1.5 carts. If the remaining elements weigh in the vicinity of 2,200 lbs/1,000 kg, then only two carts remain for the קְרָשִׁים.

## Allotment of Weight to Four Carts

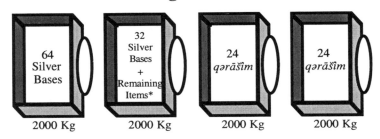

| 64 Silver Bases | 32 Silver Bases + Remaining Items* | 24 *qərāšîm* | 24 *qərāšîm* |

| 2000 Kg | 2000 Kg | 2000 Kg | 2000 Kg |

* Includes 60 courtyard columns/bases
and 9 columns/bases for Tabernacle's
screen and *parōket*

Figure - 10

With a maximum weight for two carts of 8,800 lbs/4,000 kg divided among 48 frames, this leaves an maximum weight for each frame of 183.6 lbs/83 kg, significantly below Kennedy's 444 lbs/200 kg frame.

Given the limitations of Kennedy's frame theory, it seems the best reconstruction for the קְרָשִׁים adheres to the understanding of Josephus and Philo: namely, that they were thin boards.[59] This

---

[56] Note that some of the heaviest objects, such as the Ark, mercy seat, and other furniture, are transported by hand, not by cart. This is presumably because they are holier than the outer framework.

[57] László Bartosiewicz, W. Van Neer, & A. Lentacker, *Draught Cattle: Their Osteological Identification and History* (Belgium, 1997): p. 18. Note the decree of Theodorus II in the 5th century C.E. which limited the loads of ox teams to c. 500 kg; see Bartosiewicz et al., p. 26 for references. For further information on the use of oxcarts in antiquity, see Stuart Piggott, *Wagon, Chariot and Carriage* (New York, 1992): pp. 13-36.

[58] Exod 38:27.

[59] Josephus, *Ant.*, III.vi.3; Philo, *Moses*, II:18. Recent proponents include

better accounts for the text's silence concerning their thickness. Furthermore, the weight is now reduced to an acceptable level. If the boards are four fingers thick, as Josephus claims, then their individual weight computes to c. 141.75 lbs/64.3 kg, a figure capable of cart transportation as claimed in Num 4:31-32; 7:8.[60] This weight also corresponds to the *qersū* at Mari, though this is likely to be coincidental.[61] The increase in weight of the Tabernacle's קְרָשִׁים from gold overlay is minimal.[62] More support for interpreting קְרָשִׁים as "thin boards" comes from Egypt, where the nested shrines encasing the coffin of Tutankhamon as well as the boards of Tiye's shrine serve as a strong parallels.[63] Each catafalque consists of a series of interlocking gold-plated wooden boards, each about four fingers thick. Bronze mortises from the tomb of Tiye finely illustrate the function of the board's יָדוֹת "arms" as a variety of mortises and tenons (Plate 56a), as does the gilded tent-frame of Hetepheres (Plate 56b).

Further understanding of the קְרָשִׁים and their associated יָדוֹת "arms" can be gained from Egyptian and Phoenician ship-building from the Old Kingdom until Roman times. The hulls and cabins of such vessels frequently consist of interlocking boards of a similar dimension to the Tabernacle's.[64] Thus it seems likely each Tabernacle קֶרֶשׁ had two tenons on the bottom to adhere to the bases, and two tenons on each side to fit each arm with "its

---

Roland de Vaux, *Ancient Israel* (New York, 1961), p. 295; and Umberto Cassuto, *Exodus* (Jerusalem, 1967): p. 357. James Strong similarly claims the planks were 1/16 cubit thick in *The Tabernacle of Israel,* Rev. Ed. (Grand Rapids, MI, 1987), p. 31. Victor (Avigdor) Hurowitz's reconstruction claims the frames were .25 cubits thick; his corner frames are placed perpendicular to the real wall, so that the .25 thickness of each wall and each corner frame account for the one cubit missing in the six standard frames on the rear wall ("The Form and Fate of the Tabernacle," p. 131). Also of this opinion is B. Jacob, *The Second Book of the Bible: Exodus,* Trans. W. Jacob (Hoboken, NJ, 1992): p. 791.

[60] This leaves a weight of 1, 913.7 kg (about one cart load) for the additional wooden and metal objects. Note that in Num 4:25-27 and 7:6-7, two wagons with four oxen are provided to transport all the coverings of the Tabernacle and the court, a load apparently much lighter than the frames.

[61] For the *qersū* at Mari, which require two men to carry, see pp. 116-18.

[62] Carol L. Meyers, *The Tabernacle Menorah,* pp. 31-34; 41-43.

[63] See Plates 36, 38, 41a, 41b.

[64] Note especially the sunken hull discovered near Kibbutz Magen Michael, currently being conserved at the University of Haifa. Here thin planks of similar dimensions to the Tabernacle's are coupled by wooden "arms."

sister." In other words, the יָדוֹת of Exod 26:19 are not those of v. 17.

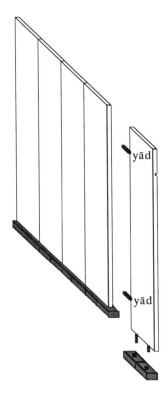

Figure 11 - Tabernacle's Thin Boards and "Arms"

These nautical parallels may further our understanding of Ezekiel's "Lament over Tyre" (Ezekiel 27). Ezekiel's meta-phorical ship consists of planks from fir trees (27:5), a mast of cedar (5), and fine linen spread out as a covering from the sun (7). This all corresponds with textual and pictorial remains of ships in antiquity. Ezek 27:6 reads: "of oaks from Bashan they made your oars; // your קֶרֶשׁ they made ivory." This provides the Hebrew Bible's only non-tabernacular use of קֶרֶשׁ. The usual translation of קֶרֶשׁ as "deck" does not fit, as an ivory deck, unlike the other components of Ezekiel's ship, is not practical; the

surface would be too slippery, not to mention costly.[65] More
likely, קֶרֶשׁ in Ezekiel refers to the boards used to construct the
ship's main cabin, existent on ship remains as well as on models
and reliefs (Plates 57a-58b).[66] These cabins metioned by Ezekiel
would not be made of ivory, but would feature decorative ivory
inlay, which is always placed on vertical surfaces, never on
floors.[67]

Menahem Haran, however, rejects understanding the Tabernacle's קְרָשִׁים as solid boards for linguistic reasons. He claims that
the Hebrew term for thin planks is לוּחֹת, like the boards
composing the altar (Exod 27:8; 38:7). Two rejoinders are
possible: first, we cannot exclude the possibility that קֶרֶשׁ and לוּחַ
are synonyms. Second, P's use of the term קֶרֶשׁ seems to be
deliberate, evoking the root used at Mari for a tent shrine and in
Canaanite mythology for El's tent.

## Two Corner Pieces and the Arrangement of the Boards

Another difficulty relating to the Tabernacle's קְרָשִׁים is the
position and shape of the two corner frames. Here again proposals
vary significantly. Most reconstruct the two corner frames as
being separated at the bottom and joined at the top, thus creating
a sort of triangular shaped frame (see for example Kennedy's
model in Plate 62).[68] Yet, these two frames need not be so very
different from the other 46 קְרָשִׁים. A simpler reconstruction that

---

[65] For "deck," see RSV; KJV has "benches."

[66] H. J. van Dijk, *Ezekiel's Prophecy on Tyre* (Rome, 1968): p. 48. For
information on ships, see George F. Bass, *A History of Seafaring Based on
Underwater Archaeology* (London, 1972): pp. 11-62. Shelley Wachsmann writes
of cabins on Phoenician ships in *Seagoing Ships and Seamanship in the Bronze
Age Levant* (College Station, TX, 1998): pp. 53-54.

[67] Note 8th-century ivory panels on a Phoenician throne from Cyprus in Eric
Gubel, *Phoenician Furniture* (Leuven, 1987): pp. 55-57; also the inlaid bed
frame from Samaria, and the ivory walls from Nineveh. While the cabin's walls
would not be composed entirely of ivory, small decorations would be inlaid
(Irene Winter, "Ivory Carving," *Ebla to Damascus*, Harvey Weiss, ed.
(Washington, 1985): pp. 339-46; pls. 172-77).

[68] Archibald R. S. Kennedy, "Tabernacle," p. 661; Victor (Avigdor) Hurowitz, 'The Form and Fate of the Tabernacle," p. 132. Note also the theory of
William B. Ridges, who constructs all 48 frames, and not just the corner pieces,
of twin boards leaning against each other at top, to form an upside-down V,
much like modern pup tents, in "On the Structure of the Tabernacle," *PEF* (1896):
p. 189.

better corresponds to known ancient woodworking practices is to interpret the corner frames as twin boards forming an "L" shape. This parallels many Egyptian wooden structures, most notably the corner frames of the tent belonging to Hetepheres (Plate 59).[69] Thus "double from below" (תֹאֲמִים) and "complete above" (תַּמִּים) in Exod 26:24 are synonymous wood-working terms for fusing boards.[70]

In addition to the thickness of the קְרָשִׁים and the shape and arrangement of the two corner pieces, another mystery in the Tabernacle's solid structure is the arrangement of the קְרָשִׁים. Thus, while most scholars place them side by side, the possibility remains that they could have overlapped. This theory will be explored in greater detail below in the section on Aharoni and Friedman's reconstruction of the Tabernacle as a whole.[71]

*Bars* (בְּרִיחִם)

> [26]And you shall make bars (בְּרִיחִם) [from] acacia wood; five for the boards of the first side of the Tabernacle. [27]And five bars for the boards of the second side of the Tabernacle; and five bars for the boards of the back-side of the Tabernacle westward. [28]And the middle (תִּיכֹן) bar in the middle (בְּתוֹךְ) of the boards; bolting (מַבְרִחַ) from end to end. [29]And the boards you shall overlay with gold and their rings you shall make gold, housings for the bars; and overlay the bars [with] gold.
>
> (Exod 26:26-29)

Verse 28 is the primary source of difficulty. How long is each bar, and is the middle bar different from the other four bars on each of the Tabernacle's sides? Most interpret the middle bar to be longer than the others. Thus in effect there are only three courses of bars on the Tabernacle's sides: the middle bar runs the entire length of each side, while the top and bottom bars meet halfway.[72]

---

[69] Also note the similarity to the coffin and sepulcher of Amenemet I, both of which have two corner boards coupled in an L shape and reinforced by metal rings (Umberto Cassuto, *Exodus* [Jerusalem, 1967]: p. 356).

[70] Alternatively, the LXX and Samaritan read תֹאֲמִים twice rather than the MT's תַּמִּים and תֹאֲמִים.

[71] See pp. 167-73.

[72] Archibald R. S. Kennedy, "Tabernacle," p. 660; Samuel R. Driver, *The Book of Exodus*, Cambridge Bible (Cambridge, 1911): p. 289.

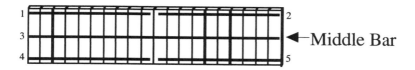

Figure 12 - Possible Arrangement for the Five Bars of the Tabernacle

This arrangement does not make sense for the Tabernacle's back side, however, as it is only a third of the length of the two longer sides. For the back side, three solid acacia bars would be preferable to breaking up the top and bottom courses. Furthermore, the top level of the boards is where the Tabernacle requires the most stability, and so upper reinforcement rather than in the middle would be architecturally preferable:

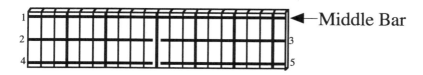

Figure 13 - Five Bars of the Tabernacle with Long Bar on Top

Another solution places the middle bar inside of the solid frames (here assumed to be massive), with the remaining four bars outside of the Tabernacle.[73]

---

[73] See William Brown, "Construction of the Tabernacle," *PEF* (1897): pp. 154-55. Richard E. Friedman's reconstruction of the Tabernacle requires a similar arrangement, where the middle bar passes between the overlapping frames. This will be examined below, pp. 167-73.

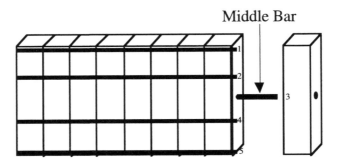

Figure 14 - Possible Arrangement of the Tabernacle's Bars

However, this only works with implausibly thick קְרָשִׁים, and the drilled-out midsection would weaken the boards; moreover, the difficulty in assembly, where tension would repeatedly stress the middle bar, makes such an arrangement unlikely. This theory further ignores all known techniques of woodworking in antiquity. But the greatest difficulty is the excessive weight of boards thick enough to house such a bar.[74]

An extreme solution comes from James Fergusson, who interprets the middle bar as a "ridgepole."[75] This theory will be examined in detail below;[76] here, suffice it to say that this is impossible based on the text, not to mention an absence of parallel constructions from the ancient Near East. Fergusson is simply retrojecting a common form of European tent into antiquity.

A better theory places the middle bar inside the Tabernacle, while the other four bars remain on the outside.

---

[74] See pp. 139-40.

[75] James Fergusson, "Temple," *William Smith's Dictionary of the Bible* III (London, 1893): pp. 1451 ff. See also Conrad Schick, *Die Stiftshütte, der Tempel in Jerusalem und der Tempelplatz der Jetztzeit* (Berlin, 1896).

[76] See p. 165.

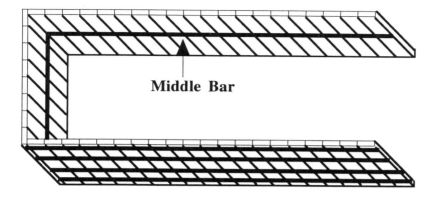

Figure 15 - Possible Arrangement of Tabernacle Bars

Hence only the middle bar is "inside" (בְּתוֹךְ) the Tabernacle. Another possible reading of verse 28 is to treat תִיכֹן and בְּתוֹךְ as synonyms. Then the text is simply redundant: "the middle (תִיכֹן) bar in the middle (בְּתוֹךְ) of the boards." This arrangement places all five bars either inside or outside the Tabernacle's boards.

Several of the aforementioned models require poles of 30 cubits. Wood anatomy, however, suggests that these bars are not composed of a single piece of solid wood. *Acacia albida* is capable of reaching heights of 30 m and thus is capable of producing such bars; nevertheless, this excessive length would render the bars brittle. More likely, they consist of several pieces fused together through mortises and tenons before they are encased in gold.

*Curtains of Fine Linen*[77] (יְרִיעֹת שֵׁשׁ מָשְׁזָר)

[1]And [for] the Tabernacle, you shall make 10 curtains [of] fine linen (שֵׁשׁ מָשְׁזָר) and blue and purple and red [wool], by the work of an artisan one shall make them [adorned with] cherubim. [2]The length of one curtain shall be 28 cubits, and the width of one curtain four cubits-- one measurement for all the curtains. [3]The five curtains shall be joined, each to its sister, and five curtains joined, each to its sister.

---

[77] The Tabernacle's inner-curtain seems likely to be composed of linen mixed with dyed wool; see A. Dillmann, *Die Bücher Exodus und Leviticus* (Leipzig, 1897); Jacob M. Myers, "Linen," and "Linen Garment," *IDB* III: pp. 134-35. I use the term "curtain of fine linen" in reference to the dominant component.

⁴And you shall make blue loops on the edge of one curtain, from the end of the juncture; and thus you shall do on the edge of the last curtain at the second juncture. ⁵Fifty loops you shall make on the one curtain, and 50 loops you shall make on the end of the curtain that is on the second junction; that the loops may correspond each to its sister. ⁶And you shall make 50 clasps of gold, and join the curtains each to its sister with the clasps, and the Tabernacle will be one.

(Exod 26:1-6)

The word מִשְׁכָּן is dually employed both for the "Tabernacle" in general and specifically for the curtain of fine linen.⁷⁸ This implies that of all the Tabernacle's components, the curtain of fine linen is the most vital and thus sacred. This curtain symbolizes the tent of Yahweh (originally, of El), itself perhaps symbolic of the heavens.

The form of the curtains is straightforward. The cherubim design is woven into the fabric.⁷⁹ Each panel measures 28 cubits in length and four cubits in width.⁸⁰ The four cubit width corresponds to the width of most looms in antiquity (Plate 60).⁸¹

The panels are coupled lengthwise to form two sections of equal dimensions, which are in turn joined to form a single piece.

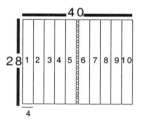

Figure 16 - The Arrangement of the Curtains of Fine Linen

---

⁷⁸ The word יְרִיעָה "curtain" has no known etymology. The root ירע is used only once verbally (Isa 15:4) and connotes fear (Cf. Arabic waraʿ "pious fear"); perhaps it is a variant of the more common yrʾ. At any rate, a connection with יריעה is most unlikely, as א and ע rarely interchange.

⁷⁹ The term שֵׁשׁ מָשְׁזָר suggests fine linen twisted, related to Arabic šazara "to twist (cord)." Thus the Tabernacle is composed of woven ply yarns.

⁸⁰ The dimensions of these panels parallel modern Bedouin tents. Four cubits in width appears to be the biggest size manageable in a hand-loom.

⁸¹ Note that Bedouin tents are composed of panels about 4 cubits wide. See Gustaf Dalman, *Arbeit und Sitte in Palästina*, vol. 5, pls. 20-23.

## Curtains of Goat-Hair (יְרִיעֹת עִזִּים)

> [7]You shall also make curtains of goats (hair), as a tent over the Tabernacle. You shall make them 11 curtains. [8]The length of one curtain 30 cubits, and width of one curtain four cubits; one measure for 11 curtains. [9]And you shall join the five curtains separately and the six curtains separately; and you shall double the sixth curtain at the front of the tent. [10]And you shall make fifty loops on the one edge of the one outer curtain at the juncture; and 50 loops on the edge of the second curtain that joins. [11]And you shall make fifty bronze clasps, and you shall make the clasps go into the loops and join the tent, and it shall be one. [12]And the remaining excess of the curtains of the tent, the half-curtain that remains, shall hang upon the back of the Tabernacle. [13]And the cubit on this side and the cubit on that side that remains in the length of the curtains of the tent, shall hang upon the sides of the Tabernacle, on this and on this to cover it.
>
> (Exod 26:7-13)

The outermost curtain is composed of goat-hair, and consists of 11 panels 30 cubits long, four cubits in width. They are joined in a similar fashion to the curtains of fine linen, except that here the halves are uneven, because one side possesses six panels rather than five.

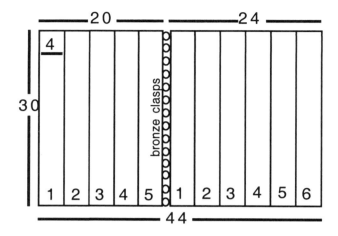

Figure 17 - Arrangement of Curtains of Goat-Hair

The primary difficulties associated with this curtain arise from verses 9, 12-13. The instructions to double the sixth curtain at the Tabernacle's front could be accomplished in two ways. The fold is made either at the halfway point of the 11th curtain's width, or alternatively at the crease between the 10th and 11th curtains.

## OUTER CURTAIN

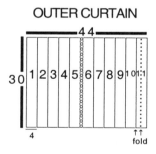

Figure 18 - Alternative Methods to Double the 6th Curtain

Additional problems are the remaining half-curtain at the Tabernacle's back side, as well as the instructions to cover the curtain of fine linen (here called the "Tabernacle") with the extra cubit of goat-hair curtain which remains on each of the Tabernacle's long sides. These issues will be addressed below.[82]

---

[82] Pp. 159-85.

*Skins* (עֹרֹת)

> <sup>14</sup>And you shall make a cover for the tent [of] ram skins dyed red
> (מְאָדָּמִים); and a cover of תְּחָשִׁים skins from above.

(Exod 26:14)

The only problem here is the identity of the Tabernacle's outermost covering of תְּחָשִׁים. Beyond the Tabernacle texts, the word appears only one other time in the Hebrew Bible: Ezek 16:10 refers to the composition of sandals. Among the many contenders for the source of this leather are badgers, seals, porpoises, narwhals, and even unicorns.[83] More viable contenders are a species of dugong in the Red Sea (Arabic *duḫas*), which although rare, can still be seen as far north as Aqabah.[84]

Alternatively, a more attractive solution (though it requires an irregular cognate equation) has been proposed by Yosef Ahituv and Hayim Tadmor, in which תְּחָשִׁים, like מְאָדָּמִים "dyed red," refers to the *color* of the leather.[85] The Akkadian cognate *dušû* is used primarily for a semiprecious stone variously shaded yellow, orange and/or red, and also sheep and goat leather dyed the same

---

[83] The KJV and AV read "badger skins." "Seal skins" are preferred by William H. Bennett, *Exodus*, Century Bible, p. 210; Samuel R. Driver, *Book of Exodus*, p. 285. Porpoise skins are favored by NJPS and Frank M. Cross, Jr., "The Priestly Tabernacle Reconsidered," p. 172. On narwhals, see Israel Aharoni, "Animals Hitherto Unknown to or Little Known from Palestine", *The Zoological Society of Egypt, Syria/Palestine*, Bulletin Supplement 6 (1944): pp. 40-41; Paula Wapnish, "Towards Establishing a Conceptual Basis for Animal Categories in Archaeology," in *Methods in the Mediterranean* (New York, 1995): p. 258.

[84] Arabic *duḫas* also denotes "dolphin." Those subscribing to תְּחָשִׁים as "dugong" include Archibald R. S. Kennedy, "Tabernacle," p. 659; Umberto Cassuto, *Exodus*, pp. 353-54. On dugong in the Red Sea, see Paula Wapnish, "Towards Establishing a Conceptual Basis for Animal Categories in Archaeology," pp. 262-63, where she discusses marine mammals in relation to Ugaritic *anḫr* and Akkadian *nāhiru*; George C. L. Bertram, "Note on the Sea Cow in the Gulf of Aqabah", *Journal of the Society for the Preservation of Fauna in the Empire* 47, (1943): pp. 21-23.

[85] Yosef Ahituv and Hayim Tadmor, "תחש," *Encyclopaedia Biblica* 8 (Jerusalem, 1982): pp. 520-21.

color as the stone.[86] This color may correspond to various solar aspects of Yahweh.

The use of an outer covering of dyed leather for a tent finds a parallel from Late Dynastic Egypt, where the mummy of Isi em Kheb was protected by a like structure (Plates 34-35).

## Veil/Canopy (פָּרֹכֶת)

> [31]And you shall make an veil/canopy (פָּרֹכֶת) [of] blue, purple, and red, and fine linen; by the work of an artisan one shall make it [adorned with] cherubim. [32]And you shall put it upon four gold-overlaid acacia pillars, their brackets gold; upon four silver sockets. [33]And you shall hang the veil/canopy under the clasps (LXX "upon the frames") and you shall bring there inside the veil/canopy (לַפָּרֹכֶת) the Ark of the Covenant; and the veil/canopy shall divide for you between the holy and between the Holy of Holies. [34]And you shall set the mercy seat upon (LXX "And you shall screen with the veil") the Ark of the Covenant in the Holy of Holies. [35]And you shall set the table outside the veil/canopy and the Menorah across from the table upon the south side of the Tabernacle and the table you shall put upon the north side.
>
> (Exod 26:31-35)

The פָּרֹכֶת, which separates the Holy of Holies from the rest of the Tabernacle, is composed in the same fashion as the curtain of fine linen, embroidered with cherubim. Most often the form of the פָּרֹכֶת is interpreted as a veil hung upon four pillars, each 10 cubits in height.[87]

---

[86] *Ibid.* Note the Targums translate תְּחָשִׁים as "colored-skins." See also *CAD*, s.v. *dušû* and *taḫaš*. On the technology of dying leather with kermes and other substances, see Alfred Lucas, *Ancient Egyptian Materials and Industries* (London, 1962): pp. 33-37; Robert J. Forbes, *Studies in Ancient Technology* V (Leiden, 1966): pp. 9; 22-46

[87] Nahum M. Sarna, *Exodus*, JPS Commentary (New York, 1991): p. 171.

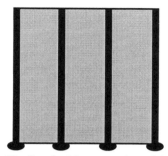

Figure 19 - Standard Interpretation of the פָּרֹכֶת

But Richard E. Friedman argues for a large canopy under which rests the Ark.

Figure 20 - Friedman's פָּרֹכֶת as a Canopy

Essential to his theory is Exod 40:3, "And you shall *cover* (וְסַכֹּתָ) over the Ark with the פָּרֹכֶת." Elsewhere it is referred to as "the *covering* פָּרֹכֶת (פָּרֹכֶת הַמָּסָךְ)."[88] There is much to be said for this interpretation; possibly the traditional interpretation of the פָּרֹכֶת as a veil arose from forcing the Temple's architecture onto the Tabernacle.[89]

---

[88] Exod 40:21; Num 4: 5. See Richard E. Friedman, "Tabernacle," p. 295 for further evidence. Lam 2:6 also refers to the Tabernacle by the word שֻׂכָּה (see pp. 9-11).

[89] According to the MT, Exod 26:33 instructs that the פָּרֹכֶת be placed under (תַּחַת) the fabric's clasps. Friedman prefers the LXX reading: the פָּרֹכֶת was placed επι των στυλων "upon the frames," reading קְרָשִׁים "frames," instead of the MT קְרָסִים "clasps." For Friedman, this means one of two things: 1) if επι is read, the פָּרֹכֶת simply goes up against the קְרָשִׁים; or 2) if תַּחַת is the preferred reading, the פָּרֹכֶת is not 10 cubits in height, but lower than the standard frames. Victor (Avigdor) Hurowitz objects that Hebrew תַּחַת always means "under," and never "lower than" (Hurowitz, "The Form and Fate of the Tabernacle," p. 136). If Friedman is correct, then the קְרָשִׁים should denote the entire structure of the

The description of the פָּרֹכֶת and the Tabernacle's furniture provides the first glimpse of the layout of the entire structure. While the exact proportions are not stated in the Hebrew Bible, and they would vary slightly depending on the overall reconstruction of the Tabernacle's form, the layout of the courtyard, Tabernacle, and furniture may adhere to the following Talmudic proportions.

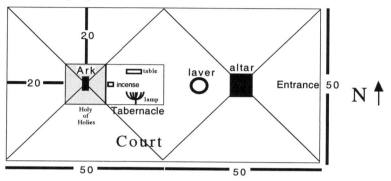

Figure 21 – Possible Ground Plan of Tabernacle and Court

## Screen/Cover (מָסָךְ)

> 36And you shall make a screen for the door of the tent [of] blue and purple and red, and fine linen; the work of an embroiderer. 37And you shall make for the screen five pillars of acacia, and overlay them [with] gold and their nails gold; and you shall cast for them five bronze sockets.
>
> (Exod 26:36-37)

The form of the Tabernacle's screen is relatively straightforward. This is a veil suspended by five pillars, each 10 cubits in height.

---

Tabernacle, just as *qrš* at Ugarit refers to El's tent, and Ezekiel's קֶרֶשׁ connotes the ship's entire cabin (pp. 146-47).

Figure 22 - Tabernacle's Screen

Though of lesser quality than the Tabernacle and the פָּרֹכֶת, the material is also composed of fine linen; however, it is decorated by embroidery rather than woven patterns (Plate 61).[90]

*Comprehensive Solutions to the Tabernacle Puzzle: Some Variations on a Standard Model*

Until recently, disputes on the form of the Tabernacle focused on relatively minor issues, as scholars agreed that the structure measured 30 cubits in length, 10 in width, and 10 in height. Debate tended to focus on whether the 10 cubit width reflects the external or internal sides of the Tabernacle's wooden frames.[91] Yet, despite this consensus, two of the three numbers were contrived. The only dimension explicitly provided by the text is the height of 10 cubits. At no place does the Hebrew Bible state that the Tabernacle's length and width measure 30 and 10 cubits respectively.

A few simple calculations underlie the hypothesis that the area of the Tabernacle spanned 30 x 10 cubits. Exod 26:16, as we have seen, instructs that the 46 frames are to be 10 cubits in height and 1 1/2 cubits in width, while the thickness is undetermined. Most scholars assume that the boards are to be situated one next to the other, with no overlap or gap. Thus, as the two side walls of the

---

[90] On the difference between מַעֲשֵׂה חֹשֵׁב "weaving" and מַעֲשֵׂה רֹקֵם "embroidery," as well as weaving and dyeing techniques, see Robert J. Forbes, *Studies in Ancient Technology* IV (Leiden, 1964). Note that unlike the curtain of fine linen and the פָּרֹכֶת, the screen has no cherubim designs.

[91] See James Strong, *The Tabernacle of Israel* (Grand Rapids, 1987): pp. 32-38.

Tabernacle consist of 20 boards each, the total length of each side measures 30 cubits (20x1.5) (Figure 23).

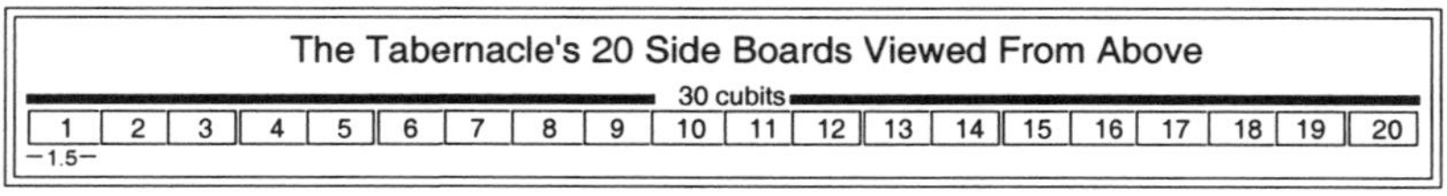

Figure 23

Establishing the width of the Tabernacle's rear wall is much more complicated. While the frames have the same width of 1 1/2 cubits, only six frames are used; thus, the whole wall may span as little as nine cubits. However, each corner of the Tabernacle contains an additional frame which may or may not differ from the standard frames in shape, because the measurements of these two corner frames are not provided.[92] So, not only the thickness of the standard frames is a variable, but also the dimensions of these two corner frames.

While a seemingly infinite number of dimensions can be calculated solely from the text's description of the frames, the placement of the curtains is an additional factor limiting the Tabernacle's size. As we have seen, the curtain of fine linen consists of 10 joined panels, each measuring four by 28 cubits. Five panels are sewn together on each side, and then these two sets are joined with golden clasps.[93] When assembled, the overall measurements of this curtain are 40 cubits in length by 28 cubits in width.[94] On top of the curtain of fine linen rests a second curtain composed of 11 goat-hair panels, each measuring four by 30 cubits.

---

[92] Exod 26:23-24. The text enigmatically instructs that these two frames be doubled from below (תֹאֲמִם מִלְּמַטָּה), while they join together on the top at the uppermost ring (וְיַחְדָּו יִהְיוּ תַמִּים עַל־רֹאשׁוֹ אֶל־הַטַּבַּעַת הָאֶחָת). See above, pp. 147-48.

[93] Exod 26:6.

[94] Exod 26:1-6.

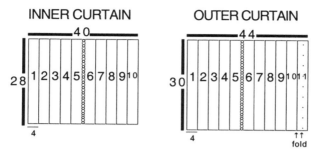

Figure 24 – Inner and Outer Curtains

Again, on one side five panels are sewn together, but now six panels constitute the opposing side. This time 50 bronze clasps join the two sections.[95] When the panels are attached, the total dimensions of the second curtain cover 30 by 44 cubits.[96] Exod 26:9 commands that in some fashion the eleventh panel of the outer curtain of goat-hair be doubled. This reduces the overall length of the outer curtain by two cubits if the panel is folded in half, or four cubits if the eleventh curtain is folded at the seam, doubling up the tenth panel (Figure 24).

These ambiguities make for a daunting puzzle, which for two thousand years has elicited a variety of solutions. For example, in Josephus's model the boards are four fingers thick. He allots the corner frames 1/2 cubit in width each, so when added to the nine cubits provided by the standard frames, a total of 10 cubits is achieved.[97] This theory partially excuses the Priestly author from neglecting to provide the thickness of the frames: they are simply thin.

---

[95] Exod 26:11.

[96] Exod 26:7-10.

[97] Josephus, *Ant.*, III.vi.3. For other proponents of this model, see above, n. 59, pp. 144-45.

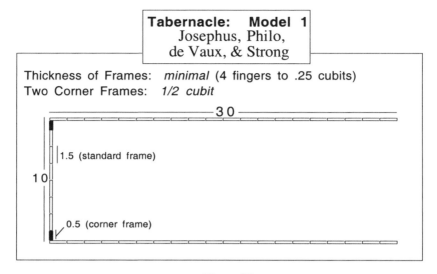

Figure 25

In regard to the outer curtain, Josephus's model works well, providing the eleventh curtain is folded at its seam with the tenth curtain. This would produce an overall length of 40 cubits for the outer fabric, four of which consist of the superimposed tenth and eleventh curtains. A 40-cubit length for the outer curtain accounts perfectly for the 30 cubits of the Tabernacle's length, with 10 cubits reserved for the Tabernacle's height. The inner curtain is more problematic. While the 40 cubit length completely covers the rear wall, its 28 cubit width falls one cubit short of covering the frames on the other two sides.

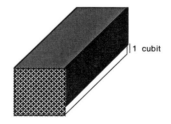

Figure 26 – Model 1 in 3 Dimensions

Proponents of this view argue that the silver bases upon which the frames rest (Exod 26:14-15) cover one cubit of each frame, and thus the fabric descends on each side to the top of each base.[98] Others suggest that the gap is intended to protect the sacred fabric from contact with the ground.[99] Nevertheless, neither of these explanations accounts for the inconsistency that in the rear of the Tabernacle, the curtain touches the ground; on the sides, the curtain is a cubit off the ground (Figure 26).

A second model suggests that the thickness of the standard frames is not minimal, but that they are in fact 1/3 to 1/2 cubit thick (Plate 62).[100]

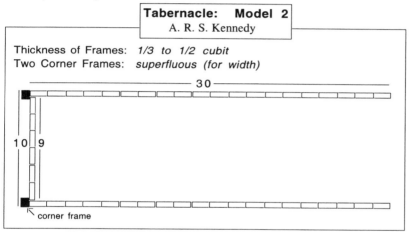

Figure 27

As in Josephus's model, the nine cubits covered by the six rear frames plus an additional 1/2 cubit on both corners produces a back wall that spans 10 cubits on the external side. The corner frames' contribution to the width of the Tabernacle is no longer necessary, so they are placed outside the structure for support. These corner frames slant in order to get the curtains off the ground.[101]

---

[98] Rashi (on Exod 26:14-15), Archibald R. S. Kennedy "The Tabernacle," p. 662, and Victor (Avigdor) Hurowitz, "The Form and Fate of the Tabernacle," pp. 131-32.

[99] Philo, *Life of Moses*, II.148.

[100] Archibald R. S. Kennedy, "The Tabernacle," p. 661.

[101] Kennedy, p. 662; R. Judah holds the same opinion in bShab 98a-b.

The preceding model's merits and difficulties in relation to the two curtains apply to this model as well because of the shared external parameters. Furthermore, a new problem is created. The interior of the Tabernacle's Holy of Holies now becomes not a perfectly symmetrical 10 cubit cube but a room 10 cubits in height, nine cubits in width, and nine and one-half cubits in depth. However, it must be admitted that thus far no ancient Near Eastern cella from the Late Bronze/Iron Age in the archaeological record forms a perfect square.

A third model that finds agreement from Rashi and the Babylonian Talmud argues that the Tabernacle's frames are one cubit thick.[102] This reconstruction concludes that the corner frames possess the same measurements as the standard frames and are simply placed alongside the six rear wall frames, providing an interior dimension of 30 cubits in length by 10 cubits in width.[103]

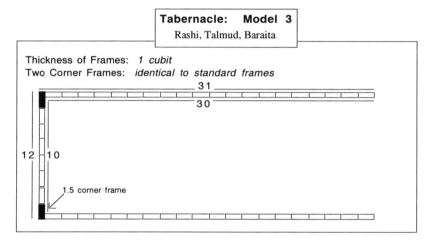

Figure 28

While the symmetry of the Holy of Holies is preserved, new problems surface regarding the curtains. For the inner covering, the 40 cubits in length fall one cubit short on the rear wall, and the 28 cubits in width fall two cubits short on each side. The outer curtain measuring 30 cubits in width likewise leaves one cubit of frame on each side exposed. For this model a curtain measuring 41 cubits in length by 32 cubits in width would be needed to cover all three sides equally.[104]

## Sloped-Roof Reconstruction with Ridgepole

A significant variation on these "standard" models, first suggested by the British architect James Fergusson and later supported by Conrad Schick, found favor in the late 19th/early 20th century.[105] This model argues that the Tabernacle roof is not flat, but sloped (Plate 63a).

To accomplish this, great liberties are taken with the text. Most notably, all but a few of the Tabernacle's fifteen bars are ignored, with the Tabernacle's "middle bar" altered into a ridgepole, spanning the length of the Tabernacle.[106] Fergusson claims that unsupported canvas spanning a distance of 15 feet is impossible and would not hold up well in the rain.[107] More astonishing, both Fergusson and Schick claim the flat-roof Tabernacle parallels no known tents.[108] On the contrary, curtains of contemporary Bedouin flat-roofed tents do span distances of 15 feet unsupported (Plate 3b), and do quite well in the rain.[109]

---

[104] Karl W. F. Bähr in *Symbolik des Mosaischen Cultus* (Heidelberg, 1837-39) attempts to get around this problem by suggesting that the coverings were hung *inside* the Tabernacle's frames. See below, p. 166. Another possibility is that the bottom cubit of the side קרשׁים was left bare deliberately, to display the silver sockets. However, as each socket most likely weighed only about 66 lbs/30 kg, they would not have been that large (for socket weight, see above, p. 144).

[105] James Fergusson, "Temple," pp. 1451 ff.; and *The Holy Sepulchre and the Temple at Jerusalem* (London, 1865): pp. 74-78; Conrad Schick, *Die Stiftshütte, der Tempel in Jerusalem und der Tempelplatz der Jetztzeit* (Berlin, 1896): pp. 6-42; "Some Remarks on the Tabernacle Controversy, *PEF* (1898): pp. 241-244. Support for Fergusson was not unanimous; see an early refutation by William Brown, "Construction of the Tabernacle," *PEF* (1897): pp. 154-55.

[106] Thus, James Fergusson claims "Five rows of bars are quite unnecessary," in "Temple," p. 1451. For Fergusson's additional misuses of the Tabernacle texts, including the invention of pillars to support the ridgepole, see William Brown, "Construction of the Tabernacle," pp. 154-55.

[107] James Fergusson, *The Holy Sepulchre and the Temple at Jerusalem*, p. 75.

[108] Conrad Schick, "Some Remarks on the Tabernacle Controversy, pp. 241-244. Note Fergusson's comment: ". . . like every tent from before the time of Moses to the present day, the tent had a ridge," *The Holy Sepulchre*, p. 76.

[109] Already pointed out by Theodore F. Wright, "The Tabernacle Roof," *PEF* (1897): pp. 225-26; "The Boards of the Tabernacle," *PEF* (1899): p. 70.

*Curtains Inside Frame*

Other scholars, most notably William Brown, adhere to the basic 30 x 10 cubit model of the Tabernacle, but envision the Tabernacle's curtains not as a tent outside the boards, but rather inside, suspended within the framework (Plate 63b).[110]

This theory enjoyed popularity early in the 20th century but has been ignored in recent literature. However, there is much to commend it. First and foremost, we have the parallel of the tent resting inside the golden catafalque of Tutankhamon.[111] Moreover, the gold-overlaid boards are now visible from the Tabernacle's courtyard. Also, the order of items described in Exodus 25-26 supports this arrangement. The Tabernacle's description begins with the Ark, followed by the table, Menorah, and then the tents of fine linen and goat-hair, and lastly the boards and their bars. That is to say, the order proceeds from the inside outward.

Nevertheless, textual difficulties hinder this interpretation. Exod 26:13 instructs that "And the cubit on this side and the cubit on that side that remains in the length of the curtains of the tent, shall hang upon the sides of the Tabernacle, on this and on this to cover it." If the curtain is on the inside, the excess would fall upon the ground. Still more problematic is the failure to mention a framework to support the tent within the Tabernacle's boards, as we find in Tutankhamon's catafalque.

*Rationale for the 30 X 10 Cubit Tabernacle*

Each of the above approaches to the form the Tabernacle reflects a calculated interest in achieving dimensions of 30 x 10 cubits. The motivation does not stem solely from the descriptions

---

Fergusson's ridgepole tent sparked a lively debate on the Tabernacle's form, with some ridiculous results, notably one by William S. Caldecott (*The Tabernacle: Its History and Structure* [London, 1904]), and another where the Tabernacle boards lean against one another, forming an inverted V frame 40 feet high (William B. Ridges, "On the Structure of the Tabernacle," *PEF* [1896]: p. 189).

[110] Karl W. F. Bähr, *Symbolik des Mosaischen Cultus*, 2 vols; Wilhelm Neumann, *Die Stiftshütte in Bild und Wort* (Gotha, 1861); Carl F. Keil, *Genesis und Exodus* (Leipzig, 1878): pp. 556-65; and Heinrich Holzinger, *Commentary on Exodus* (Leipzig, 1900).

[111] See pp. 107-09.

in Exodus regarding the size of the curtains and frames. There is also a deliberate effort to make the Tabernacle's proportions match the Second Temple in Jerusalem, assumed to be the Tabernacle's prototype.[112] Yet, the size of the second Temple remains unknown. It seems unlikely that Cyrus' command in Ezra 6:3, which orders that the dimensions are to be 60 cubits in height and width, was ever carried out.[113] Wellhausen and the majority of scholars assume that the second Temple's dimensions mirrored the first, whose dimensions are known: 60 cubits in length and 20 cubits in width.[114] Consequently for Wellhausen and his supporters, P's fabricated Tabernacle is simply half the size of both temples. Nevertheless, not only does this reconstruction assume that both the imaginary Tabernacle and the rebuilt Temple recycle Solomon's measurements, but it also ignores one of the three dimensions. Solomon's Temple towers 30 cubits in height, whereas the Tabernacle stands not 15 cubits, but 10. Why would the Priestly author fail to remain consistent with his supposed 1:2 ratio in all three dimensions?

## Another Tenable Tent: Friedman's Tabernacle

Richard E. Friedman published in *The Biblical Archaeologist* (Fall, 1980) a detailed model of the Tabernacle differing significantly from the previous reconstructions in two respects: he argued that the dimensions were only 2/3 the size previously thought; and he argued that this reduced structure may actually have stood within the Temple's Holy of Holies until its destruction in 587 B.C.E.[115]

Friedman starts with the observation that we would expect the frames' width to be an even number of cubits. Why 1 1/2? In Friedman's reconstruction of the Tabernacle, the frames overlap

---

[112] See pp. 2-3, nn. 11-12.

[113] The peculiarity of this passage's failure to provide the Temple's length may imply textual corruption. If the Second Temple were really twice the size of the first, it seems odd that the older generation would cry when viewing the new building, as recorded in Ezra 3:12-13.

[114] 1 Kgs 6:2.

[115] Richard E. Friedman, "The Tabernacle in the Temple," *BA* 43 (1980): pp. 241-48; Subsequent publications on this topic by Friedman include: *Who Wrote the Bible?* (New York, 1989): pp. 182-187, and "Tabernacle," *ABD* VI, pp. 292-300.

their neighboring frames by the 1/2 cubit. Thus the length of the structure is reduced to 20 cubits. The width, depending on the variables of frame thickness and placement of the corner frames, lies most plausibly in the range of six to eight cubits.

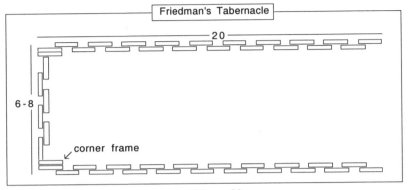

Figure 29

The above model conforms well with the two fabric coverings, but not in their typical reconstruction. Friedman folds both curtains in half at the juncture where the golden and bronze clasps connect the material. Thus, the inner curtain of fine linen becomes a double-ply fabric measuring 28 by 20 cubits. The golden clasps are placed at the Tabernacle's opening, and consequently the fabric's 28 cubit width completely covers the 10 cubit height of both the side walls as well as the Tabernacle's width of six to eight cubits. The frames of the rear wall are uncovered by the inner curtain. The second curtain of goat-hair is folded in like manner, and its bronze rings also adorn the Tabernacle's entrance. The doubled portion of this covering also measures 20 cubits in width and is placed directly upon the innermost curtain, now with an extra cubit on each of the two side walls. This extra cubit is folded inward so as to envelop the curtain of fine linen, preventing it from contacting the ground. One panel of goat-hair remains, so this eleventh curtain is folded not at the entrance, but at the Tabernacle's rear wall, in such a fashion that it meets vertically half-way between the corners, completely covering the back wall.

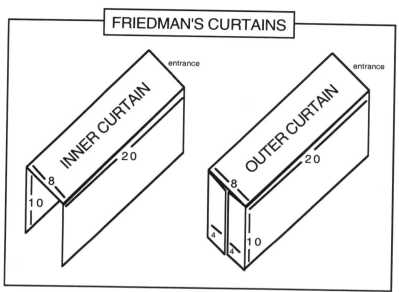

Figure 30

There are many advantages to Friedman's model. Architecturally, the doubled frames add increased stability to support the heavy fabric and withstand the elements. The arrangement in effect doubles the width of each wall, allowing for thinner frames. Aesthetically, the anterior placement of the golden and bronze rings creates a tasteful adornment not possible in the other reconstructions.[116] In addition, for the first time the fabric lies upon the frames in a uniform fashion. Whereas previous models resulted in a rear wall completely covered by fabric while the bottom cubit of each side wall remained bare, with Friedman's reconstruction the frames are totally covered by each curtain (assuming an eight-cubit width). Finally, archaeology can be invoked to support Friedman. A tenth-century Israelite shrine has been unearthed at Arad featuring striking parallels to both the Tabernacle and Temple. All three sanctuaries face east, and an altar stands immediately before their openings. While the height

---

[116] However, it must be noted that the adornment was for Yahweh and the rare human with access to the Tabernacle. Similarly, King Tutankhamon's treasure was for the pleasure and visual entertainment of those inside and for nobody outside. So normal aesthetic considerations may be overriden by the purpose of the architecture.

of the structure at Arad is unknown, its dimensions are analogous to Friedman's model, measuring 20 by 6 cubits.[117]

Still, despite the interesting parallels between the Tabernacle and the sanctuary at Arad, the analogy is not perfect. As mentioned, an eight-cubit width for the Tabernacle better corresponds to the inner curtain's width (10+8+10=28).[118] Moreover, the Arad sanctuary is a broad-room structure, meaning the entrance is placed in one of the rectangle's long walls. The Tabernacle and Temple are both long-room structures.

In 1995, Victor (Avigdor) Hurowitz wrote a harsh critique of both Friedman's model and his method.[119] Below, each point of Hurowitz's contention shall be addressed, and it will be shown that Friedman's hypothesis remains tenable.

Hurowitz invokes two major problems.[120] The first is Exod 26:9b, which reads וְכָפַלְתָּ אֶת־הַיְרִיעָה הַשִּׁשִׁית אֶל־מוּל פְּנֵי הָאֹהֶל, traditionally translated "and you shall double the sixth curtain *in front of* the Tabernacle's entrance," which would make it impossible for the goat-hair curtain's bronze rings to be placed at the front. Nevertheless, the phrase is cumbersome, and Hurowitz himself admits, "This instruction has proven difficult to exegetes . . ."[121] Moreover, the preposition מוּל can be understood to mean "opposite."[122] Friedman is thus justified in translating this verse: "and you shall double the sixth curtain *opposite* the Tabernacle's entrance."

---

[117] Richard E. Friedman ("Tabernacle," pp. 298-99) cites Yohanan Aharoni's article "The Solomonic Temple, the Tabernacle, and the Arad Sanctuary," *Orient and Occident* (ed. H. A. Hoffner, Jr.; Neukirchen, 1973).

[118] Friedman has suggested in private communication that six cubits may be the inside width and eight the exterior width due to the unknown thickness of the frames and several layers of coverings. This would make the inner dimensions match those of the Arad temple, allowing the outer surfaces to be completely covered by fabric. However, it must be noted that to date, Syro-Palestinian archaeology has not revealed two temples with identical measurements.

[119] Victor (Avigdor) Hurowitz, "The Form and Fate of the Tabernacle: Reflections on a Recent Proposal," *JQR* 86 (1995): pp. 127-51.

[120] "The Form and Fate of the Tabernacle," p. 139.

[121] "The Form and Fate of the Tabernacle," p. 137.

[122] The preposition מוּל is translated as "in front of" always in the sense of being across from something. For example, see Neh 12:38, where לְמוֹאל (=לְמוּל) means "on the opposite side." Still, we might have expected באחורי המשכן or פני המשכן לעמת in Exod 26:9.

The second and final major point of contention that Hurowitz raises with Friedman's model also involves the eleventh goat-hair curtain. The Hebrew of Exod 26:12 indicates that half (חֲצִי) of the remaining curtain is folded over the back of the Tabernacle. Hurowitz argues that "half" in this passage can only mean half of the four-cubit goat-hair panel's width, or two cubits, and thus the curtain is folded in half horizontally. This eliminates the eight cubits needed by Friedman to cover the Tabernacle's back wall. Despite Hurowitz's objection, it is possible that חֲצִי implies not half of four cubits, but half of the 30-cubit length, and thus the curtain is folded in half vertically.

**The 11th Curtain Halved Vertically (Friedman) or Horizontally (Standard)**

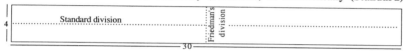

Figure 31

In this manner, half of the remaining curtain that extends upon the Tabernacle's back, is folded to join vertically the other half-curtain midway across the rear wall.[123]

Following these three points are what Hurowitz refers to as a few "additional flaws of less vital import or of a more general nature."[124] Hurowitz contends that gaps in the rear wall's frames through which one might see the covering of goat-hair in the Holy of Holies would be aesthetically unappealing in Friedman's model.[125] But Friedman's reconstruction of the פָּרֹכֶת eliminates this as a problem, as it separates all viewers from the goat-hair curtain on the rear wall.[126] Hurowitz further claims that when Friedman approximates six to eight cubits for the rear wall, "the inconsistency is revealing."[127] In fact, this reveals only Fried-

---

[123] It is also possible that חֲצִי refers to the entire single-ply 11th panel, half the thickness of the remaining, doubled fabric.

[124] Victor (Avigdor) Hurowitz, "The Form and Fate of the Tabernacle," p. 134.

[125] *Ibid.*, p. 138.

[126] See above for Friedman's reconstruction of the פָּרֹכֶת, pp. 156-58.

[127] Victor (Avigdor) Hurowitz, "The Form and Fate of the Tabernacle," p. 139.

man's unwillingness to be dogmatic when the data are ambiguous, because the corner arrangement and frame-width are uncertain.

Hurowitz raises three other minor points of contention. First, he claims that the Tabernacle's size should be determined by the outermost curtain of goat-hair, rather than the curtain of fine linen.[128] Not so; the dimensions of both curtains must be incorporated in any reconstruction of the Tabernacle. Hurowitz's second objection is that the text does not explicitly state that the curtains are to be folded in half and that the frames are to be overlapping.[129] As we have seen, many aspects of the Tabernacle are not commented on, and all reconstructions are to a degree speculative.[130] It must be remembered that the text does not say that the boards are to be placed side-by-side either. Hurowitz's last point in defense of the standard model is that the 2:1 ratio between the Tabernacle and the Temple does work, if one counts not the height of the Temple, but the height of the Holy of Holies.[131] Yet, the other two dimensions yielding the 2:1 ratio are based on the entire Temple, not just the דְּבִיר. Hurowitz cannot have it both ways.

Finally, Hurowitz indicts Friedman for "backward methodology," i.e. manipulating the geometry to fit the Tabernacle into the דְּבִיר.[132] To speculate on the motives of ancient authors such as the priestly writer is one thing, but concerning a living scholar, one ought to be more circumspect.[133] Friedman has told me, and his students can confirm this, that he arrived at his

---

[128] *Ibid.*, pp. 140-41.

[129] *Ibid.*, p. 141.

[130] For example, Hurowitz seems certain that the Tabernacle's standard frames are .25 cubits thick, and he goes on to propose that the two corner frames are either isosceles trapezoids or right trapezoids ("The Form and Fate of the Tabernacle," p. 132). There is no textual support for either of these ideas.

[131] *Ibid.*, p. 139.

[132] *Ibid.*, p. 134.

[133] The rhetoric throughout Hurowitz's article is extreme. Aside from accusing Friedman of "backward methodology" (p. 134), he refers to Friedman's arguments as "patently ridiculous" (p. 143), and writes: "Friedman's reconstruction of the Tabernacle is wrong in every detail, has not a shred of evidence in its support, does serious harm to an understanding of the structure and the texts describing it, and reflects a total disregard for the most fundamental pillars of sound exegesis, and, in particular, concern for the Hebrew language" (p. 130). Hurowitz's zeal to refute Friedman's model may have moved him to exagerate the importance of the points on which he differed.

reduced model of the Tabernacle during a course that he gave on this subject; it actually predated his theory that the Tabernacle ever stood within the Temple. And both of these ideas originated before he decided to date the priestly source to preexilic times.

In sum, contrary to Hurowitz, there is much to commend Friedman's model.

## Could the Tabernacle Have Stood in the Temple?

Over the past two decades, Friedman has taken claims for the historicity of the Tabernacle to a new level. Not only did the Temple house the Tabernacle's sacred furnishings, including the Ark, Menorah, incense altar, and table of showbread, but Friedman provocatively argues that the Tabernacle itself resided within Jerusalem's Temple. Either the Tabernacle actually stood erect in the Temple's Holy of Holies between the wings of the two olivewood cherubim, or the sacred frames and fabric of the disassembled Tabernacle were stored within the Temple's treasury, with the cherubim's wings still symbolizing its presence around the Ark.[134]

Friedman's primary evidence comes from 1 Kgs 8:4 (=2 Chr 5:5), which records that the tent of the appointed time (אֹהֶל מוֹעֵד) accompanies the Ark and the sacred vessels from the City of David into the Temple. The Tabernacle is never mentioned again in the book of Kings, but two passages in Chronicles indicate that at least until the end of Hezekiah's reign, the Tabernacle resided within the Temple. Desiring to renovate the Temple, King Joash inquires of the head Levite why the priests have not collected funds "for the tent of the testimony" (לְאֹהֶל הָעֵדוּת).[135] And in 2 Chr 29:6, Hezekiah initiates his religious reforms by acknowledging that the current generation's fathers "acted treacherously, and did the evil in the eyes of Yahweh our God, and have forsaken Him and turned their faces from the Tabernacle of Yahweh, and have given their backs." Passages such as these suggest that for over two centuries following the

---

[134] Cf. bSota 9a, where R. Hamuna says "After the First Temple was erected, the tent of the appointed time was stored away, its boards, hooks, bars, pillars, and sockets." R. Hamuna asks where they were stored, and R. Hisda replies: "Beneath the crypts of the Temple."

[135] 2 Chr 24:6.

Temple's completion, the Tabernacle continued to exist. Alternatively, the Chronicler is reading 1 Kgs 8:4 literally, just as Friedman does, and therefore has a tent in the temple. It must be noted that these references to the Tabernacle are to a degree less substantial in light of the interchange of terminology examined above in chapter one. However, as we have seen, the use of terms such as "tent" and "tabernacle" for permanent structures such as the Temple is rare compared with the frequent use of terms such as "house" and "temple" for tents.[136] Moreover, 1 Kgs 8:4-6 is not amalgamating terms, because it clearly distinguishes between the Temple and the tent of the appointed time.

Friedman then observes that the space created under the wings of the Temple's two cherubim closely corresponds to his model of the Tabernacle. The cherubim stand 10 cubits tall (1 Kgs 6:23), and each owns a pair of wings five cubits in length (1 Kgs 6:24), producing an overall wingspan of 10 cubits per cherub (Figure 32).

---

[136] See pp. 16-24.

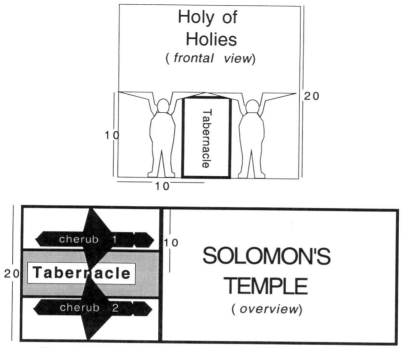

Figure 32 — Friedman's Cherubim and the Taberacle in the Temple

The cherubim face east toward the Temple's entrance, and are placed side by side so that the tips of their outer wings meet the side walls of the Holy of Holies, while the inner tips touch one another (1 Kgs 6:27). The length of Friedman's Tabernacle's fits perfectly in the 20 cubit chamber. However, the 10 cubit height and six- to eight-cubit width of the Tabernacle are more difficult to accommodate. For Friedman's model to fit, the underside of each wing must suddenly bend in an awkward fashion.[137] This is

<hr />

[137] Thus for a Tabernacle six cubits wide, the Holy of Holies' 20 cubit width would be taken up as follows: three cubits from the wall to the point at which first wing falls below 10 cubits, four cubits from this point to point where second wing reaches a 10 cubit height (including body of first cherub), six cubits housing the Tabernacle starting from the second wing's 10-cubit height to the point at which the third wing drops below a 10-cubit height, four cubits for the reduced-height wings and body of the second cherub, and finally three cubits to the opposite wall. An eight-cubit wide Tabernacle is more problematic, as the wings must reach the 10 cubit height only one cubit from the body's midpoint (Figure 32).

unlike the form of cherubim or winged creatures that exist in the Syro-Palestinian material record (Plate 64).[138]

Hurowitz objects to the Tabernacle's situation within the דְּבִיר by contesting the historicity of Chronicles. Hurowitz writes, "Much of Friedman's evidence for the Tabernacle in the Temple thesis comes from the Book of Chronicles. It is curious that not a shred of evidence comes from the older Book of Kings."[139] Ignoring the evidence of 1 Kgs 8:4 (=2 Chr 5:5), Hurowitz attacks the historical reliability of Chronicles on the grounds that it is a late work. He writes: "Any independent statement of the Chronicler must be assumed suspect unless proven otherwise."[140]

But Hurowitz uncritically attributes to the Chronicler texts that Friedman and others have argued belong to the Chronicler's source - a source that dates from the time when the First Temple was still standing.[141] Baruch Halpern has established the likelihood that among the Chronicler's sources was a historical document containing data on the Judean monarchy, ending immediately after the reign of Hezekiah.[142] Friedman suggests that this source included information pertaining to the Tabernacle.[143] Moreover, while the narrative books of the Hebrew Bible do not mention the Tabernacle after Hezekiah's reign, both Ps 74:7 and Lam 2:6-7 seem to describe its fiery destruction within the Temple at the hands of Nebuchadnezzar and his Babylonian forces in 587 B.C.E.[144] Hurowitz is again silent

---

[138] This is Helga Weippert's main criticism of Friedman's reconstruction ("Review of *Temples and High Places in Biblical Times* and *The Exile and Biblical Narrative*," *ZDPV* 199 [1984]: p. 184). Friedman has acknowledged from the beginning that his cherubim are "unlike most extant examples" ("The Temple in the Tabernacle," p. 242).

[139] "The Form and Fate of the Tabernacle," p. 142.

[140] *Ibid.*, p. 142.

[141] Hugh G. M. Williamson, *1 and 2 Chronicles* (Grand Rapids, 1982).

[142] Baruch Halpern, "Sacred History and Ideology," *The Creation of Sacred Literature*, ed. Richard E. Friedman (Berkeley, 1981): pp. 35-54.

[143] "Tabernacle," *ABD* VI, p. 294.

[144] The words "his pavilion" (שֻׂכּוֹ) and "his appointed time" (מוֹעֲדוֹ) in Lam 2:6-7 seem to be connected to the Tabernacle. See Friedman, "Tabernacle," *ABD* VI, pp. 293-94. However, this passage may simply describe the destruction of the Temple, given the interchangeability of domiciliary terms discussed above, pp. 16-24.

regarding these two explicit references to the Tabernacle within the Temple.[145]

Further evidence now supports Friedman's theory. A Hittite text attests to the placement of a tent before the gate of a temple, and more astonishingly, the tent is said to reside within the house.[146]

While Friedman's model of an erect Tabernacle in the Temple has its own difficulties, none is sufficient to render it impossible,[147] though I prefer Friedman's second option, where the Tabernacle's fabrics and boards are stored in the Temple treasury.

*A New Reconstruction of the Tabernacle*

Each of the previously examined reconstructions of the Tabernacle's form has strengths and weaknesses. No one solves all the architectural problems. Given known woodworking techniques from the ancient Near East, I prefer a reconstruction that more adequately accounts for the textual specifications. Like Friedman's reconstruction, the present theory looks at the Tabernacle's form independent of the later Temple's dimensions.

1) קְרָשִׁים, bases, and bars — The קְרָשִׁים are thin boards. This accounts for the Priestly author's silence concerning the thickness, and makes transportation feasible. Thus, if the קְרָשִׁים are

---

[145] Instead, Hurowitz attacks Friedman's use of Josephus. Josephus writes "So they carried the Ark and the Tabernacle which Moses had pitched, and all the vessels that were for ministration to the sacrifices of God, and removed them to the Temple" (*Ant.*, VIII.iv.1). Here we find Hurowitz's only mention of the critical passage in 1 Kgs 8:4: "Josephus adds absolutely nothing to what is stated in 1 Kgs 8" ("The Form and Fate of the Tabernacle," p. 143).

[146] For further detail, see Moshe Weinfeld, "Social and Cultic Institutions in the Priestly Source," p. 104.

[147] Since its initial publication, Friedman's proposal has met with various reactions. Helga Weippert, in her review of Friedman's *The Exile and Biblical Narrative*, calls the reconstruction "erwägenswert" ("Review of *Temples and High Places in Biblical Times* and *The Exile and Biblical Narrative*," *ZDPV* 199 [1984]: p. 184). Moreover, Frank M. Cross, Jr., one of the major proponents of the 30 by 10 cubit Tabernacle, concedes apropos of Friedman's theory: "It's a thoroughly defendable position (*The Wall Street Journal,* Oct 9 [1987]: pp. 1, 17). Criticism has likewise been forthcoming. Graham I. Davies, also reviewing *The Exile and Biblical Narrative*, finds Friedman's argument "unconvincing," and his measurements "arbitrary," *JTS* 34 (1983): p. 224.

each four fingers thick as Josephus argued (see figure 110), each would weigh c. 64.3 kgs/141.75 lbs. This also corresponds to the thickness of the gilded boards used to construct Tiye's shrine (figure 53), and the thickness of Tutankhamon's catafalque (figures 46 and 48). The silver bases add virtually nothing to the height.[148] Each board has four tenons: two on the bottom which fit into mortises in the bases (Exod 26:19), and two on one side to fit with mortises in the neighboring board (26:17). The poles which run along the exterior are also approximately four fingers thick (=0.2 cubits).

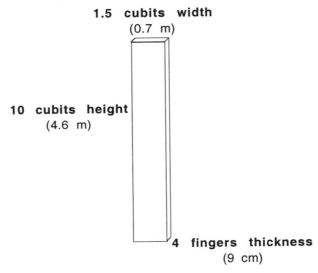

**1.5 cubits width**
(0.7 m)

**10 cubits height**
(4.6 m)

**4 fingers thickness**
(9 cm)

Figure 33 – The Form of a קֶרֶשׁ

2) Two Corner Boards — Each corner frame is composed of one קֶרֶשׁ, vertically divided in half, with the halves joined together at a right angle (Figure 34). This is done because of the allotment of silver bases. Each standard קֶרֶשׁ is supported by two bases. Each corner is composed of two boards, but are again only provided with a total of two bases (Exod 26:25). Therefore, the simplest solution is to maintain the ratio of קֶרֶשׁ to base, and divide each

---

[148] Exod 38:27 records that the 96 silver bases of the קְרָשִׁים and the four silver bases of the פָּרֹכֶת weigh 100 talents (= c. 3000 kg). Thus each individual base weighs about 30 kg, not enough to extend the Tabernacle's overall height more than a cm or two.

corner קֶרֶשׁ in half, and join them together. Furthermore, this
method of construction finds a strong parallel in the corner
frames of Hetepheres's tent (Plates 46, 59). Exod 26:24 states that
the corner boards shall be double (תֹאֲמִם) from below and joined
(תַמִּים) on top. These two terms are interpreted as woodworking
synonyms, both meaning that the two boards composing each
corner are coupled both at the bottom and at the top.[149]

However, the widths of each corner are not uniform, due to the
four finger thickness of the boards (again, see figure 34). Thus,
one side is .75 cubits (1/2 of a קֶרֶשׁ), while the other side is .95
cubits, resulting from the .75 cubit width plus the four finger
thickness (4 fingers = 0.2 cubits).

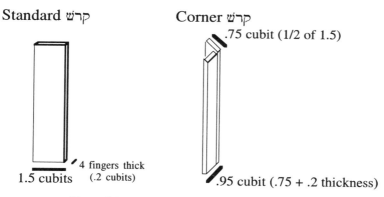

Standard קֶרֶשׁ     Corner קֶרֶשׁ

.75 cubit (1/2 of 1.5)

4 fingers thick
(.2 cubits)

1.5 cubits

.95 cubit (.75 + .2 thickness)

Figure 34 – Proposed Corner Frames of the Tabernacle

In our model, we put the longer dimension (.95 cubit) on the side
walls. This means that the corner frames add .75 cubit to the back
wall's width, and .95 cubit to the overall length. When assembled,
the Tabernacle's back wall measures 10.5 cubits while the side
walls each measure 30.95 cubits (30 cubits from the 20 boards
plus .75 cubits from corner boards plus 0.2 cubits thickness)
(Figure 35). This is similar to the traditional 30 x 10 model,
except that the back now gains .5 cubits and the sides .95 cubit
from the proposed corner pieces. The text is silent concerning the
dimensions of the bars. We propose they are four fingers thick,
and thus slightly increase the overall exterior dimensions of the

---

[149] See p. 138 above for a textual variant (Samaritan and LXX read תֹאֲמִם for
תַמִּים)

Tabernacle. Now, the final dimensions of the Tabernacle that the curtains will cover is as follows:

Height=10 cubits
Length=31.15 cubits (30 cubits + .95 corners + 0.2 bars)
Width=10.9 (9 cubits + 1.5 from 2 corners + 0.4 from 2 bars)

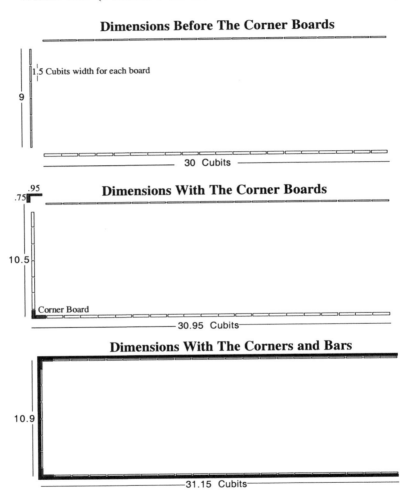

Figure 35 – Dimensions of the Tabernacle

3) Fabric — The curtain of linen measures 40 x 28 cubits (Exod 26:1-6). The curtain of goat-hair is 44 x 30 cubits (Exod 26:7-9).

The sixth curtain of goat-hair is folded in half (Exod 26:9) at the Tabernacle's entrance, and thus produces an overall dimension for the outer curtain of 42 x 30 cubits (Figure 36).

## Folding the Sixth Curtain

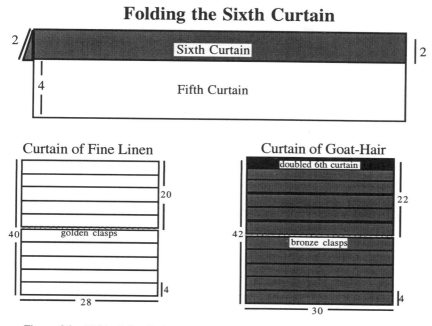

Figure 36 – Fold of the Sixth Curtain and the Dimensions of the Curtains

When the curtains are laid one on top of the other, now one cubit of the curtain of goat-hair remains on each of the Tabernacle's long sides, as dictated by Exod 26:13. Moreover, on the Tabernacle's back, half of a curtain (2 cubits) hangs beyond the curtain of fine linen, as stated in Exod 26:12. The lay of the curtains is depicted in Figure 37.

# Lay of Both Curtains

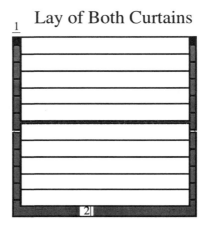

Figure 37 – The Curtain of Linen on Top of the Goat-Hair Curtain

This arrangement of the curtains best adheres to the textual specifications. The way that the curtains lie upon the boards is shown in Figure 38.

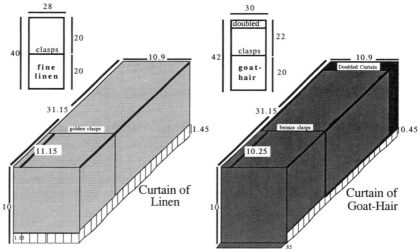

Figure 38 – Proposed Tabernacle Boards With Curtains

The benefits of this model are that it arises from the simple reading of the text, and it uses known woodworking techniques from antiquity. However, like all models of the Tabernacle, there is a problem. Now there is .85 cubit of the curtain of goat-hair left on the ground, a feature that would be unlikely. This excess curtain could be folded inward to envelope the curtain of fine linen. But why would this not be done uniformly on the other two sides?

It seems the best way to overcome this problem is to alter the placement of the fold of the sixth curtain. If, instead of folding it directly in half as shown in Figure 36, the sixth curtain is folded 0.7 cubits from its juncture with the fifth curtain, it now lies more uniformly upon the Tabernacle's boards and bars.

## Folding the Sixth Curtain

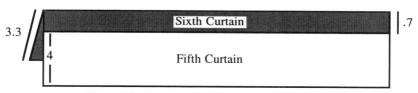

Figure 39 – Proposed Folding of the Sixth Curtain

## Lay of Both Curtains

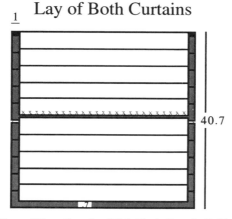

Figure 40 – Lay of Two Curtains With Sixth Curtain Folded at 0.7 Cubits

This leaves a uniform .45 cubits of the boards uncovered on each of the three sides of the Tabernacle, as seen in Figure 41.

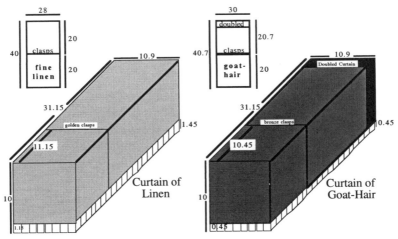

Figure 41 – Curtains on Boards with Sixth Curtain of Goat-Hair Folded at 0.7
Cubits

While this arrangement is preferable in that the curtains end
uniformly at .45 cubits off the ground, fidelity to the text is
sacrificed to a degree. While one cubit still remains on the two
sides of the Tabernacle (Exod 26:13), now the sixth curtain is not
evenly doubled (26:9), and instead of half a curtain remaining in
the back (26:12), now there is 0.7 curtain extending beyond the
curtain of linen.

*Will the Real Tabernacle Please Stand Up: The Quest for an
Unobtainable Solution and Other Conclusions*

In conclusion, despite P's unprecedented attention to the detail
concerning the Tabernacle's form, the precise shape continues to
be unknown. While some models, such as the sloped-roof, are
easily discarded, not even the best reconstructions solve all of the
architectural and textual difficulties. The main point is, however,
that the many parallels to the Tabernacle in form and function
support its historicity; the Tabernacle as described by the Priestly
author likely existed in early Iron Age Israel.

This book's final chapter explores the biblical expression "T o
your tents, O Israel!" in the context of the many tent functions
previously examined (domestic, military, love, religious). Similar

calls to tents in Egypt and Ugarit support the idea that it was a widespread formula to disband assemblies in societies in which tents at one time were the dominant form of habitation. Thus, by examining this expression, greater insight into the important role tents played in the ancient Near East will be revealed.

CHAPTER NINE

# TO YOUR TENTS, O ISRAEL! THE LEGACY OF A TENT HERITAGE IN AN ARCHAIC PROCLAMATION OF DISBANDMENT

> The phrase "To your tents, O Israel!" is enigmatic, as for house-dwelling urbanites, a call to tents is unexpected. The many functions of tents in the Hebrew Bible and ancient Near East previously explored provide insight into this biblical proclamation, as do parallels from Ugarit and Egypt. It will be shown that the expression "To your tents, O Israel!" is part of a widespread legal formula for disbanding councils in the ancient Near East.

## To Your Tents, O Israel! Some Possible Interpretations

Sheba's rebellion against King David in 2 Sam 20:1 begins by sounding the trumpet, followed by the proclamation: "There is no portion for us in David, and no inheritance in the son of Jesse. Every man to his tents, O Israel!" Years later, the Israelites reject Rehoboam's regal claim with a similar idiom: "What portion have we in David? And no inheritance in the son of Jesse. To your tents, O Israel! Now see to your own house, David!" (1 Kgs 12:16=2 Chr 10:16). This formula for political rejection seems out of place in the monarchical period, as the majority of the population are not tent-dwellers; rather, they live in houses.

Difficulties in understanding this enigmatic call to tents began at an early date, as 2 Sam 20:1 and 1 Kgs 12:16 are two of the more famous cases where scribal corrections were posited by early Rabbinic tradition. Rather than read לְאֹהָלֶיךָ "to your tents," this interpretation claims לֵאלֹהֶךָ "to your gods" is the original reading, suggesting that Israel had apostatized.[1] Further evidence of difficulty comes from the LXX, which translates the MT phrase

---

[1] See Peter R. Ackroyd, *II Samuel*, Cambridge Bible Commentary (London, 1977): p. 188; Samuel R. Driver, *Notes on the Hebrew Text of the Books of Samuel* (Oxford, 1890): p. 340.

"Now see (רְאֵה) to your own house" as "Now shepherd (βοσκε/
רְעֵה) your own house."[2] This reading corresponds to the use of
tents by pastoral herders, as well as to the image of the king as
shepherd. While these two emendations are quite unlikely, they
suggest that the original expression was problematic for early
interpreters.

Modern interpretations of "To your tents, O Israel!" do not
emend the text, but they still significantly vary. For example,
Robert H. Smith understands the phrase as a call to return to
desert origins.[3] There is much merit to this suggestion, as tents
symbolize an egalitarian past, whereas the king epitomizes the
stratified trappings of urbanism.[4] Nevertheless, events that occur
after the proclamation do not support this interpretation. The
people do not return to a tent-dwelling life, but continue to live in
urban houses. More important, in 1 Kings 12, a new king is
quickly anointed (12:20), proving that the people intended no
abandonment of monarchy *per se*.

Alternatively, John Gray understands the tents in the
proclamation not as a symbol for a former way of life, but as "the
tents where the representatives of the tribes camped during the
tribal gathering at Shechem."[5] Thus the call to tents would
parallel Achilleus' sulking in his hut at the onset of Homer's
*Iliad*.[6] We have seen that tents are a big part of ancient military
campaigning, and it is likely that many of the tribal representatives gathered at Shechem were dwelling in tents. However,
these tents are not mentioned in the surrounding passages.

Albrecht Alt argues that at Dtr's late date of composition,
"tent" had become synonymous with "house."[7] The two terms
certainly blend in usage, as we have seen in Chapter 1. Yet, the
fact that the call to tents in 1 Kings 12 is followed by the utterance
"Now see to your own *house* (בית), David," suggests more than a

---

[2] Note also Targum Jonathan, which corresponds to the LXX, using the verb
מלוך.

[3] Robert H. Smith, "Arabia," *ABD* I, p. 327.

[4] On the symbolism of tents and praise for their inhabitants in the Hebrew
Bible, see pp. 7-9; 35-38.

[5] John Gray, *II Kings* (Philadelphia, 1963): p. 306.

[6] As pointed out by Baruch Halpern.

[7] Albrecht Alt, "Zelt und Hütten," *Kleine Schriften zur Geschichte des Volkes
Israel* III, pp. 239-42.

semantic conflation. The people are playing with the opposition between "tent" and "house."

A superior interpretation is presented by Abraham Malamat, who understands the phrase as a formula for assembly disbandment.[8] Malamat's case is improved through examining the events that follow the proclamations. In 2 Samuel 20, only Judah remains loyal to David, while the Israelites follow Sheba. Eventually David's forces catch up with Sheba, besieging him and his subjects within the walls of Abel. Upon Sheba's death, Joab blows the trumpet, and the followers of Sheba withdraw from Abel, and Joab's troops disband "every man to his tent" (2 Sam 20:22). This clarifies that the meaning of the proclamation is not martial; it simply means that the rebellion is over, and now the people will go home. Also in 1 Kgs 12:16=2 Chr 10:16, the call to tents is followed by the phrase "so Israel departed to their tents." Thus again, it is not a call to arms, nor a call to desert wanderings. It is an archaic vestige of former days of tent-dwelling, legally signifying the end of the assembly.

Other passages not discussed by Malamat bolster his case. Joshua 22 tells of the allotment of territories for the Transjordanian tribes at Shiloh. When Reuben, Gad, and half of Manasseh leave the collective assembly for their land, they go "to their tents."[9] Also in 1 Sam 13:2, when Saul has more soldiers than he needs, he sends the remainder "each to his tent." And again, Solomon gathers an assembly for a feast when the Temple is completed, and when the celebration has ended, his subjects "blessed the king, and went to their tents" (1 Kgs 8:66). In these examples, the end of the gathering is signified by an idiom involving movement towards tents.

The interpretation of "To your tents, O Israel" as a formula for assembly disbandment finds further support in Judges 20, where the Israelites gather at Mizpah to collectively punish the inhabitants of Gibeah for the murder of the Levite's concubine.[10]

---

[8] Abraham Malamat, "Organs of Statecraft in the Israelite Monarchy," *BA* 28 (1965): p. 39-40. See also Georg Fohrer, "Der Vertrag zwischen König und Volk in Israel," *ZAW* 71 (1959): p. 8.

[9] Josh 22:4, 6-7. Josh 22:9 makes it clear that the tents referred to are not simply the tent-encampments gathered at Shiloh, but their newly acquired homes.

[10] This passage is mentioned by Malamat, p. 40.

The people express their unity by stating, "None of us will go to his tent, nor will any turn back to his house" (Jug 20:8). Thus the call to tents is not a declaration of war, but the opposite. The refusal to return to tents signifies that the tribes are standing as a united front.

### To Your Tents, O Israel, O Ugarit, and O Egypt! The Meeting is Adjourned

Two Late Bronze extra-biblical sources, one from Ugarit and one from Egypt, further confirm Malamat's interpretation.[11] An Ugaritic divine council is summoned to bestow their blessings on Kirta. The assembly ends with the following words:

> *tbrk · ilm · tity*
> *tity · ilm · lahlhm*
> *dr · il · lmšknthm*
> The gods bless, they go
> The gods go to their tents
> The circle of El to their tabernacles.[12]

Thus, just as in the biblical passages, the meeting is adjourned by retreating to tents. While El lives in a tent, the majority of the pantheon inhabit permanent temples. Thus, it is again noteworthy that the gods do not retreat to houses.[13]

A New Kingdom Egyptian text strongly resembles both the biblical and Ugaritic passages. In the "Contest of Horus and Seth," the Ennead quarrels and following some name-calling, the text reads "And they [gods] went to their tents (*'imw*). The great god [Re] slept in his pavilion (*sḥ*)."[14] Again, nearly all of the

---

[11] See Michael M. Homan, "To Your Tents, O Egypt, Canaan, and Israel: An Ancient Formula for Council Disbandment," *UF* 31 (2000): pp. 237-40.

[12] *CAT* 1.15.III.17-19. Elsewhere Kothar departs for his tent (*ahl*), also called a tabernacle (*mškn*) in *CAT* 1.17.V.32.

[13] Note the contrary formula from a ritual text at Mari, in which after a donkey sacrifice inside tent frames (qé-er-su-ú), the divine assembly departs to their houses and the king to his palace (*Florilegium Marianum* III.4.ii.7-14).

[14] For translation see Miriam Lichtheim, *Ancient Egyptian Literature* (Berkeley, 1976): p. 216, and *ANET* p. 15. For the Egyptian text see Alan H. Gardiner, *Late Egyptian Stories* (Brusells, 1932): p. 41 (3,13). This text is notably absent in discussions of divine assemblies. See for example E. Theodore Mullen, Jr., *The Assembly of the Gods* (Missoula, MT, 1980): pp. 3-4, who

Egyptian pantheon live in temples, so the gods going to tents is peculiar.

It now seems clear that departing to tents is a widespread formula for disbanding assemblies, divine at Ugarit and Egypt, secular in the Hebrew Bible. The parallel is part of a larger set of correspondances in the terminology of public gatherings. For example, both the Ugaritic and biblical examples employ the root *y'd* for the assembly, at Ugarit *m'd*, at Shechem הָעֵדָה.[15]

In all three literatures, first the masses are dismissed, and then the higher-ranking leaders. At Ugarit the ordinary gods depart to their tents, then the head of the pantheon El and his entourage go to their tabernacles. At Egypt, the ordinary gods go to their tents, then Re the head of the pantheon sleeps in his pavilion. And in 1 Kgs 12:16, the call for the citizens of Israel to depart for their tents is followed by the call for the king to look after his own house.[16]

When these texts were composed, all three societies were dominantly urban. However, all three societies claimed a heritage of nomadic tent-dwelling. Israel's tent-dwelling past has been examined previously.[17] At Ugarit, the elder head of the pantheon, El, lives in a tent while the younger gods dwell in houses. In any case, a nomadic tent-dwelling heritage is often assumed for the Northwest Semitic peoples, including the citizens of Ugarit.[18] In Egypt, Min has many similarities to Ugaritic El: he is seen as the eldest god, the early head of the Egyptian pantheon, and he also continues to live in a tent.[19] Thus it seems that the widespread call

---

states that the Canaanite/Hebrew concept of divine assembly stems from Mesopotamia with no Egyptian parallels. Also John A. Wilson, "The Assembly of a Phoenician City," *JNES* 4 (1945): p. 245, who calls attention to the Phoenician assembly (*mw'd*) in the Egyptian text of Wenamun but is again silent on the Contest.

[15] 1 Kgs 12:20. 2 Chr 10:3 leaves out "assembly," using instead "all Israel." For the Ugaritic assembly, see E. Theodore Mullen, Jr., *The Divine Council in Canaanite and Early Hebrew Literature*.

[16] In 2 Sam 20:1, however, nothing is said about David departing to or looking after any sort of domicile. However, two verses later, David does return to his house in Jerusalem, where he deals with the concubines violated by Absalom (2 Sam 20:3).

[17] See chapter 3, pp. 29-45.

[18] See pp. 94-99.

[19] See pp. 109-110.

to return to tents as a formula for assembly disbandment is a survival from a nomadic, egalitarian past, a verbal fossil still remembered.

## Conclusion

Tents played an integral role in the ancient Near East. Their vast quantity and importance have been examined above from both historical and archaeological perspectives. More specifically, the historicity of the claim of a tent-dwelling heritage made by various authors of the Hebrew Bible has been strengthened. Tents served many purposes in ancient Israel, including domestic, military, nuptial, and religious. Most, if not all of these aspects are evoked in the cry, "To your tents, O Israel."

# BIBLIOGRAPHY

Ackerman, Susan. *Warrior, Dancer, Seductress, Queen: Women in Judges and Biblical Israel.* New York: Doubleday, 1998.

Ackroyd, Peter R. *The Second Book of Samuel.* Cambridge Bible Commentary. Cambridge: Camridge University Press, 1977.

Adams, Russell B. "Romancing the Stones: New Light on Glueck's 1934 Survey of Eastern Palestine as a Result of Recent Work by the Wadi Fidan Project." *Early Edom and Moab: The Beginning of the Iron Age in Southern Jordan.* Piotr Bienkowski, ed. SAM 7 (Sheffield: J. R. Collis, 1992): 177-86.

Aharoni, Israel. "Animals Hitherto Unknown to or Little Known from Palestine." *The Zoological Society of Egypt, Syria/Palestine.* Bulletin Supplement 6 (1944): 4-41.

Aharoni, Miriam. "Arad." *The New Encyclopedia of Archaeological Excavations in the Holy Land* (Jerusalem: IES, 1993): 82-87.

Aharoni, Yohanan. "The Solomonic Temple, the Tabernacle and the Arad Sanctuary." In *Orient and Occident: Essays presented to Cyrus H. Gordon.* H. A. Hoffner, Jr., ed. AOAT 22 (Neukirchen: Butzon and Bercker Kevelaer, 1973): 1-7.

——. "New Aspects of the Israelite Occupation of the North." In *Near Eastern Archaeology in the Twentieth Century.* Essays in Honor of Nelson Glueck (Garden City, NY: Doubleday, 1970): 254-67.

——. "Arad: Its Inscriptions and Temple." *BA* 31 (1968): 2-32.

——. "Trial Excavation in the 'Solar Shrine' at Lachish." *IEJ* 18 (1968): 157-69.

Aharoni, Yohanan, and Amiran, Ruth. "Excavations at Tel Arad." *IEJ* 14 (1964): 131-47.

Ahituv, Yosef, and Tadmor, Hayim. "חרם." *Encyclopaedia Biblica* 8 (Jerusalem, 1982): 520-21 (Hebrew).

Ahlström, Gösta W. *Who Were the Israelites?* Winona Lake: Eisenbrauns, 1986.

Albright, William F. "Abram the Hebrew." *BASOR* 163 (1961): 36-54.

——. "The Furniture of El in Canaanite Mythology." *BASOR* 91 (1943): 39-44.

——. *Archaeology and the Religion of Israel.* Baltimore: Johns Hopkins University Press, 1942.

——. "The Names Shaddai and Abram." *JBL* 54 (1935): 183-84.

Alt, Albrecht. *Die Landnahme der Israeliten in Palästina.* Leipzig: Universität Leipzig, 1925. Reprinted and Translated by R. A. Wilson in *Essays on Old Testament History and Religion* (Oxford: Basil Blackwell, 1966): 133-69.

——. "Zelte und Hütten." *Alttestamentliche Studien.* Fs. F. Nötscher. Bonn: Peter Hanstein, 1950. Reprinted in *Kleine Schriften zur Geschichte des Volkes Israel* Vol. 3. Munich: Beck'sche, 1959: 233-42.

Andrae, Walter. *Das wiedererstandene Assur.* 2nd edition, B. Hrouda, ed. Munich: Beck, 1977.

Arnaud, Daniel. *Emar VI: Les textes sumérians et accadiens.* Paris: E.R.C., 1986.

Arnold, Patrick M. "Gibeon." *ABD* II (1992): 1010-12.

Attridge, Harold W., and Robert A. Oden, Jr. *Philo of Byblos*. CBQ Monograph Series 9. Washington, D.C.: Catholic Biblical Association of America, 1981.

——. *The Syrian Goddess*. Missoula: Scholars Press, 1976.

Avner, Uzi. "Settlement, Agriculture and Paleoclimate in 'Uvda Valley, Southern Negev Desert, 6th-3rd Millennia BC." *Water, Environment, and Society in Times of Climatic Change*. A. S. Issar and N. Brown, eds. (Netherlands: Kluwer Academic, 1998): 147-202.

Avner, Uzi, Israel Carmi, and Dror Segal. "Neolithic to Bronze Age Settlement of the Negev and Sinai in Light of Radiocarbon Dating." *Late Quaternary Chronology and Paleoclimates of the Eastern Mediterranean*. Ofer Bar-Yosef and Renee S. Kra, eds. (Cambridge, MA: American School of Prehistoric Research, 1994): 265-300.

Badawy, Alexander. "Min, the Cosmic Fertility God of Egypt." *Mitteilungen des Instituts für Orientforschung* 7 (1959): 163-79.

Bähr, Karl W. F. *Symbolik des Mosaischen Cultus*. 2 vols. Heidelberg: J. C. B. Mohr, 1837-39.

Baillet, Maurice, Jozef T. Milik, and Roland de Vaux. *Discoveries in the Judaean Desert of Jordan III: Les "Petites Grottes" de Qumrân*. Oxford: Clarendon, 1962.

Bar-Yosef, Ofer, and Anatoly Khazanov, eds. *Pastoralism in the Levant: Archaeological Materials in Anthropological Persectives*. Madison: Prehistory Press, 1992.

Barfield, Thomas. *The Nomadic Alternative*. Englewood Cliffs, NJ: Prentice Hall, 1993.

Barth, Jacob. *Die Nominalbildung in den semitischen Sprachen*. Leipzig: Hinrichs, 1894.

Bartlett, John R. "Biblical Sources for the Early Iron Age in Edom." *Early Edom and Moab: The Beginning of the Iron Age in Southern Jordan*. Piotr Bienkowski, ed. SAM 7 (Sheffield: J. R. Collis Publications, 1992): 13-19.

Bartosiewicz, László, W. Van Neer, and A. Lentacker. *Draught Cattle: Their Osteological Identification and History*. Belgium, 1997.

Basilav, Vladimir N., and O. Naumova. "Yurts, Rugs, and Felts." *Nomads of Eurasia*. Seattle: University of Washington Press, 1989.

Bass, George F. *A History of Seafaring Based on Underwater Archaeology*. London: Thames and Hudson, 1972.

Baumgartel, Elise J. "Herodotus on Min." *Antiquity* 21 (1947): 145-50.

Baumgarten, Albert. *The Phoenician History of Philo of Byblos: A Commentary*. Leiden: E. J. Brill, 1981.

Bennett, Crystal M. "Biblical Traditions and Archaeological Results." *The Archaeology of Jordan and Other Studies*. Lawrence Geraty and Larry G. Herr, eds. (Berrien Springs: Andrews University Press, 1986): 77-80.

——. "Excavations at Buseirah, Southern Jordan, 1974." *Levant* 7 (1975): 1-19.

Bennett, William Henry. *Exodus*. Century Bible 2. Edinburgh: Jack, 1908.

Benz, Frank L. *Personal Names in the Phoenician and Punic Inscriptions*. Rome: Biblical Institute Press, 1972.

Bertram, George C. L. "Note on the Sea Cow in the Gulf of Aqabah." *Journal of the Society for the Preservation of Fauna in the Empire* 47 (1943): 21-23.

Bezold, Carl. *Ninive und Babylon*. Leipzig: Velhagen und Klafing, 1903.

Bidwell, Robin. *Travellers in Arabia*. New York: Hamlyn, 1976.

Bienkowski, Piotr. "Iron Age Settlement in Edom: A Revised Framework." *The World of the Aramaeans: Biblical, Historical, and Cultural Studies in Honour of Paul Dion*. P. M. M. Daviau and M. Weigl, eds. (Sheffield: Sheffield Academic Press): In press.

———. "The Beginning of the Iron Age in Southern Jordan: A Framework." *Early Edom and Moab: The Beginning of the Iron Age in Southern Jordan*. Piotr Bienkowski, ed. SAM 7 (Sheffield: J. R. Collis Publications, 1992): 1-12.

Biran, Avraham. *Biblical Dan*. Jerusalem: IES, 1994.

Blackman, Aylard M., and Michael R. Apted. *The Rock Tombs of Meir*. Vol. V. ASE 28. Oxford: Oxford University Press, 1953.

Bleeker, Claas J. *Die Geburt eines Gottes*. Leiden, E. J. Brill, 1956.

Bleibtreu, Erika. "Grisly Assyrian Record of Torture and Death." *BAR* Jan/Feb (1991): 52-61; 75.

Blenkinsopp, Joseph. *Gibeon and Israel*. Cambridge: Cambridge University Press, 1972.

Blunt, Anne. *Bedouin Tribes of the Euphrates*. Vol. II. London: John Murray, 1879.

Bohec, Yann le. *The Imperial Roman Army*. London: B. T. Batsford, 1994.

Bonnet, Hans. "Min." *Reallexikon der ägyptischen Religionsgeschichte* (Berlin: Walter de Gruyter, 1952): 461-67.

Borowski, Oded. *Agriculture in Iron Age Israel*. Winona Lake, IN: Eisenbrauns, 1987.

Bowman, Raymond A. "An Aramaic Religious Text in Demotic Script." *JNES* 3 (1944): 219-31.

Breasted, James H. *Ancient Records of Egypt*. Chicago: University of Chicago Press, 1906.

———. *The Battle of Kadesh*. Chicago: University of Chicago Press, 1903.

Briggs, Charles A. *The Book of Psalms*. ICC. New York: Charles Scribner's Sons, 1906.

Brockelmann, Carl. *Grundriss der vergleichenden Grammatik der semitischen Sprachen*. 2 Vols. Berlin: Reuther and Reichard, 1908-13.

Broneer, Oscar. "The Tent of Xerxes and the Greek Theater." *University of California Publications in Classical Archaeology* I:12 (1944): 305-12.

Broshi, Magen, and Hanan Eshel. "How and Where Did the Qumranites Live?" *The Provo International Conference on the Dead Sea Scrolls*. D. W. Parry and E. C. Ulrich, eds. (Leiden: E. J. Brill, 1997).

———. "Response to J. Patrich." *Qadmoniot* 115 (1998): 67.

———. "The Archaeological Remains on the Marl Terrace Around Qumran." *Qadmoniot* 114 (1997): 129-33.

Brovarski, Edward. "The Doors of Heaven." *Orientalia* 46 (1977): 107-15.

Brown, John P. "Peace Symbolism in Ancient Military Vocabulary." *VT* 21 (1971): 1-23.

Brown, William. *The Tabernacle*. Edinburgh: Oliphant, Anderson, and Ferrier, 1899.

———. "Construction of the Tabernacle." *PEF* (1897): 154-55.

Brunner-Traut, Emma. *Die altägyptischen Scherbenbilder*. Wiesbaden: Franz Steiner Verlag, 1956.

Büchler, Adolf. "The Induction of the Bride and Bridegroom into the חופה in the First and Second Centuries in Palestine." *Livre d'hommage a la mémoire du Samuel Poznanski* (Leipzig, 1927): 82-132.

Budde, Karl. "The Nomadic Ideal in the Old Testament." *The New World* 4 (1895): 726-45.

Buhl, Frants. "Maḥmal." *The Encyclopaedia of Islam* VI, New Edition (Leiden: E. J. Brill, 1986): 44-46.

Buisson, Robert du Mesnil du. *Études sur les dieux phéniciens hérités par l'empire romain* Leiden: E. J. Brill, 1970.

Burckhardt, Johann L. *Bedouins*. 2 Vols. London: Colburn and Bentley, 1831.

——. *Arabic Proverbs*. London, 1830.

——. *Travels in Arabia*. London: H. Colburn, 1829.

Busink, Th. A. *Der Tempel von Jerusalem*. Leiden: E. J. Brill, 1970.

——. "Les origines du temple de Salomon." *Jaarbericht Ex Oriente Lux* 17 (1963): 165-92.

Butzer, Karl W., et al. *Ancient Egypt: Discovering its Splendors*. Jules B. Billard, ed. Washington, D. C.: National Geographic Society, 1978.

Caldecott, William. S. *The Tabernacle: Its History and Structure*. London: Religious Tract Society, 1904.

Carter, Howard. *The Tomb of Tut-ankh-amen*. 2 Vols. New York: George H. Doran, 1927.

Carter, Howard, and Alan H. Gardiner. "The Tomb of Ramesses IV and the Turin Plan of a Royal Tomb." *JEA* 4 (1917): 130-58.

Cassuto, Umberto. *Commentary on Exodus*. Translated from Hebrew by I. Abrahams. Jerusalem: Magnes Press, 1967.

Chang-Ho, C., Jr. "A Note on the Iron Age Four-Room House in Palestine." *Orientalia* 66 (1997): 387-413.

Charpin, Dominique, and Jean-Marie Durand. *Florilegium marianum* III. Paris: SEPOA, 1997.

Chéhab, Maurice. *Monnaies greco-romaines et phéniciennes*. Paris: Librairie d'Amérique et d'Orient, 1977.

Clapham, Lynn R. *Sanchuniathon: The First Two Cycles*, Unpublished Harvard University Dissertation (1969).

Clements, Ronald E. *God and Temple*. Oxford: Basil Blackwell, 1965.

Clermont-Ganneau, Charles. "L'Heracleion de Rabbat-Ammon Philadelphia et la déesse Asteria." *Recueil D'Archéologie Orientale* 7 (1905): 147-55.

Clifford, Richard J. *The Cosmic Mountain in Canaan and the Old Testament*. Cambridge: Harvard University Press, 1972.

——. "The Tent of El and the Israelite Tent of Meeting." *CBQ* 33 (1971): 221-27.

Cogan, Mordechai, and Hayim Tadmor. *II Kings*. Anchor Bible 11. Garden City, NY: Doubleday, 1988.

Cohen, Rudolph. "Excavations at Kadesh-barnea." *BA* 44 (1981): 93-107.

Cole, Alan. *Exodus*, Tyndale OT Commentary. Leicester: Inter-Varsity Press, 1973.

Comay, Joan. *The Temple of Jerusalem*. New York: Holt, Rinehart and Winston, 1975.

Conder, Claude R. *Tent Work in Palestine*. London: Richard Bentley and Son, 1878. 2 Volumes.

Cook, Stanley A. *The Religion of Ancient Palestine in the Light of Archaeology*. London, Oxford University Press, 1930.

Cooper, Jerrold S. *The Curse of Agade*. Baltimore: Johns Hopkins, 1983.

Coote, Daniel B., and Daniel Robert Ord. *The Bible's First History*. Philadelphia: Fortress Press, 1989.

Creswell, Keppel A. C. *Early Muslim Architecture*, revised edition. London: The American University in Cairo Press, 1989.

Cribb, Roger L. "Mobile Villagers: The Structure and Organisation of Nomadic Pastoral Campsites in the Near East." *Ethnoarchaeological Approaches to Mobile Campsites*. C. S. Gamble and W. A. Boismier, eds. (Ann Arbor: International Monographs in Prehistory, 1991): 380-86.

———. *Nomads in Archaeology*. Cambridge: Cambridge University Press, 1991.

Cross, Frank M., Jr. "The Priestly Tabernacle in the Light of Recent Research." *Temples and High Places in Biblical Times*. A. Biran, ed. (Jerusalem: HUC, 1981): 169-82.

———. *From Epic to Canon*. Baltimore: John Hopkins University Press, 1998.

———. *Canaanite Myth and Hebrew Epic*. Cambridge, Massachusetts: Harvard University Press, 1973.

———. "The Priestly Tabernacle." *The Biblical Archaeologist Reader I*. D. N. Freedman and G. E. Wright, eds. (Garden City, NY: 1961): 201-28.

———. "The Tabernacle: A Study from an Archaeological and Historical Approach." *BA* 10 (1947): 45-68.

———. and Freedman, David Noel. *Studies in Ancient Yahwistic Poetry*. Missoula, Montana: Scholars Press, 1975.

Crüsemann, Frank. *The Torah: Theology and Social History of Old Testament Law*. Translated by Allan W. Mahnke. Minneapolis : Fortress Press, 1996.

Cumont, Franz. "La double Fortune des Sémites et les processions àdos de chameau." *Études Syriennes* (Paris, 1917): 263-76.

Dahood, Mitchell. *Psalms III*. AB 17A. Garden City, NY: Doubleday, 1970.

Dalman, Gustaf. *Arbeit und Sitte in Palästina*. Hildesheim: Georg Olms Publisher, 1928. 7 volumes.

Davies, G. Henton "Tabernacle." *IDB* IV (New York: Abingdon Press, 1962): 498- 506.

Davies, Graham I. "*The Exile and Biblical Narrative*: A Review." *JTS* 34 (1983): 222-26.

Davies, Norman de G. *Two Ramesside Tombs at Thebes*. New York: Metropolitan Museum of Art, 1927.

———. *Rock Tombs of Amarna*. Vol. V. London: EEF, 1908.

Davis, David, and Amos Kloner. "A Burial Cave of the Late Israelite Period on the Slopes of Mt. Zion." *Qadmoniot* 41 (1978): 16-19 (Hebrew).

Davis, Theodore M. *The Tomb of Queen Tîyi*. London: Constable and Co., 1910.

Dawson, Warren R. "Making a Mummy." *JEA* 13 (1927): 40-49.

Delcor, Mathias. "Astarte." *Lexicon Iconographicum Mythologiae Classicae* III.1 (Munich: Artemis, 1986).

Desroches-Noblecourt, Christiane. *Ramsès le Grand*. Paris: Galeries Nationales du Grand Palais, 1976.

Desroches-Noblecourt, Christiane, S. Donadoni, and E. Edel. *Grand Temple d'Abou Simbel: Bataille de Qadech*. Cairo: Centre de documentation et d'études sur l'ancienne Égypte, 1971.

Dever, William G. "Israelite Origins and the 'Nomadic Ideal': Separating Fact from Fiction." *Mediterranean Peoples in Transition*. Fs. Trude Dothan (Jerusalem: IES, 1998): 220-37.

———. "Will the Real Israel Please Stand Up? Part 1." *BASOR* 297 (1995): 61-80.

———. "Will the Real Israel Please Stand Up? Part 2." *BASOR* 298 (1995): 37-58.

———. "Israel, History of (Archaeology and the 'Conquest')." *ABD* III (1992): 545-58.

——. "Cultural Continuity, Ethnicity in the Archaeological Record, and the Question of Israelite Origins." *Eretz Israel* 24. Avraham Malamat Volume (Jerusalem: IES, 1993): 22-33*.

——. "Pastoralism and the End of the Urban Early Bronze Age in Palestine." In *Pastoralism in the Levant*. O. Bar-Yosef and A. Khazanov, eds. Madison, WI: Prehistory Press, 1992): 83-92.

——. "Archaeological Data on the Israelite Settlement," *BASOR* 284 (1991): 77- 90.

——. "Palestine in the Second Millennium B.C.E.: The Archaeological Picture." *Israelite and Judaean History*. J. Hayes and J. M. Miller, eds. (Philadelphia: Westminster, 1977): 70-120.

——. "The Beginning of the Middle Bronze Age in Syria-Palestine," in *Magnalia Dei: The Mighty Acts of God*. Fs. G. E. Wright. Garden City, NY: Doubleday, 1976.

Dietrich, Manfried, Oswald Loretz, and Joaquín Sanmartín. *The Cuneiform Alphabetic Texts: From Ugarit, Ras Ibn Hani and Other Places*. Münster: Ugarit-Verlag, 1995.

Dijk, H. J. van. *Ezekiel's Prophecy on Tyre*. Rome: Pontifical Biblical Institute, 1968.

Dillmann, August. *Die Bücher Exodus und Leviticus*. Leipzig: Hirzel, 1897.

Dion, Paul E. "YHWH as Storm-god and Sun-god." *ZAW* 103 (1991): 43-71.

Drew, Philip. *Tensile Architecture*. New York: Granada, 1979.

Drioton, Étienne. "*Das ägyptische Reinigungszelt*: A Review." *ASAE* 40 (1940): 1007-14.

Driver, Godfrey R. "Supposed Arabisms in the Old Testament," *JBL* 55 (1936): 101-20.

Driver, Samuel R. *Notes on the Hebrew Texts of the Books of Samuel*. Oxford: Clarendon, 1890.

Dupont-Sommer, André. "Nubes tenebrosa et illuminans noctem." *Revue de l'histoire des religions* 125 (1942-1943): 10.

Dus, Jan. "Noch zum Brauch der 'Ladewanderung.'" *VT* 13 (1963): 126-32.

Edzard, E. O. "Altbabylonische *nawûm*." *ZA* 53 (1959): 168-73.

Eickelman, Dale F. "Being Bedouin: Nomads and Tribes in Arab Social Imagination." *Changing Nomads in a Changing World*. J. Ginat and A. M. Khazanov, eds. (Brighton: Sussex Academic Press, 1998): 38-49.

Eilberg-Schwartz, Howard. *God's Phallus*. Boston: Beacon Press, 1994.

Einhard. *Vie de Charlemagne*. Ed. and Trans. by L. Halphen. Paris: H. Champion, 1923.

Emery, Walter B. *Excavations at Saqqara, 1937-1938: Ḥor-aḥa*. Cairo: Government Press, 1939.

Ephʿal, Israel. *The Ancient Arabs*. Leiden: E. J. Brill, 1982.

Erman, Adolf, and Hermann Grapow. *Wörterbuch der aegyptischen Sprache* I. Leipzig: J. C. Hinrichs, 1926.

Esin, Emel. *Mecca the Blessed, Medinah the Radiant*. London: Elek Books, 1963.

Ewald, Heinrich. "Abhandlungen über die phönikischen Ansichten von der Weltschöpfung und den geschichtlichen Wert Sanchuniathons." *Abhandlungen der königlichen Gesellschaft der Wissenschaften zu Göttingen* 5 (1851): 1-68.

Faegre, Torvald. *Tents: Architecture of the Nomads*. Garden City, NY: Anchor Books, 1979.

Fahd, Toufic. *Le Panthéon de L'Arabie centrale á la veille de L'Hégire*. Paris: LOPG, 1968.

Fahn, Abraham, and Ella Werker. *Wood Anatomy and Identification of Trees and Shrubs from Israel and Adjacent Areas*. Jerusalem: The Israel Academy of Sciences and Humanities, 1986.

Faulkner, Raymond O. "The Battle of Kadesh." *Mitteilungen des deutschen Archäologischen Instituts Abteilung Kairo* 16 (1968): 93-111.

Fecht, Gerhard. "Ramses II und die Schlacht bei Qadesch." *Göttinger Miszellen* 80 (1984): 41-50.

Feilberg, Carl G. *La tente noire*. Kobenhavn: Lunos Bogtr, 1944.

Fergusson, James. "Temple." *William Smiths' Dictionary of the Bible*. III (London: John Murray, 1893): 1451 ff.

———. *The Holy Sepulchre and the Temple at Jerusalem*. London: John Murray, 1865.

Feugère, Michel. *Les armes des Romains*. Paris: Errance, 1993.

Finkelstein, Israel. *Living on the Fringe*. Sheffield: Sheffield Academic Press, 1995.

———. "The Great Transformation." *The Archaeology of Society in the Holy Land*. T. E. Levy, ed. (NY: Facts on File, 1995): 349-62.

———. "Pastoralism in the Highlands of Canaan in the Third and Second Millennia B.C.E." *Pastoralism in the Levant*. O. Bar-Yosef and A. Khazanov, eds. (Madison, WI: Prehistory Press, 1992): 133-42.

———. *The Archaeology of the Israelite Settlement*. Jerusalem: IES, 1988.

———. *'Izbet Ṣarṭah*. Oxford: B.A.R., 1986.

———. "Shiloh Yields Some, But Not All, Of Its Secrets," *BAR* 12 (Jan/Feb 1986): 22-41.

Finkelstein, Israel, and A. Perevolotsky. "Processes of Sedentarization and Nomadization in the History of Sinai and the Negev." *BASOR* 279 (1990): 67-88.

Finkelstein, Israel, Shlomo Bunimovitz, and Zvi Lederman. *Shiloh: The Archaeology of a Biblical Site*. Tel Aviv: Tel Aviv University Press, 1993.

Finkelstein, Jacob J. "The Genealogy of the Hammurapi Dynasty." *JCS* 20 (1966): 95-118.

Flannery, Kent V. "The Origins of the Village as a Settlement Type in Mesoamerica and the Near East." *Man, Settlement, and Urbanism*. Peter J. Ucko, Ruth Tringham and G. W. Dimbleby, eds. (London: Duckworth, 1972): 23-53.

Fleming, Daniel E. "More Help From Syria: Introducing Emar to Biblical Studies." *BA* 58 (1995): 126-47.

———. "Mari's Large Public Tent and the Priestly Tent Sanctuary." *VT* 50.4 (2000): 484-98.

Flight, John W. "The Nomadic Ideal in the OT." *JBL* 42 (1923): 158-226

Fohrer, Georg. "Der Vertrag zwischen König und Volk in Israel." *ZAW* 71 (1959): 1-22.

Forbes, Robert J. *Studies in Ancient Technology* IV. Leiden: E. J. Brill, 1964.

———. *Studies in Ancient Technology* V. Leiden: E. J. Brill, 1966.

Fowler, Jeaneane D. *Theophoric Personal Names in Ancient Hebrew*. JSOTSS 49 Sheffield: JSOT, 1988.

Frankfort, Henri. *Kingship and the Gods*. Chicago: University of Chicago Press, 1948.

Freedman, David Noel, "Early Israelite Poetry and Historical Reconstructions." *Symposia for ASOR's 75th Anniversary*. F. M. Cross, ed. (Cambridge, MA: ASOR, 1979): 85-96.

——. "Early Israelite History in the Light of Early Israelite Poetry." *Unity and Diversity: Essays in the History, Literature, and Religion of the Ancient Near East*. H. Goedicke and J. J. M. Roberts, eds. (Baltimore: Johns Hopkins): 3-35.

——. "The Refrain in David's Lament Over Saul and Jonathan." *Ex Orbe Religionum* 21 (1972): 115-26.

Fretheim, Terence E. "The Priestly Document: Anti-Temple?" *VT* 18 (1968): 313- 29.

Friedman, Richard E. "The Tabernacle." *ABD* VI (1992): 292-300.

——. *Who Wrote the Bible?* Englewood Cliffs, NJ: Prentice Hall, 1987.

——. "The Tabernacle in the Temple." *BA* 43 (1980): 241-48.

Fritz, Volkmar. "Conquest or Settlement? The Early Iron Age in Israel." *BA* 50 (1987): 84-100.

——. "The Israelite 'Conquest' in Light of Recent Excavations at Khirbet el-Meshâsh," *BASOR* 241 (1981): 61-73.

Gaballa, Gaballa Ali. *Narrative in Egyptian Art*. Mainz: Zabern, 1976.

Gardiner, Alan H. *The Kadesh Inscriptions of Ramses II*. Oxford: Griffith Institute, 1960.

——. *Late-Egyptian Stories*. Brussels: FAR, 1932.

Gaster, Theodor H. "The Furniture of El in Canaanite Mythology." *BASOR* 93 (1944): 20-23.

Gesenius, Wilhelm. *Hebrew Grammar*, 2nd English edition. Oxford: Clarendon, 1910.

——. *Thesaurus Philologicus Criticus Linguae Hebraeae et Chaldaeae Veteris Testamenti*. Lipsiae: Vogelii, 1829.

Ghazi, Muhammad F. "Remarques sur l'armée chez les Arabes." Ibla, 1960.

Gitin, Seymour. "New Incense Altars from Ekron." *Eretz-Israel* 23. Avraham Biran Volume (Jerusalem: IES, 1992): 43-49.

——. "Incense Altars from Ekron, Israel, and Judah." *Eretz-Israel* 20. Yigael Yadin Volume (Jerusalem: IES, 1989): 52-67.

Gitin, Seymour, and Trude Dothan. "The Rise and Fall of Ekron of the Philistines." *BA* 50 (1987): 197-222.

Giveon, Raphael. *The Impact of Egypt on Canaan*. Orbis Biblicus et Orientalis 20. Göttingen: Vandenhoeck and Ruprecht, 1978.

——. *Les bédouins Shosou des documents égyptiens*. DMOA 18. Leiden: E. J. Brill, 1971.

——. "The Shosu of the Late XXth Dynasty." *JARCE* 8 (1970): 51-53.

Glueck, Nelson. *The Other Side of the Jordan*. New Haven: ASOR, 1940. Reprinted by ASOR in 1970.

Goedicke, Hans. *The Report of Wen Amun*. Baltimore: Johns Hopkins University Press, 1975.

Goldsworthy, Adrian K. *The Roman Army at War*. Oxford: Clarendon, 1996.

Gooding, David W. *The Account of the Tabernacle: Translation and Textual Problems of the Greek Exodus*. Cambridge: Cambridge University Press, 1959.

Goodwin, Godfrey. *A History of Ottoman Architecture*. Baltimore: Johns Hopkins Press, 1971.

Gordon, Cyrus. *Ugaritic Textbook.* Analecta Orientalia 38. Rome: Pontifical Biblical Institute, 1965.

Görg, Manfred. "Aaron-von einem Titel zum Namen?" *BN* 32 (1986): 11-17.

Gottwald, Norman. *The Tribes of Yahweh.* New York: Orbis, 1979.

Graf, David F. "The Origin of the Nabataeans." *Aram* 2:1 (1990): 45-75.

Graf, Karl H. *Die geschichtlichen Bücher des Alten Testaments.* Leipzig: T. O. Weigel, 1866.

Gray, John. *I and II Kings.* OT Library 11/12. Philadelphia: Westminster, 1963.

Grdseloff, Bernhard. *Das ägyptische Reinigungszelt.* Cairo: Institut Français D'Archeologie Orientale, 1941.

Greenberg, Moshe. *Ezekiel 1-20.* AB 22. Garden City, NY: Doubleday, 1983.

————. *The Ḫab/piru.* AOS 39. New Haven: AOS, 1955.

Gressman, Hugo. *Altorientalische Texte und Bilder zum Alten Testament.* Vol. II. 2nd edition. Berlin, 1927.

————. *Mose und seine Zeit.* Göttingen: Vandenhoeck and Ruprecht, 1913.

Grimmelsman, Henry J. *The Book of Exodus.* Cincinnati: Seminary Book Store, 1927.

Grintz, Joshua M. "Ancient Terms in the Priestly Laws," *Leshonenu* 39 (1975): 5-20, 163-180 [Hebrew].

Gronke, Monika. "The Persian Court Between Palace and Tent: From Timur to 'Abbas I." *Timurid Art and Culture.* Lisa Golombek and Maria Subtelny, eds. (New York: Brill, 1992): 18-22.

Grunebaum, Gustave E. von. *Muhammadan Festivals.* New York, 1988.

Gubel, Eric. *Phoenician Furniture.* Leuven: Peeters Press, 1987.

Hackett, John. *Warfare in the Ancient World.* London: Sidgwick and Jackson, 1989.

Haenchen, Ernst. *The Acts of the Apostles.* Philadelphia: Westminster, 1971.

Halévy, Joseph. "Inscriptions sabéennes." *Journal Asiatique* 19 (1872): 129-266; 489-547.

Hallo, William W., ed. *The Context of Scripture.* Leiden: Brill, 1997.

Halpern, Baruch. *The First Historians.* University Park: Pennsylvania State University Press, 1996.

————. "Kenites." *ABD* IV (1992): 17-22.

————. *The Emergence of Israel in Canaan.* Chico, CA: Scholars Press, 1983.

————. "Sacred History and Ideology." *The Creation of Sacred Literature.* R. E. Friedman, ed. (Berkeley: University of California Press, 1981): 35-54.

Hamilton, Victor P. "Marriage (OT and ANE)." *ABD* IV (1992): 559-69.

Hammond, Mason. *The City in the Ancient World.* Cambridge, Mass.: Harvard University Press, 1972.

Hammond, Philip C. *The Nabataeans: Their History, Culture and Archaeology.* SMA 37. Gothenberg: Paul Aström Förlag, 1973.

Haran, Menahem. "Incense Altars—Are They?" *Proceedings of the 2nd International Congress on Biblical Archaeology,* June-July 1990 (Jerusalem: IES, 1993): 237-47.

————. "Temple and Community in Ancient Israel." *Temple in Society.* M. Fox, ed. (Winona Lake: Eisenbrauns, 1988): 17-26.

————. "Behind the Scenes of History: Determining the Date of the Priestly Source." *JBL* 100 (1981): 321-33.

————. *Temples and Temple-Service in Ancient Israel.* Oxford: Clarendon Press, 1978.

————. "The Priestly Image of the Tabernacle." *HUCA* 36 (1965): 191-226.

——. "Shiloh and Jerusalem: The Origin of the Priestly Tradition in the Pentateuch," *JBL* 81 (1962): 14-24.

——. "The Complex of Ritual Acts Performed Inside the Tabernacle." *Scripta Hierosolymitana*. Vol. 8. Chaim Rabin, ed. (Jerusalem: Magnes Press, 1961): 272-302.

——. "Otfe, Mahmal, and Kubbe—Notes on the Study of the Origins of Biblical Cult Forms: The Problem of Arabic Parallels." *D. Neiger Memorial Volume* (Jerusalem: Israel Society for Biblical Research, 1959): 215-21 (Hebrew).

Harden, Donald. *The Phoenicians*. London: Thames and Hudson, 1963.

Harmand, Jacques. *L'Armeée et le soldat à Rome de 107 à 50 avant nôtre ère*. Paris, 1967.

Hartmann, Richard. "Zelt und Lade." *ZAW* 37 (1918): 216-25.

Hasel, Michael G. *Domination and Resistance: Egyptian Military Activity in the Southern Levant ca. 1300-1185 B.C.* Leiden: E. J. Brill, 1998.

Hassan, Selim. *Excavations at Gîza IV*. Cairo: Government Press, 1943.

Hatton, Hap. *The Tent Book*. Boston: Houghton Mifflin Co., 1979.

Hatton, Howard. "The Projections on the Frames of the Tabernacle." *The Bible Translator* 42.2 (1991): 205-09.

Healey, John F. "Were the Nabataeans Arabs?" *Aram* 1:1 (1989): 38-44.

Hendel, Ronald S. *The Epic of the Patriarch*. HSM 42. Atlanta: Scholars Press, 1987.

Herr, Larry G. "The Iron Age at Tell el-ʿUmeiri." *Institute of Archaeology Newsletter* 15:1 (Philadelphia, 1995).

Herzog, Ze'ev. *Beer-Sheba* II. Tel Aviv: Tel Aviv University Press, 1984.

Hickmann, Hans. *La trompette dans l'Égypte ancienne*. Cairo: IIFAO, 1946.

Hill, George F. *Catalogue of the Greek Coins of Phoenicia*. Bologna: Arnaldo Forni, 1965.

Hillers, Delbert R. "MŠKNʾ 'Temple' in Inscriptions from Hatra." *BASOR* 206 (1972): 54-56.

Hoch, James E. *Semitic Words in Egyptian Texts of the New Kingdom and Third Intermediate Period*. Princeton: Princeton University Press, 1994.

Hoffmeier, James K. "The Structure of Joshua 1-11 and the Annals of Thutmose III." *Faith, Tradition, and History*. Alan R. Millard, James K. Hoffmeier, and David W. Baker, eds. (Winona Lake, IN: Eisenbrauns, 1994): 165-79.

——. "The Possible Origins of the Tent of Purification in the Egyptian Funerary Cult." *Studien zur altägyptischen Kultur* 9 (1981): 167-77.

——. "Tents in Egypt and the Ancient Near East." *SSEA Newsletter* vol. 7, no. 3 (May, 1977): 13-28.

Hoffner, Harry A., Jr. "The Elkunirsa Myth Reconsidered." *RHA* 76 (1965): 5-16.

——. *Hittite Myths*. Second Edition. Atlanta: Scholars Press, 1998.

Holder, Arthur G. "The Mosaic Tabernacle in Early Christian Exegesis." *Studia Patristica* 25 (1993): 101-06.

Holl, Augustin, and Thomas Levy. "From the Nile Valley to the Chad Basin: Ethnoarchaeology of Shuwa Arab Settlements," *BA* 56:4 (1993): 166-79.

Holladay, John S., Jr. "Four-Room House." *EANE* (Oxford: Oxford University Press, 1997): Vol. II, pp. 337-42.

Holzinger, Heinrich. *Exodus*. Leipzig: Mohr, 1900.

Homan, Michael M., Russell B. Adams, and Thomas E. Levy. "The Iron Age in the Jabal Hamrat Fidan (Jordan): A Preliminary Assessment of the 1997-

1999 Seasons." *Wadi Faynan Conference.* William Finlayson, ed. Forthcoming.

Homan, Michael M. "To Your Tents, O Egypt, Canaan and Israel: An Ancient Formula for Council Disbandment." *UF* 31 (2000): 237-40.

——. "Booths or Succoth? - A Response to Yigael Yadin." *JBL* 118 (1999): 691-97.

——. "A Tensile Etymology for Aaron: *'ahărōn > 'ahălōn.*" *BN* 95 (1998): 21-22.

——. "The Divine Warrior in His Tent: A Military Model for Yahweh's Tabernacle." *BR* 16.6 (2000): 22-33, 55.

Hopkins, David C. "Pastoralists in Late Bronze Age Palestine: Which Way Did They Go?" *BA* 56 (1993): 200-11.

Hösl, I. "Zur orientalischen Namenkunde: Maria - Moses - Aaron. Eine philologische Studie." *Serta Monacensia* (Leiden, 1952): 80-85.

Hurowitz, Victor (Avigdor). "The Form and Fate of the Tabernacle: Reflections on a Recent Proposal." *JQR* 86 (1995): 127-51.

——. "Temporary Temples." *Kinattūtu ša dārâti,* Raphael Kutscher Memorial Volume. (Tel Aviv: Tel Aviv University Press, 1993): 37-50.

——. *I Have Built You an Exalted House: Temple Building in the Bible in Light of Mesopotamian and North-west Semitic Writings.* JSOTSS 115. Sheffield: JSOT Press, 1992.

——. "The Priestly Account of Building the Tabernacle." *JAOS* 105 (1985): 21-30.

——. *Temple Building in the Bible in Light of Mesopotamian and North-West Semitic Writings.* Jerusalem, 1983 (Hebrew).

Hurvitz, Avi. *A Linguistic Study of the Relationship between the Priestly Source and the Book of Ezekiel.* CahRB 20. Paris: J. Gabalda et Companie, 1982.

——. "The Language of the Priestly Source and its Historical Setting: The Case for an Early Date." *PWCJS* 8 (1981): 83-94.

——. "The Use of *šēš* and *bûṣ* in the Bible and its Implications for the Date of P." *HTR* 60 (1967): 117-21.

Ingholt, Harald. "Inscriptions and Sculptures from Palmyra I." *Berytus* 3 (1936): 83-125.

Jacob, B. *The Second Book of the Bible: Exodus.* Trans. W. Jacob. German Original (unpublished) 1945. Hoboken: KTAV, 1992.

Jacobsen, Thorkild. *The Harps That Once. . .* New Haven: Yale University Press, 1983.

——. *The Treasures of Darkness.* New Haven: Yale University Press, 1976.

——. "Primitive Democracy in Mesopotamia." *JNES* 2 (1943): 159-72.

Jastrow, Marcus. *Talmud Dictionary* I. New York: Putnam, 1903.

——. *A Dictionary of the Targumim, the Talmud Babli and Yerushalmi, and the Midrashic Literature.* New York: Judaica Press, 1992.

Jaussen, Antonin Joseph. *Mission archéologique en Arabie* II. Paris: Geuthner, 1914.

Jequier, Gustave. *Le monument funéraire de Pepi II.* Cairo: IIFAO, 1938.

Juvaini, 'Ala-ad-Din 'Ata-Malik. *Genghis Khan: The History of the World Conqeror.* Seattle: University of Washington Press, 1958.

Keil, Carl F. *Genesis und Exodus.* Leipzig: Dörffling and Franke, 1878.

Kelso, James L. *The Excavations of Bethel.* AASOR 39. Cambridge: ASOR, 1968.

Kempinski, Aharon. "Some Observations on the Hyksos (XVth) Dynasty and its Canaanite Origins." *Pharaonic Egypt, the Bible and Christianity* (Jerusalem: Magnes Press, 1985): 129-38.

———. "Tel Masos," *Expedition* 20 (1978): 29-37.

Kennedy, Archibald R. S. "Tabernacle." *Dictionary of the Bible*. J. Hastings, ed. (1902): 653-668.

Khazanov, Anatoly M. *Nomads and the Outside World*. Trans. by Julia Crookenden. Cambridge: Cambridge University Press, 1984. Revised and Expanded, Madison, WI: University of Wisconsin Press, 1994.

———. "Pastoralists in the Contemporary World: The Problem of Survival." *Changing Nomads in a Changing World*. Jospeh Ginat and Anatoly M. Khazanov, eds. (Portland: Sussex Academic Press, 1998): 7-23

Kitchen, Kenneth A. "The Tabernacle-A Bronze Age Artefact." *Eretz-Israel* 24. A. Malamat Volume (Jerusalem: IES, 1993): 119-29.

———. "The Egyptian Evidence on Ancient Jordan." *Early Edom and Moab: The Beginning of the Iron Age in Southern Jordan*. Piotr Bienkowski, ed. SAM 7 (Sheffield: J. R. Collis Publications, 1992): 21-34.

———. "Two Notes on the Subsidiary Rooms of Solomon's Temple." *Eretz-Israel* 20. Yigael Yadin Volume (Jerusalem: IES, 1989): 107-12.

———. "Asiatic Wars of Ramses II" *JEA* 50 (1964): 66-67.

———. "The Desert Tabernacle" *BR* 16.6 (2000): 14-21.

Klein, F. A. 'Mitteilungen über Leben, Sitten und Gebräuche der Fellachen in Palästina." *ZDPV* 6 (1883): 81-101.

Klein, Lillian R. "A Spectrum of Female Characters in the Book of Judges." *A Feminist Companion to Judges*. Athalya Brenner, ed. (Sheffield: JSOT Press, 1993): 24-33.

Klein, Ralph W. "Back to the Future: The Tabernacle in the Book of Exodus." *Interpretation* 50 (1996): 264-76.

Knauf-Belleri, Ernst A. "Edom: The Social and Economic History." *You Shall Not Abhor an Edomite for He is Your Brother*. Diana Vikander Edelman, ed. (Atlanta: Scholars Press, 1995): 93-117.

Knobel, August. *Die Bücher Exodus und Leviticus*. Leipzig: Hirzel, 1857.

Koester, Craig R. *The Dwelling of God: The Tabernacle in the Old Testament, Intertestimental Jewish Literature, and the New Testament*. CBQMS 22. Washington, DC: CBA, 1989.

Kraeling, Carl H. *The Synagogue*. Hoboken: KTAV Publishing, 1979.

Kramer, Samuel N. *Sumerian Mythology*. Philadelphia: University of Pennsylvania Press, 1972.

Krauss, Samuel. "Der richtige Sinn von 'Schrecken in der Nacht.'" *Occident and Orient*, Moses Gaster 80th Anniversary Volume (London: Taylor's Foreign Press, 1936): 323-30.

Kuentz, Charles. *Le bataille de Qedech*. Cairo: IIFAO, 1928.

Kupper, Jean-Robert. *Les nomades en Mésopotamie au temps des rois de Mari*. Paris: University of Liège, 1957.

Kuschke, Arnulf. "Der Tempel Salomons und der 'syrische Tempeltypus.'" *Das Ferne und Nahe Wort*, Fs. Rost. ZAW 105 (1967): 124-32.

Lacau, Pierre. "L'érection du mât devant Amon-Min." *Chronique D'Égypte* 55 (1953): 13-22.

Lambdin, Thomas O. "Egyptian Loan Words in the Old Testament." *JAOS* 73 (1953): 145-55.

Lammens, Henri. "Le culte des bétyles et les processions religieuses chez les arabes préislamites." *Bulletin de l'Institut français d'archéologie orientale* 17 (1919); Reprinted in *L'Arabie occidentale avant l'Hégire* (Beirut: Imprimerie Catholique, 1928): 101-79.

Lancaster, William. *The Rwala Bedouin Today.* 2nd edition. Prospect Heights, IL: Waveland Press, 1997.

Lane, Edward W. *Arabic-English Lexicon.* New York: Frederick Ugar Publishing, 1863.

———. *The Manners and Customs of the Modern Egyptians* II. London: Charles Knight, 1842.

Langlamet, François. "Absalom et les concubines de son père." *RB* 84 (1977): 161- 209.

Lawrence, Thomas E. *The Seven Pillars of Wisdom.* Garden City, NY: Doubleday, 1926.

Laubin, Reginald, and Gladys Laubin. *The Indian Tipi: Its History, Construction and Use.* 2nd Edition. Norman: University of Oklahoma Press, 1977.

Lederman, Zvi. "Nomads they Never Were: A Reevaluation of Izbet Sarta'." *Abstracts, AAR/SBL* (1990): 238.

Lemche, Niels P. "Israel, History of (Archaeology and the 'Conquest')." *ABD* III (1992): 539-45.

———. *Early Israel.* Leiden: E. J. Brill, 1985.

Levy, Reuben. *The Social Structure of Islam.* Cambridge: Cambridge University Press, 1957.

Levy, Thomas E., and Augustin F. C. Holl. "Israelite Settlement Processes: Archaeological and Ethnoarchaeological Perspectives." *World Archaeology Congress.* New Delhi, 1994. Publication forthcoming.

Levy, Thomas E., Russell B. Adams, and Rula Shafiq. "The Jabal Hamrat Fidan Project: Excavations at the Wadi Fidan 40 Cemetery, Jordan (1997)." *Levant* 31 (1999): 293-308.

Levy, Thomas E., Russell B. Adams, et al. "Early Metallurgy, Interaction and Social Change: The Jabal Hamrat Fidan (Jordan) Research Design and 1998 Archaeological Survey: Preliminary Report." *Studies in the History and Archaeology of Jordan VII.* G. Biseh, ed. (in press).

Lewis, Norman N. *Nomads and Settlers in Syria and Jordan, 1800-1980.* Cambridge, Cambridge University Press, 1987.

L'Heureux, Conrad E. *Rank Among the Canaanite Gods: El, Ba'al and the Rephaim,* HSM 21. Missoula: Scholars Press, 1979.

Lichtheim, Miriam. "The Report of Wenamun." *The Context of Scripture.* W. H. Hallo, ed. (Leiden: E. J. Brill, 1997): 90-91.

———. *Ancient Egyptian Literature* II. Berkeley: University of California Press, 1976.

Lie, Arthur G. *The Inscriptions of Sargon II.* Paris: Geuthner, 1929.

Lind, Millard C. *Yahweh is a Warrior.* Scottsdale, PA: Herald Press, 1980.

Lipiński, Edward. "The 'Phoenician History' of Philo of Byblos." *Bibliotheca Orientalis* 40 (1983): 306-08.

———. "El's Abode." *OLP* 2 (1971): 13-69.

Livingstone, Alasdair. *Mystical and Mythological Explanatory Works of Assyrian and Babylonian Scholars.* Oxford: Clarendon Press, 1986.

Loffreda, Stanislao. "Capernaum." *NEAEHL* Vol. 1: 291-95.

Lucas, Alfred. *Ancient Egyptian Materials and Industries.* Fourth Edition. Revised and Enlarged by J. R. Harris. London: Edward Arnold, 1962.

Mace, David R. *Hebrew Marriage*. London: Epworth Press, 1953.

Maier, Johann. *The Temple Scroll*. JSOTSS 34. Sheffield: University of Sheffield, 1985.

———. "The Architectural History of the Temple in Jerusalem in the Light of the Temple Scroll." *Temple Scroll Studies*. G. J. Brooke, ed. JSPSS 7. Sheffield: Sheffield Academic Press, 1989.

Malamat, Abraham. "Organs of Statecraft in the Israelite Monarchy," *BA* 28 (1965): 34-65.

Manor, Dale W. "Massebah." *ABD* IV (1992): 602.

Marx, Emanuel. *Bedouin of the Negev*. New York: Praeger, 1967.

Mas'udi. *The Meadows of Gold: The Abassids*. Trans. and Ed. by Paul Lunde and Caroline Stone. London: Kegan Paul Int., 1989.

Matthews, Victor H. *Pastoral Nomadism in the Mari Kingdom*. Cambridge, MA: ASOR, 1978.

Matthiae, Paolo. "Some Notes About Solomon's Palace and Ramesside Architectural Culture." *L'impero ramesside*. Vicino Oriente 1. S. Donadoni, ed. (Rome: Università degli studi di Roma, 1997): 117-30.

May, Herbert G. "The Ark - A Miniature Temple." *AJSL* 52 (1936): 215-34.

Mazar, Amihai. *Archaeology of the Land of the Bible*. New York: Doubleday, 1990.

McCarter, P. Kyle, Jr. *1 Samuel*, AB 8. Garden City, NY: Doubleday, 1980.

———. *II Samuel*. AB 9. Garden City, NY: Doubleday, 1984.

McEwan, Calvin W. "The Syrian Expedition of the Oriental Institute of the University of Chicago." *AJA* 41 (1937): 8-16.

McKenzie, John L. *Second Isaiah*. AB 20. Garden City, NY: Doubleday, 1968.

Meek, Harold A. *The Synagogue*. London: Phaidon, 1995.

Meissner, Bruno. "Ein altbabylonisches Fragment des Gilgamosepos." *MVAG* (Berlin, 1902): 1-16.

Mendenhall, George E. "The Amorite Migrations." *Mari in Retrospect*. Gordon D. Young, ed. (Winona Lake, IN: Eisenbrauns, 1992): 233-41.

———. *The Tenth Generation*. Baltimore: Johns Hopkins University Press, 1973.

———. "The Hebrew Conquest of Palestine," *BA* 25 (1962): 66-87.

———. "Amorites." *ABD* I (1992): 199-202

Meyer, Eduard. *Die Israeliten und ihre Nachbarstämme*. Halle: Max Niemeyer, 1906.

Meyers, Carol L. "Lampstand." *ABD* IV (1992): 141-43.

———. *The Tabernacle Menorah*. ASOR Dissertation Series 2. Missoula, Montana: Scholars Press, 1976.

Michaelis, Wilhelm. "σκηνη; σκηνοποιος" *Theological Dictionary of the New Testament* 7 (Grand Rapids, MI: Eerdmans, 1997): 368-94.

Milgrom, Jacob. "Priestly ('P') Source." *ABD* V (1992): 454-61.

———. *Numbers*. JPS Torah Commentary. Philadelphia: JPS, 1990.

———. "The Shared Custody of the Tabernacle and a Hittite Analolgy." *JAOS* 90 (1970): 204-09.

Millard, Alan R. "Mesopotamia and the Bible." *Aram* 1:1 (1989): 24-30.

———. "La prophétie et l'écriture: Israel, Aram, Assyrie." *Revue de l'histoire des religions* 202 (1985): 125-45.

Miller, Patrick D., Jr. "El the Warrior." *HTR* 60 (1967): 411-31.

———. *The Divine Warrior in Early Israel*. HSM 5. Cambridge, MA: Harvard University Press, 1973.

Milton, Joyce. *Sunrise of Power: Ancient Egypt, Alexander and the World of Hellenism*. Boston: Boston Publishing Co., 1986.

Moens, Marie-Francine. "The Procession of the God Min to the *ḥtjw*-Garden." *Studien zur altägyptischen Kultur* 12 (1985): 61-73.

Möhlenbrink, Kurt. *Der Tempel Salomos*. Stuttgart: W. Kohlhammer, 1932.

Moon, Cyris H. *A Political History of Edom*. Emory University Dissertation. (1971).

Moorehead, W. G. *The Tabernacle*. Grand Rapids: Kregel, 1957.

Morgenstern, Julian. "The Ark, the Ephod, and the Tent of Meeting." *HUCA 17* (1942): 153-266; *HUCA* 18 (1943): 1-52.

———. "The Book of the Covenant." *HUCA* 5 (1928): 1-151.

———. "The Tent of Meeting." *AOS Journal* (1918): 125-39.

Moritz, Bernhard. "Edomitische Genealogien." *ZAW* 44 (1926): 81-93.

Mullen, E. Theodore, Jr. *The Assembly of the Gods: The Divine Council in Canaanite and Early Hebrew Literature*. HSM 24. Missoula: Scholars Press, 1980.

Munro, Irmtraut. *Das Zelt-Heiligtum des Min*. Münchner Ägyptologische Studien 41. Munich: Deutscher Kuntstverlag, 1983.

Musil, Alois. *The Manners and Customs of the Rwala Bedouins*. New York: AGS, 1928.

Myers, Jacob M. "Linen; Linen Garment." *IDB*. III (1962): 134-35.

Naʾaman, Nadav. "Habiru and Hebrews: The Transfer of a Social Term to the Literary Sphere." *JNES* 45 (1986): 271-88.

Naveh, Joseph. "Phoenician Ostraca from Tel Dor." *Solving Riddles and Untying Knots*. Fs. J. C. Greenfield. Z. Zevit, S. Gitin, and M. Sokoloff, eds. (Winona Lake: Eisenbrauns, 1995): 459-64.

Negev, Avraham. *Nabatean Archaeology Today*. New York: New York University Press, 1986.

Nelson, Russell D. *Studies in the Development of the Text of the Tabernacle Account*. Harvard University Dissertation. Cambridge, MA: Harvard University Press, 1986.

Netzer, Ehud. "Domestic Architecture in the Iron Age." *The Architecture of Ancient Israel*. Aharon Kempinski and Ronny Reich, eds. (Jerusalem: IES, 1992): 193-201.

Neumann, Wilhelm. *Die Stiftshütte in Bild und Wort*. Gotha: Friedrich Andreas Perthes, 1861.

Newberry, Percy E. *Beni Hasan* I. London: Egypt Exploration Fund, 1893.

Noth, Martin. *Könige*. Neukirchen: Neukirchener Verlag, 1968.

———. *Exodus*. OTL. Philadelphia: Westminster Press, 1962.

———. *The History of Israel*. Translated by S. Godman. New York: Harper, 1958.

———. *Die israelitischen Personennamen*. Stuttgart: Kohlhammer, 1928.

Oden, Robert A., Jr., and Harold W. Attridge. *Philo of Byblos: The Phoenician History*, CBQMS 9. Washington, DC: Catholic Biblical Association of America, 1981.

———. *Studies in Lucian's De Syria Dea*. Missoula, Montana: Scholars Press, 1977.

O'Kane, Bernard. "From Tents to Pavilions: Royal Mobility and Persian Palace Design." *Ars Orientalis* 23 (1993): 249-68.

Otten, Heinrich. "Ein kanaanäischer Mythus aus Boğazköy." *Mitteilungen des Instituts für Orientforschung* 1 (1953): 125-50.

Ottosson, Magnus. "The Iron Age of Northern Jordan." *History and Traditions of Early Israel*. Studies Presented to E. Nielsen. VTS 50. André Lemaire, ed. (Leiden: E. J. Brill, 1993): 90-103.

Paran, Meir. *Literary Features of the Priestly Code: Stylistic Patterns, Idioms and Structures*. Hebrew University Dissertation (1983).

Parrot, André. *Le temple de Jérusalem*. Neuchâtel: Delachaux and Niestlé, 1954.

——. *Le "refrigerium" dans l'au-delà*. Paris: Geuthner, 1937.

Patai, Raphael. *Sex and Family in the Bible and the Middle East*. Garden City, NY: Dolphin, 1959).

Patrich, Joseph. "The Enigma of Qumran: Four Archaeologists Assess the Site." *BAR* 24:1 (Jan/Feb 1998): 25-37, 78-84.

——. "Was There An External Residence Area at Qumran?" *Qadmoniot* 114 (1997): 129-33.

Piankoff, Alexandre. *The Shrines of Tut-Ankh-Amon*. Bollingen Series 40.2. New York: Pantheon Books, 1955.

Piggott, Stuart. *Wagon, Chariot, and Carriage*. New York: Thames and Hudson, 1992.

Polotzky, Hans J. "The Battles of Megiddo and Kadesh." *The Military History of the Land of Israel in Biblical Times*. Jacob Liver, ed. (Israel Defense Forces Publishing, 1973): 17-26 (Hebrew).

Pope, Marvin H. "The Status of El at Ugarit." *UF* 19 (1987): 219-230.

——. *Song of Songs*. AB 7C. Garden City, NY: Doubleday, 1977.

——. "The Scene on the Drinking Mug from Ugarit." *Near Eastern Studies in Honor of W. F. Albright*. Hans Goedicke, ed. (Baltimore: Johns Hopkins University Press, 1971): 393-405.

——. *Job*. AB 15. Garden City, NY: Doubleday, 1965. Second (third) enlarged and revised edition, 1973.

——. *El in the Ugaritic Texts*. VTS 2. Leiden: Brill, 1955.

Postgate, J. Nicholas. "Nomads and Sedentaries in the Middle Assyrian Sources." *Nomads and Sedentary Peoples*. J. S. Castillo, ed. (Mexico: D. F. Colegio de México, 1981).

Price, Martin J., and Bluma L. Trell. *Coins and Their Cities*. London: V. C. Vecchi and Sons, 1977.

Pritchard, James B. *Ancient Near Eastern Texts Relating to the Old Testament*. Princeton: Princeton University Press, 1969.

——. *The ancient Near East in Pictures Relating to the Old Testament*. Princeton: Princeton University Press, 1969.

Propp, William H. C. *Exodus 1-18*. AB 2A. New York: Doubleday, 1999.

——. "On Hebrew śāde(h), 'Highland.'" *VT* 37 (1987): 230-36.

Quibell, James E. *The Ramesseum*. London: Bernard Quaritch, 1898.

Rabe, Virgil W. "The Identity of the Priestly Tabernacle." *JNES* 25 (1966): 132-34.

Rabin, Chaim. "The Song of Songs and Tamil Poetry." *Studies in Religion* 3 (1973): 205-19.

Raswan, Carl R. *The Black Tents of Arabia*. Boston: Little, Brown, and Co., 1935.

Reeves, Nicholas. *The Complete Tutankhamun*. London: Thames and Hudson, 1990.

Reisner, George A. *A History of the Giza Necropolis II: The Tomb of Hetep-Heres*. Completed and Revised by William S. Smith. Cambridge: Harvard University Press, 1955.

Renan, M. Ernest. "Mémoire sur l'origine et le caractère véritable de l'Histoire phénicienne qui porte le nom Sanchoniathon." *Mémoires de L'institut Impérial de France* 23 (1858): 241-334.

Rendsburg, Gary A. "Late Biblical Hebrew and the Date of P." *JANES* 12 (1980): 65-80.

Ridges, William Brryman. "On the Structure of the Tabernacle." *PEF* (1896): 189.

Riemann, Paul A. *Desert and Return to Desert in the Pre-Exilic Prophets.* Harvard University Dissertation. 1964.

Risch, Erna. "United States Army in WWII: The Technical Services." *The Quartermaster Corps: Organization, Supply, and Services.* Vol. I. Washington: Office of the Chief of Military History, 1953.

Roaf, Michael. *Cultural Atlas of Mesopotamia.* New York: Facts on File, 1990.

Rogers, Robert W. "Letter of March 31, 1883." *Academy* (1883): 221 ff.

Ronzevalle, Sébastien. "Le Prétendu 'Char d'Astarté.'" *Mélanges de l'Université S. Joseph* 16 (1932): 51-63.

Rosen, Steven A. "Nomads in Archaeology: A Response to Finkelstein and Perevolotsky." *BASOR* 287 (1992): 75-85.

Rosenberg, Stephen. "The Tabernacle Archetype." *Journal of the Visual Arts* vol. 3, no. 4 (Winter 1960-61): 22-25.

Rothenerg, Beno. "מקדש הכורים בבקעת תמנע." ישראל-עם וארץ 19 (Tel-Aviv, 1983-84): 85-122.

———. *Timna.* London: Thames and Hudson, 1972.

———. "Les mines du roi Salomon." *Bible et Terre Sainte* 25 (Jan 1960): 4-10.

Rothenberg, Beno, and Jonathan T. Glass. "The Midianite Pottery." *Midian, Moab, and Edom.* JSOTSS 24. Eds John Sawyer and David Clines (Sheffield: JSOT, 1983): 65-124.

Rowton, Michael B. "Economic and Political Factors in Ancient Nomadism." *Nomads and Sedentary Peoples.* J. S. Castillo, ed. (Mexico: D. F. Colegio de México, 1981): 25-36.

———. "Enclosed Nomadism." *JESHO* 17 (1974): 1-30.

Rubenstein, Jeffrey L. *The History of Sukkot in the Second Temple and Rabbinic Periods.* Atlanta: Scholars Press, 1995.

Russell, John M. *Sennacherib's Palace Without Rival at Nineveh.* Chicago: Chicago University Press, 1991.

Russell, Kenneth W. *Ecology and Energetics of Early Food Production in the Near East and North Africa.* University of Utah Dissertation (1986).

Rycaut, Paul. *The History of the Turkish Empire From the Year 1623 to the Year 1677.* London: Basset, Clavell, Robinson, and Churchill, 1687.

Ryckmans, Gonzaque. *Les Noms propres sud-sémitiques I: Répertoire analytique.* Bibliothèque du Muséon 2. Louvain: Bureaux du Muséon, 1934.

Said, Edward W. *Orientalism.* New York: Vintage, 1979.

Sameh, Waley-el-dine. *Daily Life in Ancient Egypt.* New York: McGraw-Hill, 1964.

Sarna, Nahum M. *Exodus.* JPS Commentary. New York: JPS, 1991.

———. *Exploring Exodus.* New York: Schocken, 1986.

Saulcy, Félix de. *Numismatique de la Terre Sainte.* Paris: Rothschild, 1874.

Säve-Söderbergh, Torgny. *Private Tombs at Thebes I: Four Eighteenth Dynasty Tombs.* Oxford: Oxford University Press, 1957.

Sawaya, Z. "Cronos, Astarté: deux légendes phéniciennes inédites sur des monnaies de Byblos." *Bulletin de la Société Française de Numismatique* 53 (Mai, 1998): 93-99.

Schäfer, Heinrich. "Lederbespannung eines Holzkästchens," *ZÄS* 31 (1893): 105-07.

Scharr, Kenneth W. "The Architectural Traditions of Building 23A/13 at Tell Beit Mirsim." *Scandinavian Journal of the Old Testament* 2 (1991): 75-98.

Schick, Conrad. "Some Remarks on the Tabernacle Controversy." *PEF* (1898): 241-44.

———. *Die Stiftshütte, der Tempel in Jerusalem und der Tempelplatz der Jetztzeit.* Berlin: Weidmann, 1896.

Schmitz, Philip C. "Phoenician Religion." *ABD* V (1992): 357-63.

Schneider, Thomas. *Asiatische Personennamen in ägyptischen Quellen des Neuen Reiches,* Orbis Biblicus et Orientalis 114. Freiburg: Universitätsverlag Freiburg, 1992.

Schroeder, Christoph. "'A Love Song: Psalm 45 in the Light of Ancient Near Eastern Marriage Texts." *CBQ* 58 (1996): 417-32.

Schulman, Alan R. "*Mhr* and *Mškb,* Two Egyptian Military Titles of Semitic Origins." *Zeitschrift für ägyptische Sprache und Altertumskunde* 92 (1966): 123-32.

Schult, Hermann. "Der Debir im salomonischen Tempel." *ZDPV* 80 (1964): 46-54.

Scott, Alexander. "Notes on Objects from the Tomb of Tut-Ankh-Amen." *The Tomb of Tut-Ankh-Amen.* Volume 2. Howard Carter, ed. (New York: Cassell, 1927): 197-213.

Segert, Stanislav. "Preliminary Notes on the Structure of the Aramaic Poems in the Papyrus Amherst 63." *UF* 18 (1986): 271-99.

Seligman, Brenda Z. "Sacred Litters Among the Semites." *Sudan Notes and Records* I:4 (1918): 269.

Selms, Adrianus van. *Marriage and Family Life in Ugaritic Literature.* London: Luzac and Co., 1954.

Seyrig, Henri. "Antiquités Syriennes: Divinités de Sidon." *Syria* 36 (1959): 48-56.

Seyrig, Henri, Robert Amy, and Ernest Will. *Le temple de Bêl à Palmyre.* Paris: Geuthner, 1968-1975.

Sheffer, Avigail, and Amalia Tidhar. "Textiles and Textile Impressions on Pottery." *The Egyptian Mining Temple at Timna.* B. Rothenberg, ed. (London: Institute for Archaeo-Metallurgical Studies, 1988): 224-32.

Shiloh, Yigal. "A Group of Hebrew Bullae from the City of David." *IEJ* 36 (1986): 16-38.

———. "The Four-Room House, Its Situation and Function in the Israelite City." *IEJ* 20 (1970): 180-90.

Shmueli, Avshalom. *Nomadism About to Cease.* Tel Aviv: Reshafim, 1980 (Hebrew).

Shryock, Andrew J. "Popular Genealogical Nationalism: History Writing and Identity Among the Balqa Tribes of Jordan." *Comparative Studies in Society and History* 37:2 (April, 1995): 325-57.

Silva, Jorge L. da. *The Implications of the Arad Temple for the Question of Dating P.* Ann Arbor: U.M.I., 1992.

Smith, J. Payne. *A Compendious Syriac Dictionary.* Oxford: Clarendon Press, 1903.

Smith, Mark S. *The Early History of God.* San Francisco: Harper, 1990.

——— . "Mt. *ll* in *KTU* 1.2.I.19-20." *UF* 18 (1986): 458.

Smith, Robert H. "Arabia." *ABD* I (1992): 324-27.

Smith, W. Robertson. *Kinship and Marriage in Early Arabia.* London: A. and C. Black, 1903.

Soden, Wolfram von. *Akkadisches Handwörterbuch.* 3 Vols. Wiesbaden: O. Harrassowitz, 1965-1981.

Sokoloff, Michael. *A Dictionary of Jewish Palestinian Aramaic of the Byzantine Period.* Jerusalem: Bar Ilan University Press, 1990.

Spalinger, Anthony J. "Some Notes on the Battle of Megiddo and Reflections on Egyptian Military Writing." *MDAIK* 30 (1974): 221-29.

Speiser, Ephraim A. "Preliminary Excavations at Tepe Gawra." *AASOR* 9 (1927-1928): 17-94.

Spencer, John R. "Aaron." *ABD* I (1992): 1-6.

——— . "Hophni." *ABD* III (1992): 285-86.

——— . "Phinehas." *ABD* V (1992): 346-47.

Spina, Frank A. "Israelites as *gērîm.*" *The Word of the Lord Shall Go Forth.* Fs. D. N. Freedman. Winona Lake, IN: Eisenbrauns, 1983.

Stager, Lawrence E. "Archaeology, Ecology, and Social History: Background Themes to the Song of Deborah." *VTSup* 49 (1987): 221-34.

——— ."The Song of Deborah," *BAR* 15 (1989): 50-64.

——— . "Merneptah, Israel and Sea Peoples: New Light on an Old Relief." *EI* 18 (1985): 56-64.

——— ."The Archaeology of the Family in Ancient Israel." *BASOR* 260 (1985): 1-35.

Starcky, Jean, and Michel Gawlikowski. *Palmyre.* Paris: Librairie d'Amérique et d'Orient, 1985.

Steckoll, Solomon H. "Preliminary Excavation Report on the Qumran Cemetery." *Revue de Qumran* 6 (1968): 323-44.

Steiner, Richard C. "An Aramaic Text in Demotic Script." *The Context of Scripture.* W. H. Hallo, ed. (Leiden: E. J. Brill, 1997): 309-27.

Stierlin, Henri, and Christiane Ziegler. *Tanis.* Paris: Éditions du Seuil, 1987.

Stillman, Nigel, and Nigel Tallis. *Armies of the Ancient Near East.* Sussex: Wargames Research Group, 1984.

Stockton, Eugene D. "Phoenician Cult Stones." *Australian Journal of Biblical Archaeology* 2 (1974-1975): 1-27.

Stone, Ken. "Sexual Practice and the Structure of Prestige: The Case of the Disputed Concubines." *SBL Seminar Papers.* E. H. Lovering, Jr., ed. (Atlanta: Scholars Press, 1993): 554-73.

Strong, James. *The Tabernacle of Israel in the Desert.* Providence, RI: Harris, Jones, 1888. Revised Edition. Grand Rapids, 1987.

Stuart, H. Villiers. *The Funeral Tent of an Egyptian Queen.* London: John Murray, 1882.

Sukenik, Eleazar L. "Did the Synagogue of Capernaum Have a Fixed Torah-Shrine?" *Kedem* II (1945): 121-22 (Hebrew).

——— . *Ancient Synagogues in Palestine and Greece.* London: Oxford University Press, 1934.

Svarth, Dan. *Egyptisk Møbelkunst fra Faraotiden.* Denmark: Skippershoved, 1998.

Talmon, Shemaryahu. "The 'Desert Motif' in the Bible and in Qumran Literature." *Biblical Motifs*. Alexander Altmann, ed. (Cambridge, MA: Harvard University Press, 1966): 31-63.

Thompson, Thomas L. *The Historicity of the Patriarchal Narratives: The Quest for the Historical Abraham*. BZAW 133. Berlin: Walter de Gruyter, 1974.

Thubron, Colin. *The Ancient Mariners*. Alexandria, Virginia: Time-Life Books, 1981.

Tournefort, Joseph P. *A Voyage into the Levant*. 2 Vols. London: D. Browne, 1718.

Travlos, John. *Pictorial Dictionary of Ancient Athens*. New York: Hacker Art, 1980.

Trever, John C. "Aloes." *IDB* I (NY: Abingdon, 1962): 88.

Trumbull, H. Clay. *The Threshold Covenant*. New York: Charles Scribner's Sons, 1896.

Tufnell, Olga. *Lachish III: The Iron Age*. Oxford: Oxford University Press, 1953.

Ussishkin, David. *The Conquest of Lachish by Sennacherib*. Tel Aviv: Tel Aviv University Publications, 1982.

———. "The 'Camp of the Assyrians' in Jerusalem." *IEJ* 29 (1979): 137-42.

———. "Solomon and the Tayinat Temples." *IEJ* 16 (1966): 104-10.

Van Seters, John. *Abraham in History and Tradition*. New Haven: Yale University Press, 1975.

Vaux, Roland de. *Ancient Israel*. Translated by John McHugh. New York: McGraw- Hill, 1961.

Virolleaud, Charles. *La déesse 'Anat*. Paris: Geuthner, 1938.

Wainright. G. A. "Some Celestial Associations of Min." *JEA* 21 (1935): 152-70.

Wapnish, Paula. "Towards Establishing a Conceptual Basis for Animal Categories in Archaeology." *Methods in the Mediterranean*. David B. Small, ed. (New York: E. J. Brill, 1995): 233-73.

Ward, William A. "Shasu." *ABD* V (1992): 1165-67.

———. "Some Personal Names of the Hyksos Period Rulers and Notes on the Epigraphy of Their Scarabs." *UF* 8 (1975): 353-65.

Weinfeld, Moshe. "Social and Cultic Institutions in the Priestly Source Against Their Ancient Near Eastern Background." *Proceedings of the Eighth World Congress of Jewish Studies* (Jerusalem: World Union of Jewish Studies, 1983): Vol. V, pp. 95-129.

———. "Divine Intervention in War in Ancient Israel and the Ancient Near East." *History, Historiography, and Interpretation*. H. Tadmor and M. Weinfeld, eds. (Jerusalem: Magnes Press, 1983): 131-36.

Weippert, Helga. "Review of *Temples and High Places in Biblical Times* and *The Exile and Biblical Narrative*." *ZDPV* 199 (1984): 181-84.

Weippert, Manfred. Semitische Nomaden des zweiten Jahrtausends. Über die Šȝsw ägyptischen Quellen." *Biblica* 55 (1974): 265-80, 427-33.

———. *The Settlement of the Israelite Tribes in Palestine*. London: SCM Press, 1971.

———. "Erwägungen zur Etymologie des Gottesnames ʾĒl Šaddaj." *ZDMG* 111 (1961): 42-62.

Weir, Shelagh, and Widad Kawar. "Costumes and Wedding Customs in Bayt Dajan." *PEQ* 107 (1975): 39-51.

Weiss, Harvey, ed. *Ebla to Damascus: Art and Archaeology of Ancient Syria*. Washington, D.C.: Smithsonian Institution, 1985.

Wellhausen, Julius. *Prolegomena zur Geschichte Israels* 6th Edition. Berlin: Georg Reimer, 1905.
——. *Reste arabischen Heidentums*. 2nd Edition. Berlin: Reimer, 1897.
Wensinck, Arent J. "Kaʿba." *Encyclopaedia of Islam* (Leiden: E. J. Brill, 1927): Vol. II, pp. 584-92.
——. "Kaʿba." Revised by Jacques Jomier. *Encyclopaedia of Islam*. New Edition IV. (Leiden: E. J. Brill, 1978): 317-22.
Wente, Edward F. *Letters from Ancient Egypt*. Atlanta: Scholars Press, 1990.
Werker, Ella. "Wood." *The Egyptian Mining Temple at Timna*. B. Rothenberg, ed. (London: Institute for Archaeo-Metallurgical Studies, 1988): 232-35.
Westermann, Claus. *Isaiah 40-66*. Translated from German by David M. G. Stalker. Philadelphia: Westminster, 1969.
Westermarck, Edward. *Ritual and Belief in Morocco*. 2 Vols. New Hyde Park, NY: University Books, 1968.
Wetzstein, D. J. *Die poetischen Bücher des Alten Testaments*. Revision of F. Delitzsch original. Leipzig, 1875.
Wetzstein, Johann G. In Adolf Bastian, ed. *Zeitschrift für Ethnologie* (1873): 290 ff.
Wickens, Gerald E. "A Study of Acacia Albida." *Kew Bulletin 23* (1969): 197.
Williams, N. "The Master of the Royal Tents and His Records." *Journal of the Society of Archivists* 2 (October, 1960): 2-4.
Williams, Ronald J. "A People Come Out of Egypt." *VTSup* 28 (1975): 234-39.
Williamson, Hugh G. M. *1 and 2 Chronicles*. Grand Rapids: Eerdmans, 1982.
Wilson, John A. "The Assembly of the Phoenician City." *JNES* 4 (1945): 245.
Winckler, Hugo. *Die Keilschrifttexte Sargons*. Leipzig: Eduard Pfeiffer, 1889.
Winlock, Herbert E. *Models of Daily Life in Ancient Egypt*. Cambridge, MA: Harvard University Press, 1955.
Winter, Irene. "Ivory Carving." *Ebla to Damascus*. Harvey Weiss, ed. Washington, D.C.: Smithsonian Institution, 1985.
Wiseman, Donald J. "They Lived in Tents." *Biblical and Near Eastern Studies*. Fs. W. S. LaSor (Grand Rapids, MI: Eerdmans, 1978): 195-200.
Wreszinski, Walter. *Atlas zur altägyptischen Kulturgeschichte*. 3 Vols. Leipzig: Hinrichs, 1923.
Wright, G. Ernest. "The Stevens Reconstruction of the Solomonic Temple." *BA* 18 (1955): 41-44.
Wright, Theodore F. "The Boards of the Tabernacle." *PEF* (1899): 70.
——. "The Tabernacle Roof." *PEF* (1897): 225-26.
Wroth, Warwick. *Catalogue of the Greek Coins of Galatia, Cappadocia, and Syria*. Bologna: A. Forni, 1889. Reprinted 1964.
Yadin, Yigael. *The Temple Scroll: The Hidden Law of the Dead Sea Sect*. London: Weidenfeld and Nicolson, 1985.
——. *Masada*. London: Weidenfeld and Nicolson, 1966.
——. *The Art of Warfare in Biblical Lands*. NY: McGraw Hill, 1963.
——. "The Fourth Season of Excavations at Hazor." *BA* 22 (1959): 2-20.
——. "Some Aspects of the Strategy of Ahab and David." *Bib* 36 (1955): 332-51.
Yeivin, Shmuel. *American Academy for Jewish Research Proceedings* 34 (1966): 152 ff.
Yon, Marguerite. "Ugarit: History and Archaeology." *ABD* VI (1992): 695-706.
Youssef, Ahmed A. "Notes on the Purification Tent." *ASAE* 64 (1981): 155-57.

Youssef, Ahmed A., C. LeBlanc, and M. Maher. *Le Ramesseum* IV. Cairo: Centre d'Etude et du Documentation sur l'ancienne Egypte, 1977.

Zaccagnini, Carlo. "On Late Bronze Age Marriages." *Studi in Onore di Edda Bresciani*. S. F. Bondì, S. Pernigotti, F. Serra, and A. Vivian, eds. (Pisa: Giardini,1985): 593-605.

Zarins, Juris. "Pastoral Nomadism in Arabia." *Pastoralism in the Levant*. O. Bar-Yosef and A. Khazanov, eds. (Madison: Prehistory Press, 1992): 219-40.

Zevit, Ziony. "Timber for the Tabernacle: Text, Tradition, and Realia." *Eretz-Israel* 23 (1992): 136-143*.

———. "Converging Lines of Evidence Bearing on the Date of P." *ZAW* 94 (1982): 502-09.

Zobel, Hans-Jürgen. "אֲרוֹן" *TDOT* (Grand Rapids: Eerdmans, 1974): Vol. 1, pp. 363-74.

Zohar, Mattanyahu, "Pastoralism and the Spread of Semitic Languages." *Pastoralism in the Levant*. O. Bar-Yosef and A. Khazanov, eds. (Madison: Prehistory Press, 1992): 165-80.

Zohary, Michael. *Plants of the Bible*. Cambridge: Cambridge University Press, 1982.

———. *Flora Palaestina*. Part 2: Text. Jerusalem: IASH, 1972.

Zwickel, Wolfgang. "Die Kesselwagen im salomonischen Tempel." *UF* 18 (1986): 459-61.

# TEXTUAL CITATION INDEX

# SUBJECT INDEX

# CULTURE AND HISTORY
# OF THE ANCIENT NEAR EAST

ISSN 1566-2055

Plate 1a: Succoth Booth.

Plate 1b: Permanent Buildings with Tent Roof (Syria).

Plate 2a: Combination of Tent and House (Syria).

Plate 2b: Large Permanent Building with Tent Roof (Syria).

Plate 3a: Bedouin Camp Constructed of Tents, Sheet Metal, and Plastic (Wadi Kelt, Israel).

Plate 3b: Bedouin Tent (Wadi Rum, Jordan).

Plate 4a: Tents Erected for Haj Pilgrims.

Plate 4b: Tent-Mosque in Nazareth.

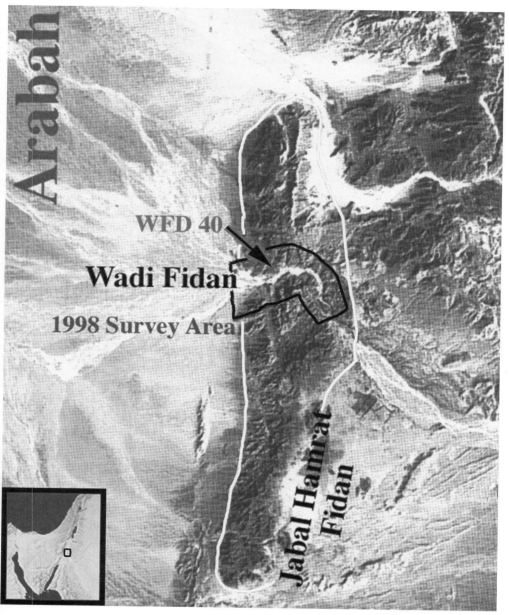

Plate 5: Aerial Photograph Showing the Jabal Hamrat Fidan (Outlined in White) with the Wadi Fidan Survey Area (Outlined in Black).

# Standard Grave Form of WFD 40

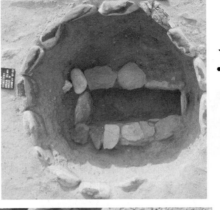

grave cist

capstones

burial

grave circles

Plate 6: Standard Grave Form of WFD 40.

# WFD 40 Grave 92

**wooden bowl**

**pomegranates**

**beads**

**copper anklets**

Plate 7: Grave 92 Burial and Associated Artifacts.

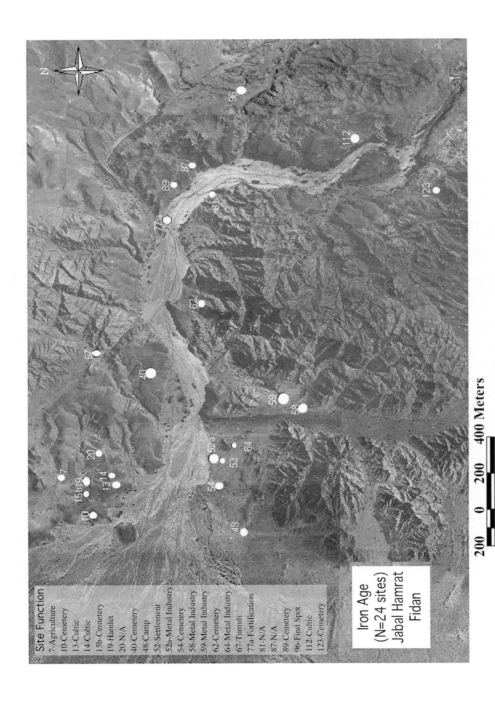

**Site Function**

7-Agriculture
10-Cemetery
13-Cultic
14-Cultic
15b-Cemetery
19-Hamlet
20-N/A
40-Cemetery
48-Camp
52-Settlement
52a-Metal Industry
54-Cemetery
58-Metal Industry
59-Metal Industry
62-Cemetery
64-Metal Industry
67-Tumuli
77a-Fortification
81-N/A
87-N/A
89-Cemetery
96-Find Spot
112-Cultic
123-Cemetery

Iron Age
(N=24 sites)
Jabal Hamrat
Fidan

200    0    200    400 Meters

Plate 9: Iron Age Sites Located in the WFD 1998 Survey

Plate 9: Three Views of WFD 48 (Large Campsite with IA Diagnostic Pottery).

Plate 10: Rameses II's Military Camp at Qedesh (Abu Simbel).

Plate 11a: Ornate Tent-pole in Egyptian Tent.

Plate 11b: Relief of Four Sons of Rameses II Fighting at Zapur

Plate 12: Relief of Sennacherib's Fortified Camp.

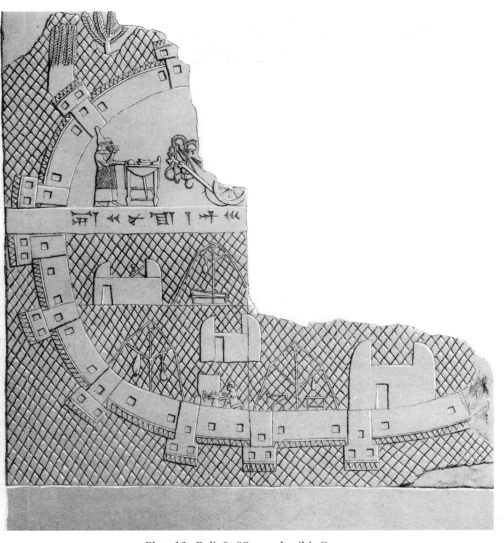

Plate 13: Relief of Sennacherib's Camp.

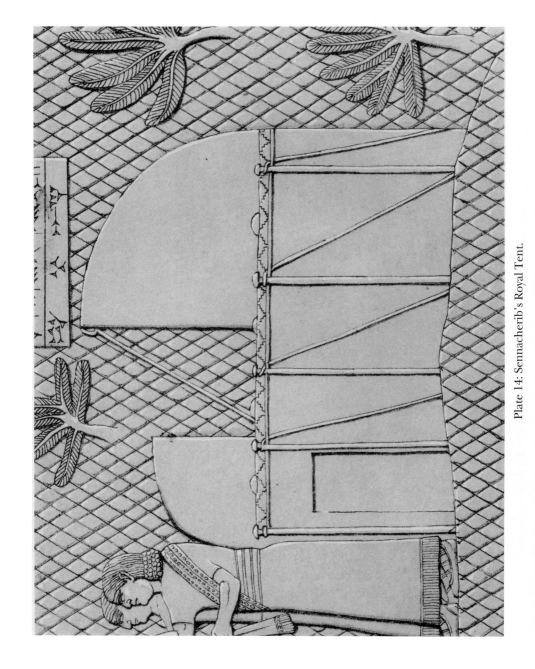

Plate 14: Sennacherib's Royal Tent.

Plate 15: Sargon II's Fortified Camp.

Plate 16: Ashurbanipal's Camp.

Plate 17: Forked-frame Tent in Camp of Ashurbanipal.

Plate 18: Burning Arab Tents from Palace of Ashurbanipal.

# THE ROMAN CAMP ACCORDING TO POLYBIUS

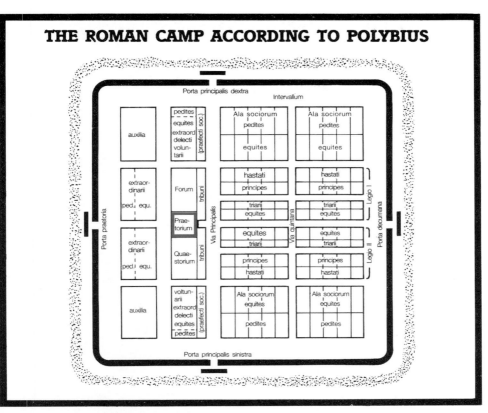

Plate 19a: The Roman Camp According to Polybius.

Plate 19b: Roman Army Tent-camp Remains at Masada.

Plate 20: Elamite Heads Stored in Assyrian Tent.

Plate 21b: *ʿutfah*.

Plate 21a: *markab*.

Plate 22: *maḥmal* in Procession.

Plate 23: *maḥmal* Returns to Cairo from Mecca.

Plate 24a: *maḥmal* Drawing.

Plate 24b: *maḥmal* Photograph.

Plate 25a: *qubba* Photograph (Palmyre).

Plate 25b: First Possible *qubba*.

Plate 26b: Third Possible *qubba*.

Plate 26a: Second Possible *qubba*.

Plate 27: Ka'ba.

Plate 28: Wheeled Shrine on Sidonian Coins (1st and 2nd Century C.E.).

Plate 29a: Shrine with Carrying Bars on Tyrian Coin (251-253 C.E.).

Plate 29b: Statue of Demeter Carried by Portable Shrine on Megarian Coin (193-221 C.E.).

Plate 29c: Statue of Hercules Carried by Portable Shrine on Coin from Philadelphia (c. 170 C.E.).

Plate 30: Wheeled Torah Ark from Capernaum.

Plate 31: Ark in Tented-wagon.

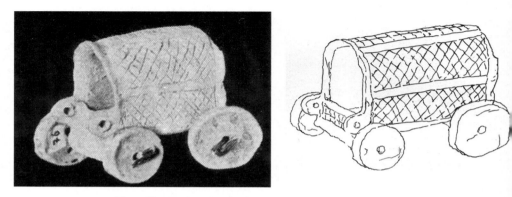

Plate 32a: Votive Wagon from Tepe Gawra with Drawing.

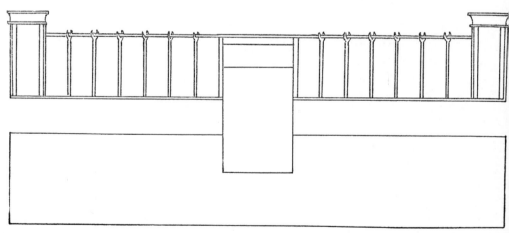

Plate 32b: The Frame of the Egyptian Tent of Purification.

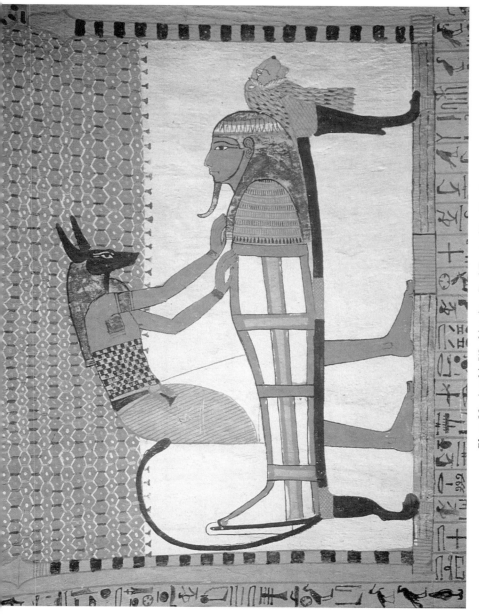

Plate 33: Anubis Working in a Red Tent of Purification.

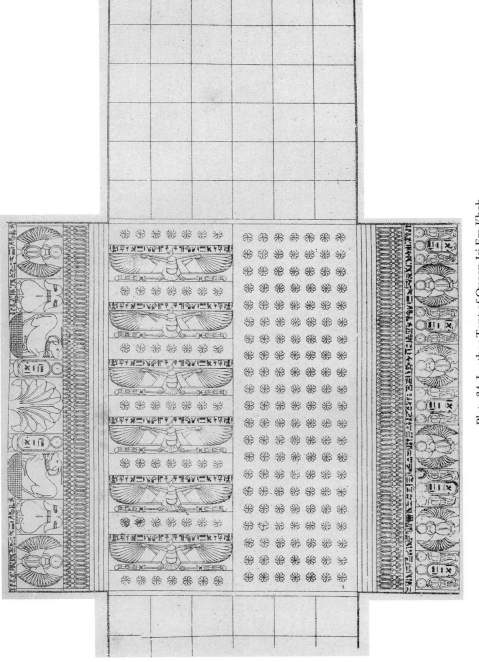

Plate 34: Leather Tent of Queen Isi Em Kheb.

Plate 35: Leather Egyptian Funeral Tent, Dyed Red, Yellow, and Green.

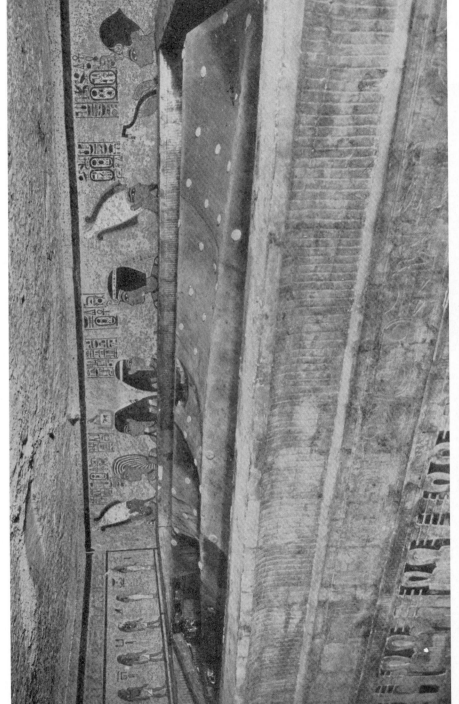

Plate 36: Tutankhamon's Pall inside Outer Catafalque.

Plate 37b: Tutankhamon's Pall Being Rolled and Removed.

Plate 37a: Tent Frame and Pall in Tomb of Tutankhamon.

Plate 38: Tutankhamon's Tent Frame inside Exterior Catafalque.

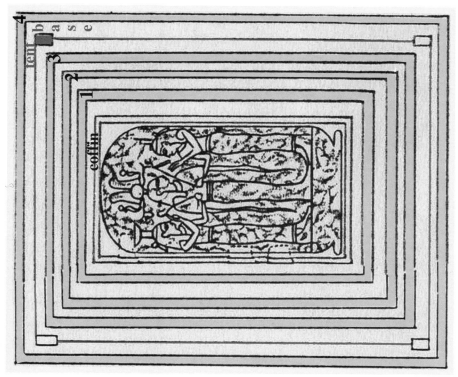

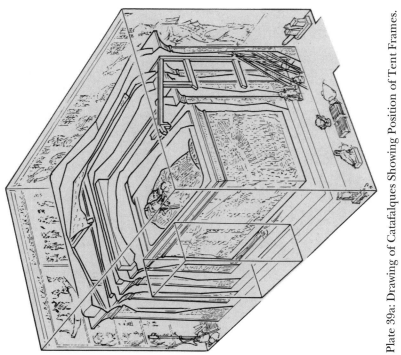

Plate 39a: Drawing of Catafalques Showing Position of Tent Frames.

Plate 39b: Plan on Papyrus of Rameses IV's Tomb Showing Possible
Tent and Floor Catafalques.

Plate 40a: Holy Barque of Amon with Catafalque.

Plate 40b: Tutankhamon's Catafalque Drawn by Court Officials.

Plate 41b: Wooden Planks as Found in Tomb of Tiye.

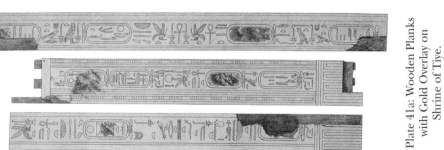

Plate 41a: Wooden Planks
with Gold Overlay on
Shrine of Tiye.

Plate 42: Tent of Min Being Constructed: Central Pole and Four Framing Poles.

Plate 43: Two Versions of Min's Tent.

Plate 44: Amarna Princesses in a Red Tent (c. 1345-1340 B.C.E.).

Plate 45: Mehu's Tent Frame over Bed.

Plate 46: Reproduction of Tent Frame, Bed, Headrest, Armchair, and Curtain Box of Queen Hetepheres I (IVth Dynasty).

Plate 47: Rameses II's Military Camp at Qedesh (Luxor).

Plate 48: Rameses II's Military Camp at Qedesh (Ramesseum).

Plate 49: Close-up of Rameses II's Military Tent at Qedesh (Abu Simbel).

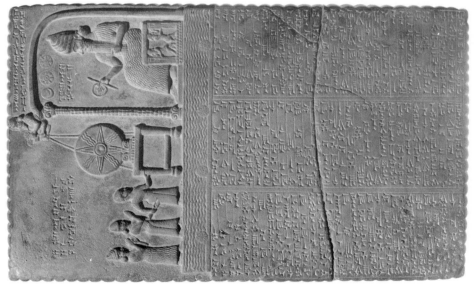

Plate 50b: Canopy at Tel Dan's Gate (Reconstructed).

Plate 50a: Sun God in Tent.

Plate 51a: Midianite Tent Shrine at Timna with *maṣṣēbôt* against Far Wall and Niche to Right.

Plate 51b: Midianite Tent Pole-hole.

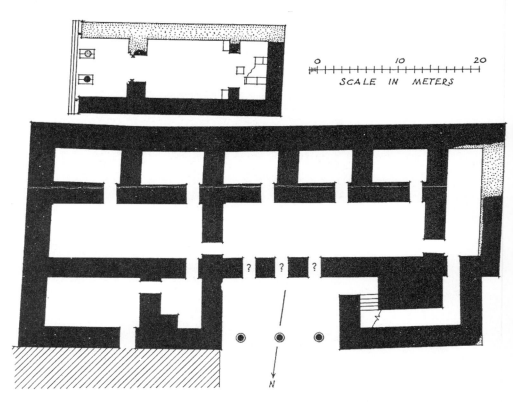

Plate 52: Temple (above) and Palace (below) at Tayinat.

Plate 53: Temple at Ain Dara.

Plate 54a: Temple at Arad.

Plate 54b: Holy of Holies at Arad.

Plate 55a: Egyptian Table for Dead Set with 12 Loaves of Bread (Slab Stela of Meretites, IVth Dynasty, reign of Khufu [2585-2560 B.C.E.]).

Plate 55b: Egyptian Model of Granary and Butchery.

Plate 56b: Examples of "Arms" in the Construction of the Tent Frame of Hetepheres.

Plate 56a: Bronze Tenons Used to Join Boards on Tiye's Catafalque.

Plate 57a: Painting of New Kingdom Barge.

Plate 57b: Model of Egyptian Boat from Tomb of Tutankhamon.

Plate 58a: Cheop's Barge.

Plate 58b: Phoenician Ship.

Plate 59: Metal Sockets and Joined Corner Pieces of Hetepheres' Tent Frame.

Plate 60: Model of Egyptian Weaving Shop (c. 2000 B.C.E.).

Plate 61: Engraving of the Tabernacle's Screen and Five Pillars (19<sup>th</sup> century).

Plate 62: Kennedy's Reconstruction of the Tabernacle.

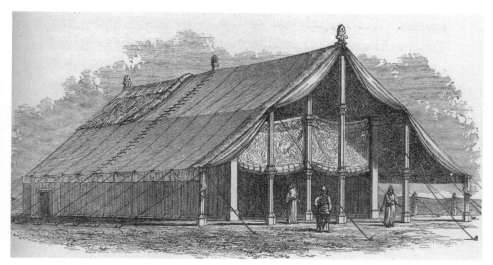

Plate 63a: Sloped-roof Tabernacle with Ridgepole.

Plate 63b: Tabernacle with Curtains inside Boards.

Plate 64: Winged Deities from Arslan Tash Protecting Sun God.